# CHURCHES OF THE VALLEY:

OR,

AN HISTORICAL SKETCH

OF

THE OLD PRESBYTERIAN CONGREGATIONS

OF

CUMBERLAND AND FRANKLIN COUNTIES, IN PENNSYLVANIA.

BY THE

REV. ALFRED NEVIN,

OF THE PRESBYTERY OF CARLISLE.

"Walk about Zion, and go round about her: tell the towers thereof. Mark ye well her bulwarks, consider her palaces, that ye may tell it to the generation following."—Ps. xlviii. 12, 13.

---

PHILADELPHIA:

JOSEPH M. WILSON,

NO. 228 CHESTNUT STREET.

1852.

C. SHERMAN, PRINTER,
19 St. James Street.

THIS VOLUME IS DEDICATED

TO THE

PRESBYTERIAN HISTORICAL SOCIETY.

# PREFACE.

---

THE early history of the old Presbyterian Churches of Cumberland Valley is fast growing dim. Many of those in whose memories interesting facts and incidents were treasured, are now dead; and others, to whom they were intrusted by tradition, are rapidly passing away.

That it is desirable to have embodied in an accessible form, the recollections and records connected with the origin and progress of these venerable congregations, none, it is believed, will question, who appreciate the ties which bind them to the past, or the duty which they owe to the future. These churches, are almost the only relics of antiquity that are to be met with in our new country, and for this reason, to say nothing of their deep religious associations besides, an effort should be made to save them from oblivion.

From the Presbyterial Records it is evident, that the

importance of such a measure was felt at an early day. In 1792, each minister was ordered to prepare a history of his own church; and in 1801, Dr. Cooper was appointed to draw up a short history of the Presbytery of Carlisle. That historical account, which was prepared according to injunction, is not now to be found. Neither is the book which contains the proceedings of Presbytery, from the year 1750 to 1759. It was borrowed, we have been told, by a gentleman in Virginia, and, after his death, was sought for in vain.

When, therefore, in connexion with these facts, it is remembered that many of the unwritten reminiscences, from which an ecclesiastical history of this valley must be compiled, are now floating in minds which age must soon enfeeble or death remove out of the body, it cannot but be acknowledged, that the work which we have undertaken, however imperfectly accomplished, has not, at least, been prematurely attempted.

It is unnecessary, perhaps, with the title of the volume in view, to state, that it was not our purpose to prepare a history of the *Presbytery* to which the congregations referred to, belong. This would have been a pleasing task. For in addition to the facts that this Presbytery, which is one of the oldest in the country, has several times changed its name and territorial limits, and has always occupied a high position, many of the churches which it now includes, though not lying within the boundaries which we have affixed to our labour, possess as much interest, are invested with as much importance, and deserve as extended a notice, as those whose rise and development we have sketched. We thought it best, however, to confine our effort principally to a more limited field; and the recollection of this, it is hoped, will prevent any expectation from our present effort, beyond what it legitimately promises.

We have, indeed, given, in a supplemental form, a very brief sketch of other congregations pertaining to the Presbytery, besides those which are embraced by the limits of Cumberland and Franklin Counties; but this was done at the suggestion of an esteemed and judicious friend, after the announcement of our plan rendered any material alteration of it impracticable; and will not, it is trusted, either be regarded as inconsistent with our primary intent, or lead to any misapprehension of it.

We are free to say, that our great object in the enterprise, has been the humble, but grateful one, of placing within the reach of those to whom veneration for departed ancestry, or long association, or present residence, has made Cumberland Valley a region of peculiar interest, such a record of its religious history as we supposed it would gratify them to read, as well as to hand down to their children. Many such there are, still worshipping where their fathers did, and meditating, at times, with deep solemnity over their last resting-place. Many more, too, are dwellers in the distant West, where, surrounded with new scenes, yet bound to old ones by ties that never can be broken, often with tender interest

> "Fond memory brings the light
> Of other days around" them.

To these, we felt assured we could not render a more acceptable service, than furnishing them with a remembrancer of the old churches with which their earliest recollections are blended, and of the old graveyards in which many of their dearest friends are buried.

In the preparation of the several sketches, great regard has been had to chronological accuracy, and, as we suppose, with about as much success as is attainable. But as the organizations of the old congregations were so nearly synchronous, we have not deemed it important to insert them in the order of time. On the Records of the Presbytery, kindly placed in our hands by the Stated Clerk, we have, of course, mainly relied for information. Several gentlemen also, however, among whom may be mentioned Dr. Moodey, Dr. M'Ginley, Hon. Geo. Chambers, Judge Clendenin, Dr. J. K. Davidson, John Cox, and L. H. Williams, Esqrs., have, by important data which they have supplied, brought us under obligations which we gratefully acknowledge. We have, too, been materially aided by Mr. I. D. Rupp's History of Cumberland and Franklin Counties. Our indebtedness to other sources, is noticed in the proper place.

We send the volume forth, confident that it is not, in many respects, what it should be, yet hoping that it may in some measure fulfil its design. We do so, likewise, with the assurance, that those who can form any idea of the difficulty of its preparation, growing out of lost and faded records, and the sameness of material to be presented, and the vagueness of traditions to be consulted, will regard it with much more readiness to appreciate any merit it may have, than to condemn the defects from which it does not claim to be free.

ALFRED NEVIN.

# CONTENTS.

## CHAPTER I.

### INTRODUCTORY.

## CHAPTER II.

### MIDDLE SPRING CHURCH.



## CHAPTER III.

### BIG SPRING CHURCH.

## CHAPTER IV.

### CHURCH AT SILVERS' SPRING.



## CHAPTER V.

### CHURCH IN MERCERSBURG.

## CHAPTER VI.

### WELSH RUN CHURCH.

## CHAPTER VII.

### CHURCH AT CHAMBERSBURG.



## CHAPTER VIII.

### CHURCH AT SHIPPENSBURG.

## CHAPTER IX.

### GREENCASTLE CHURCH.



## CHAPTER X.

### ROCKY SPRING CHURCH.

## CHAPTER XI.

### PATH VALLEY CHURCHES.

## CHAPTER XII.

### DICKINSON CHURCH.



## CHAPTER XIII.

### CHURCH AT CARLISLE.

## SUPPLEMENT.



## APPENDIX I.



## APPENDIX II.



## APPENDIX III.



## APPENDIX IV.

# CHURCHES OF THE VALLEY.

## CHAPTER I.

### INTRODUCTORY.

PENNSYLVANIA was settled more rapidly than any of the colonies. Among other causes of this, the salubrity of its climate, and the fertility of its soil, stand prominent. The speedy increase of population within its limits, however, is mainly to be attributed to the religious toleration which was secured to the colony, by its charter and its fundamental laws.

"The persecution of the Quakers and other religious denominations, during the reign of Charles II., and especially during that of his successor, the intolerance exercised by the Papists over the Protestants of Europe, and the overbearing or persecuting spirit, on religious accounts, in many of the other colonies, as contrasted with the liberality of the Quakers of Pennsylvania, who were disposed to open their arms to all denominations of professing Christians who might be inclined to settle among them, induced the flocking of men by tens, by hundreds, and by thousands, to a place where man pretended not to assume the prerogatives of Deity; nor judge, condemn, and punish in his stead."

> "What sought they thus afar?
> Bright jewels of the mine?
> The wealth of seas, the spoils of war?—
> They sought a faith's pure shrine!
> Ay, call it holy ground,
> The soil where first they trod!
> They have left unstained what there they found—
> Freedom to worship God."

We could not, perhaps, throw more light upon the early settlers in Pennsylvania, than by presenting the following extracts from reliable sources.

"Referring to those who migrated hither from the North of Ireland, and who were chiefly Presbyterians, Dr. Williamson, in his 'History of North Carolina,' says: 'The greater number of those people or their ancestors, had formerly removed from Scotland. But they were treated, after a short residence in Ireland, with much ingratitude and neglect; wherefore they sought refuge in America. The Earls of Tyrone and Tyrconnel, in the province of Ulster, having conspired against the government in the reign of James the First, fled from the kingdom to escape punishment. Some of their accomplices were arrested, condemned, and executed, but the two Earls were attainted by a process of outlawry, upon which their vast estates, about five hundred thousand acres of land, escheated to the Crown. King James resolved, if possible, to improve a country that was covered by woods, desolated by war, infested by robbers, or inhabited by ignorant adherents to the Romish Church. For this purpose he divided the escheated lands into small tracts, and those he gave to adventurers, who were to settle them within four years, with a certain number of sub-tenants. According to his advice, the preference was given, in distributing the lands, to adventurers from the west of Scotland. They were Protestants from his own country. They were industrious people, and the passage being very short, they might, with the greater ease, settle the lands according to their contracts. The establishment of prelacy in Scotland, in the year 1637, and afterwards in the year 1661, among people who had adopted the more simple form of Presbyterian worship, became the additional cause of numerous emigrations from that kingdom to the North of Ireland.

"'The superior knowledge, industry, and temperance of the Scotch farmers, in a short time enabled them to supplant the natives among whom they lived, and six of the northern counties, by the end of the seventeenth century, were chiefly inhabited by the descendants of Scottish emigrants, or the remains of Cromwell's army. That Protestant colony has been the chief support of government against all attempts to establish a Catholic prince, by treason, insurrection, or murder. Those men have been the steady and active supporters of the Hanover succession. Their faithful services, and uniform attachment to government, had placed them in the rank of good and faithful subjects, and their unshaken loyalty had entitled them to confidence and public favour. But they were treated like aliens and strangers, with marks of distrust in their civil capacity; and they were depressed in their religious capacity, by the spirit of intolerance, because they were not of the established Church of Ireland. Men who were thus degraded and vexed by incapacities and burdens, migrated in thousands to Pennsylvania ; a province in which the principles of civil and religious liberty had their full operation.'

"'In England,' says Dr. Davidson,* 'ever since the memorable St. Bartholomew's day, all eyes had been anxiously directed to the Transatlantic settlements, notwithstanding they were as yet a wilderness; and while some fled to Holland, a great number, together with many of the ejected ministers, betook themselves to New England, Pennsylvania, and other American plantations. In Scotland, fines, imprisonments, and whippings, were abundant from 1662, when the Act of Conformity was passed, until 1688, when the Act of Toleration gave relief under the Presbyterian Prince of Orange. The Western and Southern Counties, which, according to Hume, were the most populous and thriving, were the most ob-

* History of the Presbyterian Church in Kentucky.

noxious, and the severity of the persecutions surpassed, in the judgment of Bishop Burnet, the merciless rigours of the Duke of Alva. Many sold their estates and crossed over to the Scots of Ulster, where, for a time unrestricted liberty was allowed. But the arm of intolerance soon followed them to this retreat, and the hunted-down non-conformists felt that they had no resource short of absolute expatriation. In order that the fury of the prelates might have full sweep, the Presbyterians and their ejected ministers were forbidden to fly into Scotland to avoid it. Of these ejected ministers, both in Scotland and Ireland, Wodrow gives a catalogue amounting to four hundred.

"'In consequence of the persecutions of 1679,1682, and 1685, crowds of voluntary exiles sought an asylum in East New Jersey, Carolina, and Maryland. The North of Ireland shared in the general drain. The arbitrary measures pursued by James II., together with apprehensions of a general massacre by the Papists, emboldened as they were by the undisguised partiality of the king, caused such multitudes despairing of safety, to fly to foreign climes, that trade declined, and the revenue languished. Successive emigrations from the North of Ireland continued to pour into Pennsylvania in such numbers that by the year 1705, there were sufficient Presbyterian churches in that province, in conjunction with those of the provinces contiguous, to constitute a presbytery, and a few years later (1717), a synod."

Prominent among these "voluntary exiles," were the Huguenots, or French Protestants. The persecutions to which they were exposed during the reign of Louis XIV., consummated by the revocation of the Edict of Nantes in 1685, drove hundreds of thousands of those unhappy people from their native country. Though the frontiers were vigilantly guarded, upwards of five hundred thousand of them made their escape. They fled to Switzerland, Germany, Holland, and England, and large numbers of them came to this country. It is true that their principal location here, was in the Southern States, yet scattered emigrants fixed themselves in greater or less numbers, in the provinces of Pennsylvania and Maryland.

"The Welsh, also, from their numbers, deserve particular notice. The principal settlement of them at an early period, was upon the left bank of the Schuylkill. They there occupied three townships, and in a few years their numbers so increased that they obtained three additional townships."

Nor must the German settlers in Pennsylvania, by any means be overlooked in this enumeration. Their emigration commenced as early as 1682 or 1683, and very rapidly increased. From 1730 to 1740, about sixty-five vessels, well filled with Germans, arrived at Philadelphia, bringing with them ministers of the Gospel and schoolmasters, to instruct their children. From 1740 to 1755, upwards of one hundred vessels arrived, which were filled with emigrants of the same nation, and in some of which, though small, there were between five and six hundred passengers. With regard to the Germans in Pennsylvania, Mr. Andrews, in a letter dated October 14, 1730, says, "There is, besides, in this province a vast number of Palatines, and they come in still every year. Those that have come of late are mostly Presbyterian, or as they call themselves, Reformed; the Palatinate being about three-fifths of that sort of people." "There are many Lutherans and some Reformed, mixed among them. In other parts of the country, they are chiefly Reformed, so that I suppose the Presbyterian party are as numerous as the Quakers, or near it."

Such, then, were the materials, out of which the Presbyterian Church in Pennsylvania was formed. The English Puritans, many of whom, with an adventurous spirit, left their home in New England, and located in this province "were all Calvinists, and many of them Presbyterians. The Dutch were Calvinists and Presbyterians; a moiety at least of the Germans were of the same class. All the French Protestants were Calvinists and Presbyterians; and so, of course, were the Scotch and Irish. Of these several classes, the Dutch and Germans formed distinct ecclesiastical organizations, and subsist as such to the present time. In a multitude of cases, however, their descendants mingled with the descendants of other Presbyterians, and have entered largely into the materials of which our church is composed."

"As they merged their diversities of national character into that of American citizens," adds Dr.

Hodge,* "so the Scotch, Irish, French, English, Dutch, and German Presbyterians became united, in thousands of instances, in the American Presbyterian Church. Having the same views of civil government, our population, so diversified as to its origin, forms a harmonious civil society, and agreeing in opinion on the government of the church, the various classes above specified formed a religious society, in which the difference of their origin was as little regarded as it was in the state."

So far as is now known, the first Presbyterian Church that was organized and furnished with a place of worship in the American Colonies, was in the city of Philadelphia. This took place about the year 1703. The next year a Presbytery was formed, under the title of the Presbytery of Philadelphia.

As early as 1716, the Presbyterian body had so far increased, that a Synod was constituted, comprising four Presbyteries. These Presbyteries bore the following titles:—1. *The Presbytery of Philadelphia.* 2. *The Presbytery of New Castle.* 3. *The Presbytery of Snow-Hill.* 4. *The Presbytery of Long Island.*

"After the formation of the Synod, in 1716, the body went on increasing, receiving additions, not only by emigrants from Scotland and Ireland, but also from natives of England and Wales, who came to the Middle Colonies, and were thrown by cir-

* History of the Presbyterian Church, Part I., p. 69.

cumstances in the neighbourhood of Presbyterian churches, and also from natives, or their descendants, of France, Holland, and Switzerland, who preferred the Presbyterian form of worship or government. To these may be added a number from New England, who were induced by local considerations, or other circumstances, to connect themselves with the Presbyterian body."*

Up to the year 1732, at which time there were about fifteen or sixteen Presbyterian churches in Pennsylvania, the "Presbytery of New Castle" seems to have covered all the territory reaching to the Susquehanna. In September of that year the Presbytery of Donegal was organized, and to it the jurisdiction over this portion of the State was committed.

As is generally known, the limits of Lancaster, one of the first three counties organized in the province, were then so comprehensive as to embrace all the territory west and north of Chester County, between the Schuylkill, north of the boundary line of Chester, and the Susquehanna, *and all west of the Susquehanna.*

About a year or two before the erection of the Presbytery of Donegal, it was, that the first visits of the white man, with a view to residence, were made to the deep, dark forests which stretched beyond the river just named, and which abounded with

* Dr. Miller's article on "Pres. Ch. in United States," Ency. Relig. Know.

beasts of prey, and, to some extent, as the sequel proved, with still more savage men.

In 1730–1, some Irish and Scotch adventurers crossed the Susquehanna at Peixtan, Peshtank, or Paxton, and commenced settlements in the "Kittochtinny Valley," or "North Valley," at Falling Springs, and other places, till they extended from the "Long, Crooked River" to the Maryland province; about the year 1736.

As the lands west of the Susquehanna were not purchased by the Proprietary of Pennsylvania from the Indians before October, 1736, the Land Office was not open for the sale of them under existing laws, and the settlements, made on such lands before this purchase, were by special license to individuals from Samuel Blunston, or other proprietary agents, and were of limited number. After the office was open, however, for the unrestricted sale of lands on the waters of the Conodoguinett and Conococheague, at the close of 1736, the applications and grants for the district then multiplied; and the influx of settlers from Lancaster County, Ireland, and Scotland, was great, in the succeeding two or three years, nearly all of whom were Presbyterians.

Thus, by energy and intrepidity, which cannot be looked for except among men who have been schooled by difficulties and accustomed to perils, was possession taken, by our pioneer ancestry, of the rich and beautiful valley which their descendants now inherit, and which is at present embraced within the limits of

Cumberland and Franklin Counties, the former of which was established in 1750, and the latter in 1784. How changed the scene! How different an aspect this universally-admired region now wears, from that which it presented a little more than a century ago, when it stood in its wildness and its gloom!

> "Look now abroad,—another race has filled
> Those populous borders; wide the wood recedes,
> And towns shoot up, and fertile realms are tilled;
> The land is full of harvests and green meads."

One of the first arrangements made by the primitive settlers "west of the Susquehanna," was to have the Gospel preached in their midst. They had been, most of them, reared in the religious element. They had been taught to worship God. Nor was the sacred lesson of duty to the Father of Mercies, which they had received in their earlier years, forgotten by them, even amidst the hardships and perils of a life in the wilderness.

We find, accordingly, very early applications, or "supplications" (as the Records say), presented by them to the Presbytery, for ministers to be sent among them, to break unto them the Bread of Life; and in the results which soon followed the labours of these servants of God, we have the beginnings or germs of the congregations whose history is now succinctly to be given.

# CHAPTER II.

## MIDDLE SPRING CHURCH.

For some reason, probably from a regard to convenience, nearly all the old Presbyterian churches of Cumberland Valley were erected near a spring or stream of water, and from their location they derived their name. It is difficult at this late day to determine precisely why it was that *Middle* Spring received its distinctive appellation; but it is to be accounted for, as we suppose, by the equidistance of its position from Big Spring on the east, and Rocky Spring on the west, with the congregations of both of which it was originally connected, in the constitution of a pastoral charge.

Of the exact date of the origin of this congregation no record has been preserved, neither can it be ascertained from any other source. Some light, however, is thrown upon this point by the following statement, which is found in the minutes of a meeting of the Presbytery of Donegal, held at "Pacque, 8ber 17th, 1738."

"Robert Henry, a Commissioner from Hopewell, complained that the people of Falling Spring are about to encroach on Hopewell Congregation. Ordered, that representatives from both attend our next, that Presbytery may judge of said complaint."

As Big Spring was, at that time, called Hopewell, it would appear from this record that the congregation of Middle Spring, occupying an intermedial position between it and the church at Falling Spring, could not then have been organized, otherwise it, also, would be found in the same attitude of complaint. The probability, then, is, from this circumstance, and some others which need not be specified, that this congregation came into existence about the year 1740. Antecedently to this date, Middle Spring was a preaching-place, and was frequently favoured with ministerial service by neighbouring pastors, as well as by supplies under appointment of Presbytery; but not until that time was a congregation regularly organized.

We have examined with care the earliest records of the congregation now to be found, and probably the first ever written, which go back to 1742; but they consist almost exclusively of sessional proceedings. The following is a literal transcript of the title-page:

"A Session-Book, for the use of the Session of the Congregation of Middle Spring. Bought for the above-mentioned use, men. Decembris, Anno Dom. 1745. 2 Chron. xix. 8, 9: Moreover, in Jerusalem did Jehoshaphat set of the Levites, and of the priests, and of the chiefs of the fathers of Israel, for the judgment of the Lord, and for controversies when they returned to Jerusalem. And he charged them, saying, Thus shall ye do in the fear of the Lord, faithfully and with a perfect heart."

In these Records we find mention made of the following names of elders of the congregation: Allen Killough, John M'Kee, David Herron, John Reynolds, ordained 1742. John Finley, William Anderson, Robert M'Comb, ordained 1744. John Maclay, ordained 1747.

The subjoined extracts from this ancient book may be of interest. "1744. The Session condemn D. S.'s manner of expressing himself, as being very untender to his neighbour's character; and appoint the Moderator to occasion to warn their people against speaking abroad slanderous reports upon neighbours, either privately, or more publicly in company, and more especially when they have no solid grounds for, or knowledge of them;—as being very inconscientious, discovering a willingness or disposition to take up an ill report, a breach of the ninth commandment, in backbiting their neighbour, wounding to religion, having a tendency to fill the minds of people with jealousies, and thereby exposing Church judicatories, oftentimes, to reflections, as tho' they covered sin, when upon tryal they can't find guilt."

"J. R. table'd a complaint against Catherine P. his former servant, for some pieces of malconduct. The Session having examined S. R. and R. L. find from their Evidence that said P. has behaved herself undutifully in resisting her Mistress, and imprecating vengeance upon her, and ly'd in reporting that she beg'd a little Respite of her Mistress. The Session Judge that C. P. shall acknowledge her Fault to her Master and Mistress in the offence she has given them, in the Respects aforesaid, and be rebuk'd in the Session, for the contradiction she has hereby given to her religious Profession."

"1746. J. P. was cited to the Session for taking venison from an Indian, and giving him Meal and Butter for it on the Sabbath Day.

"J. P. appeared, and acknowledged that being at home one Sabbath Day, he heard a gun go off twice quickly after each other, and said he would go out and see who it was; his wife dissuading him, he said he would go and see if he could hear the Horse-bell: having gone a little way he saw an Indian, who had just killed a Fawn and dressed it: the Indian coming towards the house with him, to get some victuals, having, he said, eat nothing that morning, he saw a Deer, and shot it, and charg'd and shot again at another, which ran away; said P. stood by the Indian until he skin'd the Deer; when he had done, he told said P. he might take it in if he wou'd, for he would take no more with him, upon which, said P. and W. K., who then had come to them, took it up, and carry'd it in; when he had given the Indian his Breakfast, said Indian ask'd if he had any meal; he said he had, and gave him some; then the Indian ask'd for Butter, and asking his wife about it, he gave the Indian some; but he denies that he gave these things as a Reward for the Venison, inasmuch as they had made no Bargain about it.

"The Session Judge that J.P. do acknowledge his Breach of Sabbath in this Matter, and be rebuk'd before the Session for his Sin."

The "Moderator" referred to in the first of these extracts, was the Rev. Mr. Blair, who, it appears, was the minister of the Rocky Spring, Middle Spring, and Big Spring Congregations, and divided his time equally between them. How long Mr. Blair sustained this relation we are not able to say, but when it was dissolved, we have been informed, he went to the city of New York. This gentleman was highly esteemed by the Congregation for his piety and his learning. As a proof of their affection for him, they conveyed to him by deed, a farm belonging to them, which lay near to the church, and contained about two hundred and fifty acres. Two years after this, however, for some reason not now known, he resigned his charge, and the farm was sold. Mr. Blair was preceded in his labours at Middle Spring, by the Rev. Mr. Calls, of Ireland, and the Rev. Mr. Clarke, of Scotland, each of whom, with the sanction of Presbytery, served the Congregation about six months or a year.

At a sessional meeting, Sept. 3, 1744 we find mention made of the "Rev. Mr. Robinson" as being present. After this, notwithstanding the minutes of Session continue until 1748, there is no reference in them at all, either to preaching or a Pastor. By reason of this fact, consequently, as well as the chasm in the Minutes of Presbytery, which, as already stated, reaches from 1750 to 1759, that portion of the history of Middle Spring is a blank. Nothing can be learned of the supply of the pulpit, or of any arrangements in regard to it, until in 1760, a commissioner from the congregation lays a call before the Presbytery "requesting their concurrence to said call's being presented to the Rev. Mr. Carmichael of New Brunswick Presbytery." This call, if it was ever prosecuted, was not accepted.

We now reach the time when Dr. Cooper was called to the pastorate of Middle Spring. Of this there is the following record on the Minutes of Presbytery, May 23d, 1765. "A call was brought in from the congregation of Middle Spring to Mr. Robert Cooper, Probationer, and a supplication to the Presbytery, praying them to present said call, and to allow Mr. Cooper as their constant supply till next Presbytery, if his way be not now clear to accept their call. Said call was accordingly presented, and Mr. Cooper desir'd time to consider of it, as he cannot see his way at present clear either to accept or refuse it." "Messrs. Campble, Esq., and Benjamin Blythe, commissioners from Middle Spring Congregation, inform the Presbytery that the congregation will make good to him the sum of one hundred pounds currency per annum." Mr. Cooper accepted the call in October of the same year, and at the same time declined a call from "Tuscarora in Virginia."

The following letter concerning Dr. Cooper is from the pen of his venerable successor.

"Shippensburg, May 20th, 1852.

"REV. AND RESPECTED BROTHER,—

"In reply to your request I have to say, that my acquaintance with Dr. Robert Cooper, was not until a late period of his life. Our places of residence were fully fifty miles apart. I do not recollect that I ever had the pleasure of seeing him, until October, 1799,—two years and a half after his pastoral relation to the church at Middle Spring was dissolved, and some months after I had commenced my theological studies. This meeting was at a Presbytery convened at Derry Church, for the ordination and installation of Dr. Joshua Williams. My acquaintance with him then, was limited to what I saw and heard in the transaction of presbyterial business.

"On the following April I presented myself, and was received on trial by the Presbytery of Carlisle, nor had I any intercourse with Dr. Cooper, except at presbyterial meetings, until I was licensed to preach, October 9th, 1801. From that time I always spent at his house a portion of my time, when appointed to preach at Middle Spring, and frequently called and spent a day and night on my way to preach at other places.

"I always found him very hospitable,—a kind,

friendly, and instructive companion; and I have no doubt that he was truly pious. That he stood high in the opinion of his brethren of the Synods of New York and Philadelphia, then the supreme judicatory of the Presbyterian Church in the United States, would appear from the fact, that he was appointed on a committee, with others, among the most celebrated divines of the day, 'to take into consideration the constitution of the Church of Scotland and other Protestant churches, and, agreeably to the general principles of Presbyterian government, complete a system of general rules for the government of the Synod and the several Presbyteries under their inspection, and the people in their communion.'

"I have not heard Dr. Cooper preach very often, only a few times at Middle Spring, after my settlement there, and on a few occasions elsewhere. As to his preaching, in the latter part of his life, he appeared not to aim at display of talents and oratory, but to be instructive and practical. Before his settlement at Middle Spring, it appears, from the Presbyterial Records, that, for some reason, he was highly prized, and his preaching much sought after by the churches.

"I think I never saw but one sermon of his fully written out, and some two or three skeletons, though I have reason to believe he had, in his time, written a number in full. I do not remember ever to have seen him use any notes in the pulpit, and I believe he seldom, if ever, did. I heard him on one occasion, in a sermon, declaiming with severity against reading sermons.

"His literary attainments were very respectable, though his education was not commenced in early life. He must, I suppose, have been upwards of thirty years of age when he entered the ministry. Being gifted with a strong and sound mind, he was judicious, well-informed in Theology, a sound Calvinist, and always ready to give his views on any subject proposed. A number of young men of very respectable standing in the ministry, studied Theology under his direction; among whom were Dr. Joshua Williams, of Newville, and Dr. Herron, of Pittsburg. Except a few articles in the newspapers of the day, he never, so far as I know, published anything but a small pamphlet on Prophecy, entitled 'The Signs of the Times.'

"I may add that I am Dr. Cooper's successor in the church at Middle Spring,—the first and only pastor of it since his time. After a vacancy of six years, during which the congregation was well supplied, by members of the Presbytery and a number of very respectable licentiates, with the preaching of the gospel and the administration of Divine ordinances, a call was given to me, April 12th, 1803, which was accepted. On the 5th October, 1803, I was ordained, and installed Pastor of that church, and here I am until this day.

"The following dates I take from the Records of Presbytery:

" 'Dr. Cooper graduated at Princeton, 1763; was licensed to preach, Feb. 22d, 1765; was ordained and installed at Middle Spring, Nov. 21st, 1765; resigned his pastoral relation, Ap. 12th, 1797; departed this life, April 5th, 1805.'

"Very sincerely,

"Your friend and brother in the Gospel,

"JOHN MOODEY."

Dr. Cooper's remains are buried in the "Lower Graveyard" of the church, and on his tombstone is this inscription:—

"In memory of Rev. Robert Cooper, D.D., Pastor of the Congregation of Middle Spring nearly forty years, who departed this life A.D. 1805, aged 73 years. Also, his surviving partner, Elizabeth Cooper, who deceased A.D. 1829, aged nearly 86 years.

"De quibus qui nunc vivunt et audiverunt venerantur, qui contemporales noverunt, plerique mortui sunt."

As there is some discrepancy between the statement of Dr. Moodey, as to the length of time Dr. Cooper was pastor of Middle Spring, and the record of this that is made on his tombstone, it is probable that in the latter case the time is estimated from the date of Dr. Cooper's acceptance of the call, to his *death*, instead of to the dissolution of his pastoral relation, as it should have been.*

* The following extract from a letter from Jonathan K. Cooper, Esq., of Peoria, Ill. (a grandson of Dr. Cooper), is here in place.

As we have already had occasion to notice, the Rev. John Moodey, a native of Dauphin County, in this State,—who, after he graduated in Princeton College in 1796, studied Theology under the direction of the Rev. James Snodgrass,—succeeded Dr. Cooper as pastor of Middle Spring. Mr. Moodey was called, and ordained, and installed, in 1803, and there he has ever since remained, notwithstanding the frequent sundering of pastoral relations that has taken place around him.

Dr. Moodey, who was born July 4th, 1776, is now, of course, far advanced in life. To him have been allotted, by a kind Providence, more than threescore years and ten. He stands as the representative of a generation which will soon have entirely disappeared. But one now lives in connexion with the Presbytery, that belonged to it at his reception; and most of the oldest members of his congregation are either those whom he baptized in their

"The cause of my grandfather's retiring from the active duties of his charge was, as perhaps you are aware, a strange, brooding melancholy (occasioned, as it was found, by a dropsical habit of body), which, for a season, whelmed his mind in gloom, and made him doubt, not merely his fitness for the station he filled, but the sufficiency of the hope in which he had himself trusted. With returning health, his confidence and hope were restored, and he experienced again a bright sunshine of the soul, during which he travelled extensively, and preached in the newly-settled and mountainous parts of Pennsylvania and Virginia, as a sort of missionary, still residing, however, on his farm in the bounds of Middle Spring, and, I presume, occasionally officiating."

infancy, or whose memory cannot reach beyond his ministry. Few, indeed, remain, who witnessed his installation. They have nearly all been removed by death, and now sleep either in the graveyard of the church in which they worshipped, or in some distant part of the country in which they settled and died.

To say of the pastoral relation which has for half a century subsisted at Middle Spring, that it has been marked with peace, would be but to affirm what truth demands. To say, also, of Dr. Moodey, that his long life has been one of Christian consistency and large usefulness, would be only to utter a testimony which none that have known him would hesitate to endorse. For fifty years he has gone in and out before his people, preaching to them, though always changing, a gospel that changes not, and exhibiting to them an example of calm, steady, and trustful devotion to the service of God. As a preacher, he has ever had an excellent reputation, and been regarded as a logical, instructive, and able expounder of the truth as it is in Jesus. With him there never have been the flourishes of oratory, or flashes of fancy, or efforts after novelty, which so often attract without permanently pleasing; but his ministry has ever been characterized by a plain, manly, and solemn exhibition of the Word, and a bringing of things new and old out of his treasure, which have saved his acceptableness in the pulpit from anything like abatement. He is now, as he ever has been, universally esteemed in the community in which his days have been chiefly spent; and when it shall please God to allow him to sink into the ground which he has seen so often broken for others, all will acknowledge that a faithful servant of the Most High has gone to his reward.

The following statistics, with which we have been furnished by Dr. Moodey, will be read with interest:

"In my church there have been 1165 baptisms; of these there were 44 white adults, one a female above fifty years of age, and 4 adults and 3 infants of colour. In other churches, where, by Presbyterial appointments, I have preached, and administered, or aided in administering, the Lord's Supper, I have baptized 139 infants and 8 adults: 3 of the last were persons of colour. Whole number of baptisms, 1312.

"During my pastoral relation with Middle Spring, there have been added to the list of our communicants, 655. A few of these have been received on certificate; but by reason of death, removal, and church extension, the number increases but slowly. The largest number added at any one time was 24; and on every occasion, with one exception, there have been more or less added.

"I have officiated at the solemnization of 587 marriages. The numbers who have sprung from our congregation and become preachers of the gospel are very gratifying."

We now proceed to notice the *church* at Middle Spring. Those who are familiar with this locality, three miles north of Shippensburg, remember well the green slope to the right, on which the building stands; the graveyard in the rear; the beautiful wood, stretching back, with its refreshing shadows; "the old mill-dam," a few rods to the left of the road, calmly reflecting the light of heaven; the fountain of fresh water bubbling up close by; the murmuring stream, which rolls on under the thick overhanging foliage; and the "Lower Graveyard," a little to the north, along which that stream flows in its course, chaunting its sweet requiem for the dead.

It was in that graveyard the first church in that region was built. Anxious for a place of worship, the early settlers met to devise a plan for this purpose; and the result of their consultation was the erection of a log-building, near the gate of the graveyard, about thirty-five feet square. This was about the year 1738. Soon this edifice, in which, for a while there was preaching only four or five times a year, was found to be too small to accommodate the people, and it was demolished, and another of the same material erected on the same spot. This was considerably larger, being about fifty-eight feet long and forty-eight feet wide. In a little while it became necessary again that the house of worship should have its capacity extended; and this desideratum was effected by removing three sides of the building then in use, and embracing a little more space on either side, which was covered with a roof, something in the form of a shed. Up the sides of these additions to the main edifice, and over the roofs, were fixed wooden steps, by which access was gained into the gallery. This arrangement was made for want of room in the interior of the building for the construction of a stairway. Of the internal appearance of this ancient structure we are not able to give any very definite information. We have been told, however, that the pulpit, which was of walnut, was a remarkably neat piece of workmanship for that day. This interesting relic, which, with other portions of the building at the time it was torn down, was purchased by Samuel Cox, Esq., was converted into a table, which is yet in the possession of his son, John Cox, Esq., who still lives in the old homestead.

In this church, for many years, the growing congregation worshipped; and during this time the graveyard was filled with the dead. This sacred spot, which consists of about an acre of ground, is enclosed by a substantial stone wall, and stands by the roadside, teaching its solemn lesson to the passer-by. Of the epitaphs upon the few tombstones which it contains, we give the following:—

"Here lies the body of John Reynolds, Esq., who departed this life on the twentieth day of October, 1789, aged 40 years.

"This modest stone (what few vain marbles can)
May truly say, 'Here lies an honest man.'"

"Interred here is the body of Capt. Samuel Kearsley, a veteran survivor of the Revolution which procured the Independence of America, who departed this life on the 22d of March, A.D. 1830, in the 81st year of his age.

> "In profession a Christian,
> A soldier intrepid,
> In body and mind vigorous,
> Fearless of man,
> But who confessed that Wisdom's beginning is God's fear."

About the year 1781, the old stone church was erected, whose site, as is well known, was just beside that of the present building. This was still larger than its predecessor (being fifty-eight by sixty-eight feet), and was necessarily so, by reason of the rapid increase of population. About the same time that this church was built, and which, for its day, was one of more than ordinary elegance, the graveyard immediately in its rear, was located. This was done, not only because the old receptacle of the dead was well filled, but also because its soil was of a gravelly description, and its lower section, by reason of its nearness to the stream, was subject to frequent inundation.

The present building at Middle Spring, which was erected in 1848, and demanded by the dilapidated condition of the former one, is a neat brick edifice, one story high, with a gallery for a choir, and capacity to accommodate about four hundred persons. It was with many a deep regret that the necessity was yielded to that called for the erection of this new church; and hundreds there were who were in full sympathy with one whose earliest associations were blended with that neighbourhood, and who, returning after the absence of years, thus uttered his feelings in the contemplation of the change that was soon to occur:—

"Welcome to me once more this green churchyard,
To which, this bright May morn, have come my feet:
Ah, from the village near, still hitherward
Outdrawn I am that good old church to greet,
And these sad graves, to pay them homage meet;
What times I come back to this neighbourhood,
Long whiles between, where erst my boyhood sweet
Was sped, here o'er its joys despoiled to brood.
But though it bringeth dole the while, it doth me good.

"As now, long gone, oft sauntering have I come
Adown that stream on Sabbath mornings bland,—
In town at school, but longing much for home,—
Beneath that poplar near the church to stand,
Watching each carriage come and folks disband;
Till, see! our own wends to its trysting-place!
Then did I bound to grasp each welcome hand;
To catch the beaming looks of each young face,
A father's anxious smile, a mother's soft embrace!

"They come not now, who gave that spot its zest.
Parent and brothers, sisters, all are gone
To newer homes, far settled in the West,—
No more to walk, on holy days, this lawn.
Yet one here rests. O, most reverèd one!
Dear parent mine! Say, is thy spirit near,
To whose green mound here have I first been drawn?
Mark'st thou my sorrowing step and briny tear,
To think I loved thee not the more when thou wast here?

"That old stone church! Hid in these oaks apart,
I hoped Improvement ne'er would it invade;
But only Time, with his slow, hallowing art,
Would touch it, year by year, with softer shade,
And crack its walls no more, but, interlaid,
Mend them with moss. Its ancient sombre cast
Dearer to me is than all art displayed
In modern churches, which, by their contrast,
Make this to stand forlorn, held in the solemn Past.

"Ah, now, they tell me, they will raze it low,
And build a lowlier, neater church instead;
And well, no doubt, it is it should be so.
But me not joy it brings, but drearihead:
For still my thoughts, like fondest ivy spread,
In memory green, do clasp that old church-pile;
And round a softer, holier light is shed,
Than that through stainéd glass on chequered aisle:
Oh, must it then be torn, on me no more to smile?"

In "that old stone church" there was, for many long years, a very large congregation. Its boundaries reached six or eight miles in several directions. When the Sabbath dawned, every road and avenue might be seen thronged with those who were assembling for worship,—some on foot, some on horseback, and some in carriages. The spacious house was crowded. Even the galleries, above which "the swallow had built a nest for herself, where she might lay her young," was filled. Loud throughout the surrounding forest might be heard the praises of God. At "intermission," the people gathered together in little circles. Some wandered to the cemetery, to sigh over the departed loved ones, and drop a tear upon the sweet-briar that bloomed by their graves. Some flocked to the "spring," to quaff its sparkling waters. Others met to exchange salutations and friendly greetings. The interval past, the public service of the sanctuary was resumed, and in a little while a scene of happy confusion was to be witnessed:—the old, and middle-aged, and young, moving off to their homes, comfortable, at least, in the consciousness that, whatever other sins might be laid to their charge, they had not neglected the assembling of themselves together. Pleasant days were those at Middle Spring!

Here we cannot resist the temptation to give, somewhat at length, an admirable description of the old church, which, though written in 1847, has but recently been published, and from which we have presented an extract already.*

"Its pews of obdurate pine, straight-backed and tall—
Its gallery, mounted high three sides around—
Its pulpit, goblet-formed, half up the wall,
The sounding-board above, with acorn crowned,
And Rouse's psalms, that erst therein did sound
To old fugue tunes, to some the thoughts might raise
Of folks antique that certes there were found—
Ah no! I wote in those enchanting days,
There beauty beamed, there swelled the richest notes of praise.

"What though no dainty choir the gallery graced,
And trolled their tunes in soft, harmonious flow;

---

* Poem by Prof. W. M. Nevin:—"*The Guardian.*" May, 1852.

One pious clerk, tall formed and sober faced,
With book enclutched, stood at his desk below,
And with his pitch all people's voice did go;
If not full blent, certes in soul sincere,
Up from their hearts their praises they did throw,
Nor cared they e'en, of some deaf dame, to hear,
At close, the voice in suit, lone quavering in the rear.

"Out from that pulpit's height, deep-browed and grave,
The man of God ensconced, half bust was shown,
Weighty and wise, he did not thump nor rave,
Nor lead his folks, upwrought, to smile nor moan.
By him, slow cast, the seeds of truth were sown,
Which, lighting on good soil, took lasting hold.
Not springing eftsoons, then to wilt ere grown,
But, in long time, their fruits increased were told :
Some thirty, sixty some, and some an hundred fold.

"Ah, then, in our pew, my cousin Bess,
Happy I was downseated by thy side,
With youngsters more, in middle stowed, the less,
Where, sex from sex, we did our kin divide.
High boarded up no face without we spied,
Save of his Reverence high, or some ybent
Out o'er the balustrade of gallery wide.
Thus were our minds from vanities safe pent,
And kept the text, I wote, and each commandement.

"And when, through summers, thou hadst tall up grown,
Above that pew did peer thy witching grace,
Like some red rose out o'er its wall, full blown,
Is seen abroad, unweeting of its case.
And thy full voice, within that holy place,
Was heard all others through, richest, I ween;
And not a daintier foot nor lovelier face,
When all out came the service times between,
Nor on this shaded knoll nor by yon spring was seen.

"Nurtured thou wast hard by yon mountain's height,
Which now the distance does in azure steep;
Whose base with laurels, moss, and fern is dight,
Where through its gap the gladsome waters leap.
The scene there doth its verdure ever keep;
And with its joys was thy young spirit stirred;
And thy dark eye mirrored its beauty deep;
And in its glens thy mellow voice was heard,
Sweeter than dash of stream or song of mountain bird.

"Ah, can it be that slumbering thou art laid,
Hard by this high, in yon low burial plot,
In quiet bed trimmed by the sexton's spade,
With grass o'ergrown, and violets thither brought
By hands bereaved! Yes, sorrow deep was wrought,
And still for thee is felt a lasting gloom;
For just when thy rich heart and sprightliest thought
Were shedding us, like rose, their prime perfume,
Then snapped, thou sudden fell'st into that early tomb!

"In this high burial-ground, in that below,
No massive structure stands of sculptured stone;
No column's shaft, off broke, that it might show
Youth's vigour downwards all untimely thrown.
But humble slabs and headstones many strown,
Simply the names and years and worth avow
Of those here laid. 'Tis well. They covet none.
In life they were plain men of honest brow,
They sought no honours then, nor do they seek them now.

"Here were they gathered every good Lord's day,
From town, from hamlet, and from country wide,
In pleasant groups, but meek and staid alway,
They showed not often levity nor pride;
Yet sooth in some gay maids some pranks were spied,
Misled by dress and spirits over light,
Out by yon firs, with beaux convened aside,

They laughed and joked; yes, some did shrill outright!
And that it was God's day they had forgotten quite.

"But these were few: and for that breach, I wote,
At home their mothers did them well aread.
Others all o'er this place in solemn thought,
Stood lone, or spoke with sanctimonious heed.
Yet this to take full many had no need,
For they were grave in grain. Who would might scan,
Still were they upright found in word and deed.
They knew, but most they felt, the gospel plan,
And loved their God supreme, and next their fellow-man.

"Blest sight it was to mark that godly flock,
At intermission, grouped throughout this wood.
Each log, each bench, each family upping-block,
Some granddame held amidst her gathered brood.
Here cakes were shared, and fruits, and counsel good;
Devoutly spoken 'twas of crops and rain;
Hard by the church the broad-brimmed elders stood,
While o'er that slope did flow a constant train
Of bevies, springward bound, or coming back again.

"Ah! luckless wight, whom gallantry did press,
Fast by that spring, to stoop him often low,
And serve, with cup up-dipped, and bland address,
The gathered fair, whose multitude did grow!
One whom he most affects, and did bestow
Her first the cup, hath drunk, and off does walk;
Her then to follow fain he must forego,—
With some far happier swain he marks her talk,
While he must stoop, and grin, and water all the flock.

"Here too, like me, some lonesome wight of yore
Did stand apart, and these memorials scan,
And blighted hopes and buried loves deplore,
And feel, in sooth, how frail a thing is man.

Hither the widow came, weeping and wan,
To muse on him of late her joy and pride.
Ah! now no more she mourns the solemn ban
Which did her then from her loved spouse divide—
Now does she sleep herself all sweetly by his side.

"These ask no ponderous tombs, yet sooth to tell,
Above doth lie the turf, too bleak and bare;
For they did love their homes and country well,
And still of these fresh garlands they should share.
Here should the rose its ruddiest clusters wear,
The willow droop, the cedar winters brave;—
But, ah! few hands are left for this to care.
So mote the briar spring, and o'er each grave
Spread out its vernal blossoms. This they seem to crave."

That the congregation of Middle Spring is not now as large as formerly, is well known. Germans have settled in the region from which it once derived its numerical strength, and consequently have limited the Presbyterian population from which accessions might be expected. Other congregations, too, have sprung up in the neighbourhood, which have served to weaken the old one from which they proceeded. We regard it as one of the evils of the times, that congregations have, in late years, been so much multiplied; for, to say nothing of the fact that attendance upon public worship has not increased by being rendered more convenient, it is undeniable that, in this way, venerable and vigorous churches have had their strength and influence seriously impaired, whilst the new organizations erected around them, have also, in most instances, been doomed to a feeble and embarrassed existence. Such a course, however, was pursued in regard to Middle Spring, and it certainly has not contributed to its prosperity. The present members of the Session of the Church are as follows: Joseph M. Means, Abraham S. McKinney, David S. Runsha, Robert S. McCune, James Kelso, Robert McCune, and Samuel Wherry.

## CHAPTER III.

### BIG SPRING CHURCH.

AMONG the primitive Presbyterian ministers of Pennsylvania, were several of the name *Craighead*. One of these, whose Christian name is not given on the Records of Presbytery, was installed as pastor of the congregation of Pequea, in Lancaster County, in 1733. Another (Alexander) settled at Middle Octarara, in the same county, about the same time. The name of a third (Thomas) appears on the Presbyterial Records in 1735. These last two gentlemen were the first preachers of the Gospel in the regions beyond the Susquehanna. In 1734 the former was appointed by the Presbytery to "supply over the river." The year following, "a supplication from the settlement over the river desiring supplies," he was again appointed to act in the same capacity. In the same year, Mr. Thomas Craighead was sent to "supply the people of Conodoguinot." This gentleman was a cousin of Mr. John Craighead, who settled at an early date on Yellow Breeches Creek, near Carlisle, and who was the father of the Rev. Mr. Craighead, afterwards pastor of the church at Rocky Spring.

The Rev. Thomas Craighead was the first pastor of Big Spring Congregation, or Hopewell, as it was then called. He entered into this relation with it in 1738. In regard to his salary, it is only recorded that, "A list of subscriptions being produced, the commissioners agreed that Mr. Craighead shall have the benefit of all future subscriptions." Previously to this settlement, it would seem that Mr. C. was stated supply at Carlisle and Silvers' Spring (or Upper and Lower Pennsborough); for in 1738 it was ordered by Presbytery, "that the two Societies in Pennsburg pay to Mr. Craighead the two-thirds of sixteen pounds, for the half year that he was appointed to supply there, and that the people of Mr. Craighead's congregation make up the other third."

About the time of Mr. Craighead's settlement at Hopewell, there was some difficulty existing between that congregation and the one at Upper Pennsborough, in relation to the proposed erection of a meeting-house by the former. The nature and issue of this difficulty, the subjoined extracts from the Presbyterial Records will serve, in some degree, to explain.

June 22d, 1737. "A supplication from the people of Hopewell being presented, requesting the concurrence of Presbytery to draw a call to Mr. Thomas Craighead, the Presbytery, finding some inconvenience in reference to the situation of one of their houses, don't see cause to concur with them at present, but do appoint Mr. Black to supply at Pennsboro' on the last Sabbath of July, and on the week following to convene that people and the people of Hopewell, at James McFarlan's, in order to inquire if Pennsboro' will agree that Hopewell build a meeting-house at Great Spring, — and make a report thereof at our next."

Aug. 31, 1737. "Mr. Black reports that he supplied at Pennsboro', and convened the people and those of Hopewell on the Monday following, and heard them confer about the meeting-house proposed to be built at Great Spring, but the parties did not agree about the same."

Subsequently, "Presbytery voted, by a great majority, not to alter the bounds of the congregation of Pennsboro'," and "disapproved the people of Hopewell building a meeting-house just on the border of Pennsborough congregation."

Mr. Craighead, though called in 1737, was not installed until October, 1738. This service was conducted by the Rev. Alexander Craighead, an "edict," by order of Presbytery, having been sent "to be published timeously before." Mr. Craighead died in June of the ensuing year. In relation to this event, Thomas Craighead, Jr., of Whitehill, Cumberland County, has thus written in a letter, dated Dec. 16, 1845, and published in Mr. I. D. Rupp's "History of Dauphin, Cumberland, Perry, Bedford, Adams, and Franklin Counties:"

"At Big Spring, protracted meetings were held for public worship. So powerful, it is said, were the influences of the Spirit, that the worshippers felt loth, even after having exhausted their stores of provision, to disperse. I have heard it from the lips of those present, when Thomas Craighead delivered one of the parting discourses, that his flow of eloquence seemed supernatural,—he continued in bursts of eloquence, while his audience was melted to tears; himself, however, exhausted, hurried to pronounce the blessing, waving his hand,—and as he pronounced the words, Farewell, farewell! he sank down, and expired without a groan or struggle. His remains rest where the church now stands, the only monument of his memory."

After Mr. Craighead's demise, Mr. James Lyon, of Ireland (and, at the time of his invitation, under the care of the Presbytery of New Castle), supplied the pulpit at Hopewell for some months. After his term of service had expired, Big Spring was connected with Rocky Spring and Middle Spring, as a charge. We learn this from the sessional records of the last-mentioned congregation, which state (1742) that "the minister and elders of Big Spring, Middle Spring, and Rocky Spring, met at Middle Spring, in order to settle the division of the minister's labours among the three congregations." The arrangement agreed upon at this meeting was "that the minister's labours be equally divided in a third part to each place, as being most for the glory of God and good of his people." It was also, "upon the motion of the elders of Big Spring, left to them, the people, and *Mr. Blair*, to converse among themselves in respect to the subscriptions of the Big Spring Congregation." How long Mr. Blair sustained the pastoral relation to these three congregations we have no means of determining.

The next point at which it is possible to write with any confidence of the regular occupancy of the pulpit at Big Spring, is 1759. In that year the Rev. George Duffield was installed over Carlisle and Big Spring. According to the terms of his call, one-third of his time was to be given to Big Spring, and two-thirds to Carlisle. In 1761, an effort was made by the former congregation to obtain the half of Mr. Duffield's labours; but this effort was not sanctioned, for reasons which were regarded as satisfactory by Presbytery, and among which was an apprehension that Mr. Duffield's constitution would not be able to endure, any length of time, the fatigue of being the one-half of his time at Big Spring.

Mr. Duffield's successor at Big Spring was the Rev. William Linn. The congregation at this time seems to have increased sufficiently to justify them in securing the time and labour of a pastor for themselves alone. When, precisely, Mr. Linn was called to this pastorate, cannot be ascertained; for it was registered in that portion of the Records of Presbytery which cannot be found. It was, however, there is strong reason to believe, before the year 1778. In 1784, Mr. Linn applied to Presbytery to have his relation to the congregation dissolved, in order that he might accept the Presidency of Washington Academy, in Somerset County, Maryland; and his request was granted.

After being two years vacant, the church at Big Spring found a pastor in the Rev. Samuel Wilson, who continued with them until he was removed by death, in March, 1799. There is yet in the possession of Mrs. Doctor Sharp, of Newville,—who is the only surviving child of the Rev. Mr. Wilson,—the call which was given to her father. This is rather an interesting document in several respects; and therefore we cheerfully comply with the request of several members of the congregation, communicated by a venerable member of the Session, that it be published in our volume.*

In 1801, the Rev. Joshua Williams was called to Big Spring. His installation took place April 14th, 1802. On that occasion Dr. Davidson delivered a discourse from Acts xx. 27, and Dr. Cooper delivered a charge. The salary promised was "two hundred pounds annually." Dr. Williams died on the 21st of August, 1838, at his residence in Westpennsborough Township.

The following extracts from two obituaries of him which were published will serve to give some idea of his history and character. We most sincerely regret that we have not been able to furnish an equally full and satisfactory account of his worthy predecessors.

* See Appendix I.

"Dr. Williams had not the advantage of entering at an early age on a course of studies preparatory to the ministry. He was graduated at Dickinson College, in the year 1795, then under the presidency of Dr. Nesbit. His theological studies were pursued chiefly under the direction of Dr. Robert Cooper. In the year 1798, in the thirtieth year of his age, he was licensed to preach the Gospel by the Presbytery of Carlisle. The year following, he received a call from the United Congregations of Derry and Paxton, which he accepted, and was ordained to the work of the ministry, and installed pastor of said charge, by the Presbytery of Carlisle, in the autumn of the same year. After having served the people of this, his first charge, for about four years, he received a call from the Presbyterian Church at Big Spring, left vacant by the death of the Rev. Samuel Wilson, which he judged it to be his duty to accept; and accordingly he gave up the charge of his former congregations, and was installed pastor of the latter in the year 1802. Under the labours of a prolonged pastorate, his general health declined, and a complication of infirmities reduced his physical strength. His nervous system, especially, became disordered, and as a consequence, he often suffered great mental depression. A year or two previous to his release from his pastoral charge, under the impression that he was unable to perform, as they should be done, the duties of a pastor, he proposed resigning his charge. But the congregation earnestly remonstrated against his doing so, and assured him of their being well satisfied with such services as his feeble state of health permitted him to render. About the year 1829, at his earnest request, the pastoral relation between him and the congregation of Big Spring was dissolved. From the day of his installation till his resignation, he lived and laboured among his people with uninterrupted harmony and growing interest.

"After retiring from his pastoral charge, Dr. Williams did not at all abandon the duties of his office as a minister of the Gospel, but continued, as his health permitted and opportunity was afforded, serving vacant congregations in the bounds of the Presbytery, and frequently assisting his brethren on special occasions. In these labours of love he seemed to take great interest, often crossing mountains and riding to a distance into neighbouring counties, to preach the Gospel to the destitute. Dr. Williams's last illness was only of about four days' continuance. He had at various times expressed his fears of the dying struggle; but in his own case death seemed wholly disarmed of all his terrors. His end was peaceful, without a disturbed feature. On the morning of the 21st of August, 1838, he seemed literally to fall asleep in Jesus. The next day a very large concourse of persons (most of whom had been formerly the people of his charge), together with eight or ten ministers, attended the funeral, and testified their very great regard for him, whom they had so much reason to love and to venerate. His remains were deposited in the Big Spring Churchyard, nearly in view from the sacred desk where he had so long preached to that people the Gospel of God, which brings life and immortality to light.

"In the death of Dr. Williams, the Church lost an able and faithful advocate of the truth. His retired situation and unobtrusive disposition were, no doubt, the occasion of his being less publicly known than he justly merited. His talents and attainments as a minister of the Gospel were such as always to command the highest respect from all who knew him. He was naturally possessed of strong and vigorous intellectual powers. His judgment was sound and discriminating. He had a remarkable taste and aptitude for metaphysical discussions, which, however, never seem to have led him into erroneous speculations on the doctrines of religion.

"As a steward of the mysteries of God, Dr. Williams was well instructed, and furnished for every good work, above most others in the sacred office. His mind was richly stored with theological knowledge: with every part of Scripture he seemed familiar, and could quote any passage to which he wished to refer, with great readiness and accuracy. He employed much of his time in reading instructive authors, and always with a view to the furnishing of his mind the more thoroughly, for the duties of his office, and for his own personal edification.

"As a preacher of the Gospel, Dr. W. was grave

and solemn in his manner, and highly instructive in his discourses. His usual method in his sermons was to explain his text, if it needed explanation, then state the subject, or doctrine illustrated, and confirm this by Scripture and argument. And to make the truth bear upon the hearts of his audience, his first object was to instruct, then to persuade; believing that truth is in order to righteousness, and that there can be no correct Christian practice, till the mind be enlightened, and the heart sanctified through the truth of the Word of God.

"In his manners and conversation, this excellent man was courteous and affable, yet always dignified. He was truly a lover of hospitality. It gave him great pleasure to have his brethren in the ministry visit him. Nor were such occasions suffered to pass without improvement. Very few men, we are assured, ever possessed, in the same degree with Dr. W., the happy faculty of communicating solid instruction in social conversations. Some useful subject was always introduced, and discussed in such a manner as to be at once interesting and instructive. The great doctrines of the Cross, which he professed to believe, and which he preached, were not held by him as mere theoretical subjects, without a salutary and practical influence on his own heart. It was seldom, except to very intimate friends, that he would freely unfold his religious experience, but then it was manifest that his mind was deeply imbued with the precious truths of the Gospel, that he had felt intensely the power of that Word of God which he preached to others. But he has fought a good fight; he has finished his course, he has kept the faith, and now we confidently trust he is in possession of that Crown of Righteousness which the Lord, the righteous Judge, will give to all them that love his appearing."

Soon after the withdrawment of Dr. Williams from the church at Big Spring (1830), the Rev. Robert McCachren, a native of Chester County, and a licentiate of the Presbytery of Newcastle, was called to be its pastor. This call he accepted, and in this relation he continued until it was resigned in October, 1851. Mr. McCachren's labours among that people were not without encouraging success. The number of members added to the congregation during his connexion with it, was four hundred and eighty-five. During the second year of his ministry the church was favoured with a season of the revival of religion, which resulted in an accession of seventy-three to the list of communicants. Some of the precious fruits of that awakening remain there to this day. Mr. McCachren since his resignation has not accepted of another charge, but still resides in Newville, and has the supervision of a classical academy of that place.

From him we have learned that the earliest elders of Big Spring, now known, were, John Carson, John McKeehan, John Bell, David Ralston, Sr., Thomas Jacobs, Alexander Thompson, William Lindsay, Atcheson Laughlin, all of whom served under the ministry of the Rev. Samuel Wilson, and some of them part of the time of his successor. The session at present consists of the following members: Robert McElwain, William Ker, Samuel Davidson, James McIlhenny, William Green, James Fulton, Samuel McKeehan.

It is with Newville, as with other localities in Cumberland Valley—in gazing upon it the mind is filled with amazement at the mighty change which has taken place. The time is almost within the memory of some who live, when the dark shadows of the gloomy forest fell upon all that region, and the savage Indian roamed over the surrounding hills and valleys; but now the eye is there called to survey a thriving village in which there are three churches for the worship of God, the circumjacent country highly cultivated and thickly inhabited, with a moral and religious population, the rushing railcar bearing the traveller along with dizzying speed, and the quiet magnetic wires annihilating both time and space with the electric celerity of their communication.

The first church erected at Big Spring, stood in the graveyard now in use by the congregation, within a few rods of the present building, and was erected about the year 1738. From all the information we can obtain in regard to it, it was a plain log building, such as we have described as being the first places of worship for several of the surrounding congregations, and like them it had a "study" attached to it. It seems to have been the opinion of our fathers that the minister of the sanctuary, should have some place near to it, from which, at least, he could come forth into the pulpit with his mind undistracted by conversation with the members of his flock, and his heart elevated by its communing with heaven. And we are free to acknowledge that we have no disposition to differ from this idea. Surely such an arrangement much better comports with the sacredness and effectiveness of the service to be performed, than does that which now so generally prevails.

At what time precisely the present edifice at Big Spring was erected, we are not able to say, but it was in all probability during the early part of the ministry of the Rev. Mr. Wilson. Until the year 1842, it was a plain stone building, having three doors, with the pulpit on the north side, and pews with high straight backs, and, on the whole, indicating far more regard for the essential than the comfortable and the ornamental; but at that time it was remodelled in modern style, and now ranks with the handsomest churches in the Presbytery. It is capable of accommodating about six hundred persons. The site which it occupies, a few rods northward from the town, is a most eligible one, and from it there is a beautiful view of the surrounding neighbourhood. Back of it, at a short distance, rolls gently along the clear and lovely stream from which it has received its name, and which for ages has been flowing on, apparently the same, whilst the crowds that have weekly been gathering on its brink, have, one after another, lain down within the sound of its murmurs, to sleep the sleep that knows no waking till the resurrection trumpet shall utter its voice.

Let us now take a view of the burial-place at Big Spring. A graveyard is always a solemn and interesting spot, whether we find it in the heart of a bustling and noisy city, where the present too much overpowers both the past and the future, or in the deep bosom of the country, where unbroken stillness reigns around, subduing the heart for the touching but wholesome lesson which it ought to learn, as the eye is fixed upon the resting-place of the dead. "While we cannot," says one, "subscribe to the doctrine of Chateaubriand, that the existence of graveyards, and our veneration for tombs, are convincing arguments for the truth of Christianity, we own that the influence emanating from the place of sepulture is by no means small; that the solemn shades of the burial-ground are congenial with a certain class of emotions which are natural to the human breast, and that there are voices thence which speak in impressive tones, for they seem to come from the very borders of the spirit-land. Hence the interest which some minds take in consecrated grounds, in God's acre, as the burial-place has been sententiously termed. Of those who have committed a friend to the last repose, there are few indeed who have not a secret sympathy for the spirit of the place." Many, very many there are who have "committed a friend" to the cemetery at Big Spring; for its enclosure, though large, is well filled with graves, and many more, doubtless, have been buried there, the visible evidence of whose sepulture has, under the wasting influence of time, entirely disappeared. Among the many graves which specially interested us in a brief visit to this consecrated spot, we have only space to refer to those of the two former pastors of the Church, the Rev. Mr. Wilson and the Rev. Dr. Williams, over each of which there is a befitting marble slab. It may be pardonable, perhaps, for us to add, that a peculiar solemnity fell upon our spirit, as the inscription, "In memory of Paul Pierce, who departed this life, June 7th, 1794, aged 78 years," reminded us of a great-grandfather, who sleeps in the tomb by the side of which we stood.

On the whole, we would say, that the graveyard of the congregation of Big Spring, is kept in such a condition as reflects credit upon those who have charge of it. The time has happily passed away in which burial-places were too generally regarded with great indifference, except to protect them from the depredations of prowling animals; and now it is gratifying to every person of good taste and correct feelings, to find in every direction, instead of tall, luxuriant grass, and crumbling tombstones, and sinking graves, cemeteries so neatly kept as at once to indicate the affection that is cherished for the mortal remains which they contain, and to make them attractive as places of profitable meditation.

# CHAPTER IV.

## CHURCH AT SILVERS' SPRING.

THE church at Silvers' Spring was first known as "the people over the Susquehanna." Afterwards (1736), as connected with the congregation at Carlisle (then called, as it would seem, the "Congregation of Conodoguinett,") it was known as the "Lower part of the settlement of Conodoguinett." Still later (1739), we find it designated as "Lower Pennsborough." The name which it now bears was received at an early date, and is to be accounted for by the fact, that the land around the stream near which the church edifice stands, was originally owned by Mr. Silvers, one of the first settlers in that region of country.

The gospel was first preached to this congregation by the Rev. Alexander Craighead, by appointment of Presbytery, in 1734, and for several years following they were supplied occasionally by the Rev. Messrs. Bartram, Thomas Craighead, Golston, and Thompson.

In the year 1739, the Rev. Samuel Thompson was installed as pastor of this church, in connexion with the church at Carlisle (or "Pennsborough," as it was then called), as the following extract from the records of Presbytery will show.

"Pennsboro', Nov. 14th, 1739.

"Mr. Anderson, at the meeting-house door, gave publick advertisement that if any could advance any lawful objection against Mr. Samuel Thompson being set apart to the work of the holy ministry, to both societies in this place, and no objection appearing, Mr. Craighead delivered a sermon from Ezek. 33, 6, and presided in the work of ordination. Accordingly, Mr. Samuel Thompson was set apart to the work of the sacred ministry by the imposition of hands, &c."

Previously to this time, Mr. Thompson seems to have laboured for a season among "the people of Conococheague," for at the next meeting of the Presbytery after the installation just referred to, "Richard O. Cahan, Joseph Armstrong, Benjamin Chambers, and Patrick Jack, publicly engaged to pay to Mr. Samuel Thompson the sum of one pound five shillings, at or before next meeting of Presbytery, as being the whole of arrears due him by the people of Canigagig." It is highly probable, also, that he officiated for some time at Pennsborough before he became pastor. This, the following extract from the Presbyterial records, before his installation at that place is noticed, will serve to show, as well as give some idea of the spirit of the times.

"The Synod, last May, having received and read a letter directed to one Alexander McKee, subscribed by Mr. Samuel Thompson, containing some things which were very offensive to the Honourable Proprietor, the Synod also have condemned said letter, and remitted the further consideration thereof, and what censure should be inflicted upon Mr. Thompson on account of writing said letter, to this Presbytery. Mr. Thompson being now present, the Presbytery took the affaire into consideration, and accordingly, Mr. Thompson being called in, with several of the People of Pennsboro', he also giving a short narrative of the Matter, did acknowledge his imprudence and inadvertency in writing said letter, tho' it was designed to signify not his own thoughts, but the thoughts of the People, and expecting that the said letter would never go any further than Alex. McKee, to whom it was directed. Commissioners also from the People of Pennsboro' gave in a supplication, wherein they took the whole blame of said letter on themselves, and declared they were provoked thereunto by their being credibly informed that some in authority had threatened to order a constable to pull Mr. Thompson out of the pulpit on the Sabbath-day, and drag him at an horsetail to Newtown. The Presbytery ordered that the Minutes of Synod be read, and finding that neither Mr. Thompson's letter nor the Synod's order in relation thereunto, are come to our hands, the Presbytery conclude that at present we can go no further than only accept of Mr. Thompson's acknowledgment which he hath already made, and sharply reprove said people for constraining him to write said letter. This conclusion unanimously agreed to, and Mr. Anderson appointed to rebuke said people."

On account of "bodily weakness," Mr. Thompson was, at his own request, dismissed from "Lower Pennsborough," in the year 1745, the Presbytery at the same time "recommending to him to be generous and industrious in preaching to the congregation, either on Sabbath-days or week-days, according to his conveniency and their necessity." In 1747, "for several reasons, but chiefly because of unhappy jealousies, on account of which he doubted he could not be farther useful in the congregation," he sought a dismission from "Upper Pennsborough," and in his desire the people, by their representatives, concurred.

After leaving this charge, Mr. Thompson settled at "Great Conewago," where he laboured until 1779, when, "on account of his infirmities by old age, which disqualified him for performing the duties of a pastor to his people," he requested Presbytery to dissolve the relation between them. In this request the congregation acquiesced, and it was granted. This acquiescence, however, was not that cold and thankless one which too often is signified when an aged servant of the Lord, who has laboured among a people for many years,—perhaps the greater part of his life,—watching over their spiritual interests with deep concern and earnest effort, and all the time receiving a bare subsistence for himself and family, has at length, with worn-out powers, to retire from his post, and is permitted to do so without any provision by his flock for his future maintenance and comfort. The people of "Great Conewago," to their credit be it known,—if credit can be awarded where only duty is done,—"afforded a gratuity for the support of Mr. Thompson, to his satisfaction."

And thus, we have not the least hesitation in saying, it ought in every case to be. There is no class of men who, in view of the expense connected with their education, and the frequent demands upon their liberality, and the amount of their labours, are so meagerly compensated as the ministers of the gospel; and therefore, though it is true that they are to look for their reward in the world above, and ought to guard against every temptation to feel "at home in the body," yet is it at the same time a sad reproach to any congregation, and sorry evidence that God's word has wrought in them as it ought, that, when a pastor's tears for long years have fallen for them, and his prayers ascended in their behalf, and theirs have been his friendly counsels and indefatigable toils, he is, under the decrepitude of a life soon to end, cast off with indifference, to suffer, perhaps, from want, which he has too much delicacy to make known, and to die with the prospect of destitution for his family, and with an exhibition of ingratitude, in the very scene of his loved labours.

In relation to this subject, we avail ourselves of an extract from an editorial article in "The Presbyterian" of July 17th, 1852, which refers to the Corporation for the "relief of poor and distressed

Presbyterian ministers, and of the poor and distressed widows and children of Presbyterian ministers." This article, which is exactly suited to our purpose, came under our notice after our views of the neglect of the duty in question had been penned.

"The Corporation offers to secure to applicants, 1. A stipulated *annuity*, payable to the widow or children of a minister after his death; 2. A stipulated *sum*, payable to the legal representatives of a minister on his decease; and, 3. A stipulated annuity for a minister in the decline of his life, to commence either at 60 or 65 years of age.

"The various provisions offered may be secured in either of four ways. 1. By the payment of a sum of money *at one time*. 2. By the payment of an *annual* premium on the 22d of May, during the life of the minister. 3. By the deposit of such a sum as, if put to interest at 5 per cent., would annually produce the amount of the annual premium, the deposit to remain during the minister's life. 4. By the deposit of a similar sum, to remain for ever in the hands of the Corporation, for the benefit of *a succession of ministers.*

"Many ministers who would not be able to deposit at one time the amount necessary to secure the payment of an annuity, might perhaps save enough to pay the annual premium. But a far better way, in most cases, would be for churches and congregations to take upon themselves the expense of such a provision for their pastor's family. A deposit might be made, which would entitle every successive pastor, of the church making it, to share its benefits, or the amount necessary to meet the annual premium could easily be raised by any energetic person in the congregation who would undertake it. Such evidences of affection by a congregation for their minister could not but have a happy effect.

"The late venerable Dr. Alexander, in a letter written near the close of his life, made some valuable suggestions on this subject. With regard to securing the provision payable after the minister's death, he says: 'Some two or three of the most active ladies in the congregation should be engaged to raise, annually, small subscriptions from females, sufficient to pay the annual premium, or if they preferred to raise a sum equal in value to the annual payment, this should be encouraged as less troublesome, and as safer for the Corporation.' The sum necessary to secure a deferred annuity to the minister himself, in advanced age, he suggests, should engage the attention of the young men."

We may add that the conditions of the Corporation have been so extended, as to include not only New and Old School Presbyterians, but the German Reformed, Reformed Dutch, Associate Reformed, Associate and Reformed Presbyterian, or Cumberland denominations.

To resume our narrative: In the year 1745, the Rev. Samuel Caven was called to "Lower Pennsborough," and continued to be its pastor, until his death, which took place, as the inscription on his gravestone in that burial-ground shows, Nov. 9th, 1750, in the 49th year of his age.

In April, 1764, the congregations of Carlisle and East Pennsborough united in a call to the Rev. John Steel, agreeing to enjoy each an equal proportion of his labours, and promising him £150 annually for his support. This call has been kindly placed in our hands by Mrs. Givin, a granddaughter of Mr. Steel, who is still living in Papertown, Cumberland County, at the advanced age of seventy-five years. In the letter in which it was forwarded to us, and which was written by her son, it is stated that Mr. Steel's papers were destroyed by fire many years ago. From the call, which we publish as interesting for its antiquity, it will be seen by those who are familiar with the locality from which it came, that many of the descendants of its signers still reside where their fathers did.* Mr. Steel died in August, 1779. Three years afterwards, "a call from the united congregations of East Pennsborough and Monaghan was presented to Mr. Samuel Waugh, together with bonds for the annual salary of one hundred and fifty pounds, and also for a gratuity of seventy-five pounds from each congregation, that from East Pennsborough to be paid in one month after his instalment, and that from Monaghan, within three years." This call was accepted by Mr. Waugh, and he continued to be pastor of the charge until his death in January, 1807. The following brief but comprehensive delineation of his

* See Appendix II.

character, by Judge Clendenin, we are happy to insert: "Mr. Waugh was a sound divine, a very acceptable preacher, and highly esteemed by his people. After I became a member of his church, I was intimately acquainted with him, and as far as my acquaintance extended, I can say of him that he was an Israelite in whom was no guile."

We also give with pleasure the subjoined extracts from a letter, in relation to Mr. Waugh, with which we have been favoured by his daughter, Mrs. Eliza W. Burd, now a resident of Bedford, Pa.

"My father was a native of Carrol's Tract, in Adams County. On April 14th, 1783, he was joined in marriage with Miss Eliza Hoge, daughter of David Hoge, Esq., a highly respectable and influential man, from whom the place called Hogestown, within one mile of Silvers' Spring Church, derived its name, years before it became a village, by reason of the fact that he and his connexions resided there, as proprietors of a large body of land. He accepted the pastorate of the congregation in 1782."

"The Lower Settlement, as it was then called, was emphatically a settlement of substantial people, who required preaching in the English language, and according to the Presbyterian form and faith. The sects which now exist in that region were unheard of at that time. A German Reformed Church, which I think still stands at Trindle's Spring, and in which there was preaching in German, was the only place of worship in all that region, out of the Presbyterian communion. At Harrisburg, my impression is, there was no settled minister for a long time, or if there was, the Susquehanna was in the way, which it was not at all times safe to cross in ferry-boats, so that from Middlesex, within three miles of Carlisle, to several miles below Harrisburg, the people attended at Silvers' Spring, as they did, also, from an equal distance north and south.

"I can in truth say, and it is but justice to do so, that my father was a very amiable and sensible man. He moved amongst the people as a father in his family, and from his mild and prudent course had great influence. In the training of his family he was very faithful, teaching us the great rule and aim of life, making us familiar with the doctrinal standards of the Church, requiring the rigid observance of the Sabbath, and giving force to all his counsels and efforts, by his unostentatious, steady, upright daily walk and his daily prayer.

"As to his pastoral labours, Silvers' Spring and Monaghan (now Dillsburg) had an equal portion of them. System and punctuality were with him cardinal points. Never did he once disappoint the people, for any cause, within my recollection. In season and out of season he met his engagements. His custom was to catechise at regular periods, throughout his charge, and not the children only, but also the heads of families—households. This was done by announcing from the pulpit certain days in the week, to meet those of a particular district, at a place named, and so he continued from week to week until the whole congregation was visited, and instructed in a pastoral way. His house was ever open to the visitation of his people, and on communion seasons four days were always set apart for religious services, during which the aged, or infirm, or distant members of the congregation, were his guests, according to their pleasure.

"My father's last sickness, which was from pleurisy, was but of six days' continuance. He was not well on Monday; on Thursday he married a couple in his own room, and on Saturday morning he died. A little while before he breathed his last (my brother Samuel having been sent for the physician, and not yet returned), he had his other children brought to his bedside, of whom my sister and myself were the oldest present. He looked upon us all, and said, "My poor girls!"—paused, and then asked, "What is the chief end of man?" This question I answered, in the words of my catechism, "To glorify God, and enjoy him for ever." After this, not another word was spoken by him; he closed his eyes, and soon calmly and peacefully expired. At the time, I did not feel that much had been said to me as I stood by the bedside of a dying father, as I had so often been asked, and answered that question before. Very different, however, has been my view, under a riper judgment and experience. A volume could not have embodied more. In no way could the momentous consequence of that weighty question have been presented, so as to secure for it a more abiding remembrance and a deeper lodgment in the soul."

The Rev. John Hayes* was Mr. Waugh's successor in the charge vacated by his decease. This connexion was formed in 1808, and dissolved by resignation in 1814.

After Mr. Hayes's resignation, the Rev. Henry R. Wilson became pastor of the church at Silvers' Spring, with the promise of a salary of $700, and made this the field of his labour until his acceptance of the call of the congregation in Shippensburg, in 1823.

The Rev. James Williamson, who followed Mr. Wilson in this relation, in 1824, resigned it in 1838.

We are thus brought down to the time of the settlement of the present pastor, the Rev. George Morris. Mr. Morris, who was "a foreign licentiate, under the care of the Presbytery of Philadelphia," was called and installed in 1839.

The present church at Silvers' Spring, which is a substantial stone building, 58 by 45 feet, was erected in the year 1783, during the incumbency of the Rev. Mr. Waugh. The warrant for the land on which it stands was granted in 1770. The congregation was incorporated by an act of Assembly, September 25th, 1786, and the Trustees named in that act of incorporation are,—Andrew Galbreath, Samuel Wallace, Daniel Boyd, John Wather, Hugh Laird, Samuel Waugh, William Mateer, Francis Silvers, and David

* For some time a Professor in Dickinson College.

Hoge. A neat and comfortable parsonage has recently been erected by the congregation.

The church edifice which preceded the present one, and which was the first meeting-house at Silvers' Spring, was, we have been informed by one who learned it from his grand-parents, a small log building, near the place where the present house stands. No record of the building of that house, or of the organization of a church in it, can be found; and, as the members of the congregation at that time are, of course, all dead and gone, it is impossible to tell with certainty when these things were done. It is, however, far more than probable, from the facts which we have already given, and from the following epitaphs, which are to be found in the cemetery, that the old log building, in which the first settlers in what is now the eastern part of Cumberland County, with its beautiful landscapes and thriving villages, assembled for the worship of God, was erected about one hundred and twenty years ago. These epitaphs we have copied from Mr. Rupp's History:—

"In memory of the Rev. Mr. Samuel Caven, who departed this life, Nov. 9, 1750, aged 49 years."

"In memory of James Wood, who departed this life, Feb. 24th, 1750, aged 41 years."

"Here lies the body of John Hamilton, who departed this life, Dec. 29th, 1747, aged 47 years."

"Here lies the body of William MacMean, who departed this life in the year 1747, aged 35 years."

We may add that these first settlers of that region

were nearly all Scotch and Scotch-Irish. "Cumberland," says Mr. Rupp, "was exclusively settled by Scotch and Scotch-Irish, with the exception of a few English. The Germans did not begin to immigrate into the lower part of the county till about 1760 or '62."

The Session of the church at Silvers' Spring, as at present constituted, consists of John Mateer, Francis Eckels, and Robert G. Young.

# CHAPTER V.

## CHURCH IN MERCERSBURG.

BY THE REV. THOMAS CREIGH.

[In November, 1851, the Rev. Mr. Creigh preached his twentieth anniversary sermon as pastor of this church. This sermon, which gave so much satisfaction to the congregation as to lead to its publication by them, has been, at our request, expanded by its respected author into the following interesting and comprehensive form, and is, with his kind permission, turned to its present use.—A. N.]

---

### PERIOD I.

FROM THE ORGANIZATION OF THE CHURCH, A. D. 1738, TO THE SETTLEMENT OF THE REV. JOHN KING, D.D., AS PASTOR, A. D. 1769.

It is a matter of sincere and deep regret that the history of the Presbyterian Church in this place had not been undertaken years ago, when the materials for its early history were more abundant than they are at the present time. From this neglect, many things connected with its early history, with which it would be interesting to be acquainted, have entirely passed away, so that it is impossible to recover them ; or the tradition by which they have been handed down, has become so vague and uncertain, that unhesitating confidence cannot be reposed in them. Discrimination has therefore been exercised in selecting from all the available sources within my reach, those facts which are supported by the best proof; and they are now collected together and arranged in the order of their occurrence.

This part of Pennsylvania began to be settled about the year, A. D. 1736, the land being taken from the proprietors by those who intended to occupy it. The inhabitants were generally Scotch-Irish, and in their 'fatherland' belonged to the Presbyterian Church. Among the first objects which claimed their attention in this their new home—among the labours and privations of a new and uncultivated country—was the organization of a Church according to the faith of their fathers. This took place, A. D. 1738, and was styled, Upper West Conococheague. And so extensive was the territory which it covered, that it embraced all the region which is now occupied by the congregations of Welsh Run, Loudon, and St. Thomas,—about fourteen miles square, or an area of nearly two hundred miles. At this early period there were but few of any other denomination of Christians in this large field. The Presbyterian Church was predominant. Its members were the first and almost the sole possessors of the soil.

Scattered over so great an extent of country, it is

not surprising that a diversity of opinion should have existed in regard to the location of the church edifice. The two most prominent places selected were, the one, near what is now known by the name of Waddell's Graveyard, and which was then opened for interments in anticipation of the building being erected there, and the other, the place where it now stands. But in the spirit of compromise, and as being the most central and eligible, the latter place was chosen. The warrant for the land was taken out by Messrs. William Maxwell and William Campbell. And thus, for more than a century, on that hallowed ground has the glorious Gospel of the Son of God been proclaimed. For centuries to come may it be occupied for the same purpose!

It was a short time before this, that the Presbyterian Church in this country began to be agitated by a religious controversy, which resulted in a separation which continued for seventeen years.* The effects of this state of things in the Church at large were felt here also. A division was the consequence. This occurred in 1741. Hence originated the congregation of Lower West Conococheague, or what is now called Welsh Run. But though a division took place, it was what their situation as a congregation required, it being much too extensive to allow frequent meetings in one place. And when effected, it was done

* For an account of this controversy, see Appendix III.

with so much Christian spirit, that both churches still adhering to the same Presbytery, were frequently represented in this judicatory by the same commissioner.

In the year 1754, this church invited the Rev. John Steel to become its Pastor. Mr. Steel having accepted the invitation, continued among them for about two years, having charge also of East Conococheague. He settled at a time when the neighbourhood was greatly disturbed by the Indians. General Braddock had been defeated; and the Indians, gathering fresh courage from this disaster, hastened to wreak their vengeance on the inhabitants of these then frontiers. It was about this time that Col. James Smith, Mr. John M'Collough, and Richard Bard, Esq., and his wife, were taken captive by them; all of whom were connected with this congregation, the latter two after their captivity; and whose thrilling narratives, as recorded in a book some time since published, called "Incidents of Border Life," give a vivid idea of the exposures and hardships and sufferings of the inhabitants at this early period.

In consequence of these frequent attacks of the Indians, the settlement was entirely broken up; the congregation was dispersed; and Mr. Steel having received an invitation from the Presbyterian Church in Carlisle to become their pastor, accepted the invitation, and there lived and laboured the remainder of his days. Mr. Steel was a man of great intrepidity of character. Often did he lead forth companies of armed men to repel the invading savages.

He was a good preacher, and a sound divine. But his labours here were of too short duration, and the country too much disturbed, to have been as greatly or as extensively useful, as he would have been under more favourable circumstances. How different is our condition from theirs! *Theirs* was one of toil and great exposure to danger—*ours* is one of comparative ease and safety. With *them*, it was a common thing to meet together to worship God with their fire-arms in their hands, and their swords at their sides—to *us*, belongs the high privilege of meeting in the house of God without fear, and of worshipping without molestation. The ancient church was enclosed by a *fortification*, erected for the safety and protection of the surrounding neighbourhood;—fit emblem of that safer, securer refuge which God has provided, in his Son, for the penitent believer, from the storms of divine wrath, and from the enemies of his soul.

After the return of the people to their desolated habitations, they again organized themselves into a congregation, and enjoyed supplies from the Donegal Presbytery, until the years 1762 and '63, when the settlement was again disturbed by the irruption of the Indians, which had once more well-nigh broken up the congregation. Yet, though few in number and labouring under great difficulties, they still clung to the church. And though it had scarcely an existence, yet did it still live, to impart consolation to them in their trying circumstances.

They seem to have identified themselves so completely with the Church, from their first settlement in these parts, that they could not live without it. They seem to have felt the truth of the promise, "They shall prosper that love thee." Hence, when driven from their homes and from the house of God, they seem to have possessed the spirit of the Psalmist, as, when under somewhat similar circumstances, he laments, "As the hart panteth after the water brooks, so panteth my soul after thee, O God. My soul thirsteth for God, for the living God; when shall I come and appear before God? My tears have been my meat day and night, while they continually say, Where is thy God? When I remember these things, I pour out my soul in me: for I had gone with the multitude: I went with them to the house of God, with the voice of joy and praise, with a multitude that kept holy day." (Psalm xlii. 1–4.) Thus were they called to pass through many changes and trials, until, in 1767, we find the Church in a more prosperous condition than it had been at any former period.

The following persons at this time composed the Session: Messrs. William Maxwell, William Smith, John M'Dowell, William M'Dowell, John Welsh, Alexander White, John M'Clelland, Jonathan Smith, William Campbell, Robert Fleming, and Samuel Templeton.

## PERIOD II.

FROM THE SETTLEMENT OF THE REVEREND JOHN KING, D.D., AS PASTOR, A. D. 1769, TO THE SETTLEMENT OF THE REVEREND DAVID ELLIOTT, D.D., AS PASTOR, A. D. 1812.

THE church having been thus brought into a more prosperous condition, and its members feeling the importance of having a settled ministry among them, in 1768 invited the Rev. John King, then a licentiate under the care of the Presbytery of Philadelphia, to preach to them with this view. Dr. King having accepted the invitation, and having laboured among them with great acceptance for several months, was at length ordained and installed pastor, August 30th, 1769. At the time of his settlement the congregation numbered one hundred and thirty families.

Dr. King commenced his ministry in exciting times. It was not long after he had entered upon the pastorate of this church, until the whole community was thrown into a ferment by the following occurrence, which seriously threatened the best interests of the church. But he was the man to meet the emergency. And he did meet it manfully and fearlessly, and the storm expended itself without any serious results. In the year 1770, Col. James Smith had been lodged in prison, in Bedford County, on the charge of murder, which had occurred in an affray which had taken place in that county. For more safe keeping he was removed to the prison at Carlisle. His friends becoming exasperated at such treatment, and calling themselves *Black Boys*, determined to go to Carlisle and attempt his rescue. Through the persuasion of the Colonel, they desisted. On their return to Conococheague they met three hundred persons who had set out on the same errand,—so great, so intense, and so general was the excitement throughout the whole settlement. It was on this occasion that Dr. King delivered the following address to his congregation. And it teaches two things: (1) that he was a man of great moral courage, to stand up and deliver such an address, under such circumstances, in the very place where this excitement was so intense, and when so many of his own congregation sympathized so deeply in the movement. And (2) that Presbyterian ministers were *then*, as they are *now*, law-abiding men. The address embodies principles in regard to subjection to the civil magistrate which are as important now as they were when they were delivered, on the occasion referred to. It may be added that Colonel Smith was honourably and justly acquitted of the charge preferred against him.*

"The distractions which have lately agitated this part of the country, and I am sorry to say, have too much prevailed in this particular settlement, are indeed a matter of no small uneasiness to me, and certainly it must appear a distressing consideration to every one that has any regard to the peace and

* See "Incidents of Border Life," pp. 67-70.

good order of society, either civil or religious. These are both divine ordinances, and as such they claim a universal regard from every one who is a subject of them. Hence, to observe persons in a riotous manner openly setting themselves against the government, and endeavouring by force and arms to prevent the due administration of justice, must be deeply afflicting to every one who pays any respect to the divine authority in this wise and useful institution. Such practices are highly criminal in themselves, not only in a civil, but also in a religious sense. For if civil government is a divine institution, if 'the powers that be are ordained of God, then whosoever resisteth that power, resisteth the ordinance of God, and they that resist shall receive to themselves damnation.' These are the express words of the inspired Apostle, in Rom. xiii. 1, 2, where he carefully inculcates subjection and other duties which we owe to magistrates. He inculcates on Christians the duty of submission even to Heathen governors who had the *rule* at the time when he wrote; and so of consequence, the obligation binds with greater firmness under Christian governors.

"The first argument he uses for this duty, is the divine appointment of it: 'For there is no power but of God; the powers that be are ordained of God.' He has, for the good of mankind, assigned different stations of rule and subjection among men, though they are all of one race, raising some above others, and clothing them with such authority whereby they bear some resemblance to himself, and accordingly, he has communicated to them his own name: 'I have said ye are gods' (Psalm lxxxii., 6); so that we see with what regard God himself speaks of magistrates and judges. He also makes use of that very power in magistracy to curb and punish those who despise it, as a strong obligation to bind us to obedience: 'For rulers are not a terror to good works,' &c. (v. 3, 4.) And further, he also adds another, of a higher necessity, that binds more strongly, and is more acceptable, that is, a necessity of conscience: 'Wherefore,' says he, 'ye must needs be subject, not only for wrath, but for conscience sake.' This is the main consideration, and which is the sum of all the rest; as if he had said: Have a reverent and conscientious respect to the ordinance of God, in the institution of government; and to the providence of God in the choice of those particular persons, he calls to the administration of it, and submit yourselves to those who are thus set over you. This you must needs do, and that 'not only for wrath, for fear of the magistrate's sword,' but out of a necessity of conscience, which makes a true willingness and an acceptable service; and where this is done, it produces an agreeable and regular motion among all superiors and inferiors, states and families, magistrates and subjects, the one commanding, the other obeying in the Lord.

"We see then that this subjection is a necessary and commanded duty incumbent upon all; and certainly Christians are to consider themselves under the strongest obligations; yea, it is so connected with religion, that I can scarcely think a person a good Christian, who is not a good civilian. A disposition to oppose, or to abet, or encourage the actual opposition to civil government, is a temper of mind contrary to the spirit of Christ, and unbecoming the Christian character. But we are still to remember that this subjection is not to infringe upon the rights of conscience, with respect to the authority and law of God, and the duty we owe to him; for the extent of all these relations and of all subjection and obedience is to be bounded by the unalterable obligations we are under to God, as supreme: 'Render therefore unto Cæsar the things that are Cæsar's,' but nothing of God's; that is neither *ours* to give, nor *his* to receive. The law of God is the first and highest rule, and binds all, both kings and subjects, high and low, under inviolable and perpetual engagements. Magistrates and judges are peculiarly under the eye of God, and as he has elevated them to a higher station than others, so he peculiarly takes notice of their conduct: as the Supreme Judge, he sits and views their proceedings, not only whether they do that which is just, but whether they judge righteously for conscience sake. They are accountable to God, and also to the laws of the land, if they go beyond their trust.

"But should they leave their station, it affords no argument for us to leave ours. Nay, if opposition should arise to such a height as to require opposition, which may sometimes happen in any government, such opposition ought to be made in a quiet, peaceable, and lawful manner, and not by force of arms, tumults, and riots, and the like. This is choosing the worst way, for no other reason but because it is the worst; for oppression itself will not justify opposition by force, until all milder measures have failed—much less is it justifiable when the circumstances of the case do not require it.

"Upon the whole, then, as I conceive it my duty to reprove sin, in whatever light it appears, and as I am convinced that the resisting a divine ordinance is a sin, and that the disgraceful conduct of the late rioters deserves that character, I conceive that no upright and well-disposed mind can take offence at what I have declared concerning it. It is a story in the mouths of those who may be called our political adversaries, that the Presbyterians are disaffected towards the government, and that their teachers instruct them so; and thus, though it is a charge upon that people in general, yet it comes sideways upon the ministers. And therefore I take this occasion publicly to declare my abhorrence and detestation of such riotous conduct, and most earnestly exhort and warn all those that hear me to abstain from it, and to avoid all those who do by any means encourage practices so destructive to the peace and good order of society—nay, so reproachful to human nature."

It was but a few years after the occurrence of the event just mentioned, until the Colonies began to be agitated, from one extreme to the other, on the subject of their connexion with Great Britain. The fires which had long been concealed were now beginning to give evidence of their existence. Great Britain had become more and more unyielding in her claims, and unrelenting; and the American Colonies had become more determined than ever to maintain their rights, and to defend them at all hazards. From these positions neither party would recede. The breach had become too wide to be healed. The crisis had been reached, and the country was in arms. The same spirit which pervaded the Colonies at large, pervaded also the minds of the people here. The feelings of patriotism had been enkindled in their bosoms, and were to know no abatement in their ardour, until they had achieved their country's independence. In producing this spirit, and in fostering it, Dr. King was second to none of the Presbyterian clergymen of his day. He not only volunteered his services, and went as chaplain to the battalion which marched from this part of the country, but many were the addresses which he delivered in behalf of the liberties of his country. It may be interesting to place on record a specimen of these addresses, which this patriotic minister made to the people during these trying times.

At a meeting of the citizens of the neighbourhood, called to deliberate on the state of affairs, he thus spoke:—"Gentlemen, the occasion of your meeting here this day is of a most serious and alarming nature. Driven by the cruel hand of violence, you are now brought to the sad alternative, either of submitting to the iron rod of oppression and slavery, or appearing under arms in the defence of your natural and sacred rights; and your sentiments are required, which of these you will choose and resolutely adhere to. Let us consider a little the occasion of these movements. Whatever secret schemes may be at the bottom, we know that actions speak loud, and from these we may judge that the heaviest chains are being prepared for us—that a plan of the most perfect slavery and oppression is laid, and is now in actual and violent execution. Say, which of your most sacred rights and invaluable franchises are not in danger by this plan? You think you have a natural right to use your own property. No! says Parliament, we have a right to tax you as we please, without your concurrence. You think you have a right to be governed by your own laws, made by your own representatives. No! says the Parliament, we have, and of right ought to have, full power to make laws and statutes sufficient to bind the Colonies and people of America in all cases whatsoever. This breaks down all your boasts of liberty at once, destroys your assemblies, and makes you absolutely subject to whatever burdens a corrupt ministry or a venal Parliament may please to lay upon you. You think you have a constitutional right to be tried, in cases of life, liberty, or property, by a jury of your vicinage. No! you must in several cases be tried in England. You think that murderers should not escape. Yes! says the Parliament, if they are engaged in our cause. Do you think your religion is safe? Not very secure, indeed, when the Popish religion is established, and the French laws are set up just in our neighbourhood. Or can you think that even your lives will be safe under a dragooning military government?

"We hold our charters, and consequently our titles to our possessions, by the plighted faith of the Crown; yet what regard is paid to this? These charters are violated at the pleasure of Parliament, and so they may go on to divest us of everything we call our own. All these things (and indeed these are but some of the cruel things) have been done by the last Parliament. And what has the present Parliament done? Instead of relieving, they have increased our burdens. We waited, and hoped for assistance from friends in England; but neither they nor we could be heard. One would say, we must confine our trade solely to Britain, Ireland, and the West Indies; another, that the people of New England must not fish on the banks of Newfoundland (that may be reserved for their peaceable neighbours, the French); and a third, to enable the King to declare us actual rebels, and treat us accordingly, thousands of men are sent over to execute the fatal sentence. The cloud is gathering thicker and thicker! Nay, it has already burst, and violence is begun. We hear pretty authentic accounts of an actual engagement.

"Now this is our lamentable situation—and what

will we do? I am ready to anticipate your answer, and say that you will firmly resolve to stand for your liberties, and, with all your force, oppose these unconstitutional exertions of power. We have been opposing them in a peaceable way, but now we are drove to the worst, and must either submit or appeal to arms—that '*ultima ratio regum*,' the last argument of kings. But some will perhaps say it is taking up arms against the King,—a grievous crime, according to the English Constitution, and contrary to the command of the Apostle, who teaches that 'every soul be subject to the higher powers.' My sentiments of this matter are these. I acknowledge King George as my rightful sovereign; I declare myself his subject, and am willing to swear allegiance to him, and I do not doubt but every one of you would declare the same; but still I do firmly believe that all allegiance is bounded by the constitution of our government, and all obedience is limited by the laws of God. It is, therefore, *constitutional* allegiance that we would declare. It is this that we plead for. It is obedience in things lawful that we are to pay, and beyond this the Apostle surely would never inculcate subjection to the earthly powers. That pernicious doctrine of passive obedience and non-resistance can stand upon no rational foundation, but is contrary thereto. It is absurd in itself, fraught with the most dangerous consequences, and only calculated for the meridian of Turkey or Tartary. The operation of it will never cease until we shall become like the slaves of Morocco, who, when their tyrant, perhaps for his sport, wounds them with a javelin, submissively employ their remaining strength to draw it out, and give it to him again, that he may give them the finishing blow.

"Now, sirs, subjection is demanded of us, but it is not the constitutional subjection which we are in duty bound to pay; it is not a legal subjection to the King they would bring us to—that we already acknowledge; but it is a subjection to the British Parliament, or to the people of Great Britain: this we deny, and I hope will always deny. They are not our lords and masters; they are no more than our brethren and fellow-subjects. They call themselves, and it has been usual to call them, the *mother country;* but this is only a name, and if there was anything in it, one would think that it should lead them to treat us like children, with parental affection. But is it fatherly or motherly, to strip us of everything, to rob us of every right and privilege, and then to whip and dragoon us with fleets and armies, till we are pleased? No! As the name does not belong to them, so their conduct shows they have no right to claim it. We are on an equal footing with them in all respects; with respect to government and privileges; and therefore their usurpation ought to be opposed. Nay, when the King uses the executive branch of government, which is in his hand, to enable one part of his subjects to lord it over and oppress another, it is a sufficient ground of our applying to the laws of nature for our defence.

"But this is the case with us. We have no other refuge from slavery but those powers which God has given us, and allowed us to use in defence of our dearest rights; and I hope he will bless our endeavours, and give success to this oppressed people; and that the wicked instruments of all these distractions, shall meet their due reward. I earnestly wish that in such troublous times, while we plead for liberty, a proper guard may be kept against any turbulent or mobbish outbreak, and that unanimity may be universal, both in counsel and action, and that we may still have an eye to the great God, who has some important reasons for such severe corrections. Let us look to the rod and him that hath appointed it; let us humble ourselves before him daily for our sins, and depend upon him for success. If he be against us, in vain do we struggle; if the Lord be for us, 'though an host should encamp against us, we need not be afraid.'

"Now from a right view of the state and circumstances of these Colonies, every man of common sense will see that in this conflict nothing is more necessary than *union*, nothing more dangerous than division; and if ever we are obliged to give up our sacred rights, it will not be by British force, but by enemies among ourselves. A state divided cannot stand, and therefore we should guard against division. Some will doubtless be so mean, as to prefer some present ease before the most lasting enjoyment, and rather than discompose themselves for the present, would submit to the vilest bondage; so sordid, as to set up their own interest in competition with the public good and this general cause, in which we are engaged. It is certain that all these are in a degree enemies to us, and should be avoided; not only such as will not act with us, but such as will not act harmoniously. Everything that tends to break the harmony should be avoided."

The following extract is from a sermon occasioned by the death of General Montgomery, preached January, 1777, from the text, "And all these things are against me." (Gen. xlii. 36.) "God's dealings with men when he is working their deliverance are often so dark and intricate, that they are apt to judge and say they are against them. This should prevent us forming hasty judgments concerning our circumstances, however dark, nay, even desperate they may be. Such judgments of matters tend to depress that spirit and weaken that activity and force which are necessary to extricate from troubles: besides, they are injurious to the right exercise of faith in the goodness and power of God, and betray an ignorance of the methods of his providence. Let us, therefore, in our circumstances guard against them. They arise from a weakness of faith, from cowardice, from principles of sense, from partial views of the matter, and from ignorance of God. To admit and to follow such a judgment in our case would be dishonourable to our cause and attended with certain ruin. For surely we have still reason for the exercise of faith and confidence in God, that he will not give a people up to the unlimited will and power of others, who have done all they could to avoid the calamity, and have so strenuously adhered to the cause of reason and humanity; —a people who have been attacked with unprovoked violence, and driven with the greatest reluctance to take up arms for their defence ;—a people whom he himself by a series of providential actings hath gradually led on to this condition. That he should give up such a people to the tyranny of masters, who impiously invade his own prerogative, and mark their proceedings with such instances of barbarity and inhumanity as nature itself abhors—let us never entertain a thought so derogatory to the honour and justice of Him who is the Judge of all the earth, and will surely do that which is right. He is the judge of right, the guardian of innocence, the protector of truth, and the defence of the oppressed. 'The Lord is the refuge for the oppressed; he will maintain the cause of the afflicted; he hath appointed his arrows against the persecutors.'

"Therefore, when these are our circumstances, we may rationally judge that God is not an unconcerned spectator, but that he sees and will reward the persecutors. Many things, indeed, seem to be against us ; a very great and powerful enemy, who have been long trained to victory; their numerous and savage allies, who, having lost their liberty, would have others in the same condition; our weakness and inexperience in war; internal enemies, which we cannot well root out; the loss of many of our friends, and a beloved and able General. But let not these destroy our hopes, or damp our spirits. To put too much confidence in man, is the way to provoke God to deprive us of them. This may perhaps be that darkness which precedes the glorious day. Nor let us judge that the cause is lost, even though we should be brought much lower still. God may have great things to do with this people. This land he made use of as a refuge for his oppressed people, and has brought them up to maturity in it; and he may now be about to make them eminent in the world, and give them a name among the nations of the earth. Should this be the case, let us not wonder that we should travail in birth; that so great a nation should be born into political life and independence with sore pangs and blood. It is agreeable to God's method to bring low before he exalteth; to humble before he raises up. Let us trust in him, and do our duty, and commit the event to his determination, who can make those things to be for us, which by a judgment of sense, we are ready to say are *against* us."

The following was addressed to Captain Huston's company, as they were about to leave their homes for the battle-field. "My brethren—I hope you will remember the designs and resolutions with which you at first consented to, and joined in, the public opposition to the tyranny of Great Britain. I hope that at this time of great necessity, you will not suffer the fire and warlike spirit to faint, and so manifest all that you have hitherto done and said, to signify nothing. It appears that even now is the critical and trying time; our enemy making their main push, and at the same time coming into such circumstances as they will be most in our power. While they continued under the cover and convoy of their ships, they were out of our reach; now, it seems, they have taken the land, and come into such circumstances as we desired. But our divided army cannot operate against their number, without an addition. You are loudly called upon to go to its assistance. Indeed, the case itself speaks so loudly, as is sufficient to rouse every spark of martial fire that may be in you.

"There is, one would think, no need of words. Your country, lives, liberties, and estates in danger, all cry most bitterly for help! And why should there be the least appearance of backwardness among you? I am glad to hear that some among you are so hearty in the cause, as by their readiness to the service, to show that they still desire to be free, and were in earnest when they said they would defend their liberties with their lives.

"The case is plain; life must be hazarded, or all is gone. You must go and fight, or send your humble submission, and bow as a beast to its burden, or as an ox to the slaughter. The King of Great Britain has declared us rebels; a capital crime. Submission therefore consents to the rope or the axe. Liberty is doubtless gone; none could imagine a tyrant king should be more favourable to conquered rebels, than he was to loyal, humble, petitioning subjects. No! No! If ever a people lay in chains, we must, if our enemies carry their point against us, and oblige us to unconditional submission. This is not all. Our Tory neighbours will be our proud and tormenting enemies. But suppose that all this were tolerable, and you might think that it might be submitted to, there is still a greater monster behind, that is, Persecution. I do not mean persecution on a religious account, though I have not the least doubt but that will also be the case. The English Government, every one knows, is favourable to Episcopacy; it has found the benefit of it, and it is to all appearance as fond of the maxim, '*No Bishop, no King*,' as ever. This was and is designed, and will no doubt be the case here, if they succeed in conquering us.

"But as sure as you sit there, you may expect a political persecution. It has ever been the case, that hard and tyrannical oaths have been imposed by conquerors in such cases; and if we are overcome, what may we expect but oaths to bind us to passive obedience and non-resistance, which no conscientious man could take; but yet, *must* take or suffer. And how miserable a case must it be to be bound by an oath to a principle of the deepest slavery, and such as cuts off the only remedy against tyranny!

"Now, gentlemen, you see what we have to expect; and surely it must appear to you intolerable, and such as must make you still adhere to the glorious struggle for liberty. To be discouraged at what has already happened, is meanly to give up the cause. Surely no one ever expected the war to be carried on with Great Britain without the loss of lives, and those who die must have their friends to lament them. This is what we expected, and though we mourn and are sorrowful for them, and for the success of the English, yet let not this discourage. I sincerely feel the distress, and pray God to enable you to be supported under it!"

An extract from a sermon preached from the text, "Be thou faithful unto death," (Rev. ii. 10,) will close these deeply interesting addresses. "My dear brethren—Since God, in the course of his providence has so ordered matters, as to require every true-hearted American to appear in defence of his liberties, it affords me great pleasure to see you stand forth, with others, in the glorious cause. We have heard your declarations on the point, we have seen your diligence in preparing, and now we see that these were not the efforts of cowardice, boasting at a distance, but that in real earnestness your hearts have been engaged in the matter. After observing in you this heroic and laudable disposition, I apprehend there need not much be said to animate you in the grand object of your present attention, and more especially as you enter upon this warfare, not from the low and sordid views which are the main object of ignorant mercenaries, but with a proper knowledge of the reasons of the contest, and I hope, too, with a consciousness of duty.

"You see an open field before you, wherein you may acquire reputation and honour to yourselves, and do a most beneficial service to your country. The cause of American Independence and Liberty, which has now called you to go forth to the scene of action, is indeed a cause in which it will be glorious to conquer and honourable to die. The victory, however dearly bought, will be but a cheap purchase; for what of all worldly goods can be of equal value to freedom from slavery, the free and lawful enjoyment and use of our own property, and the free possession of our own lives and consciences? This is an object worthy of our vigorous exertions; a prize worthy of a Christian soldier; a prize we are commanded to strive for, by the voice of Nature and the voice of God. We have now assumed the independent rank we ought to bear among the nations of the earth, and we are resolved to be free. Our enemies, with all their own and foreign force they could obtain, are attempting their utmost to make us slaves; and this appears to be the main time of the trial—the very turning-point which will decide the question, and determine either for freedom or bondage. If their designs can be baffled for this campaign, it is most probable they will despair of success, and give up the cause. At least it will be a powerfully animating motive for Americans to proceed on in that cause, with which they must at all events go through, having nothing before them but success, or the most ignominious and shameful alternative.

But though it is a worthy and honourable cause in which you now engage, you are still to consider that it is attended with danger. The instruments of death you carry in your hands, and the power of your enemies, by no means contemptible, declare it to be such. Victory can hardly be expected without blood; and in such a contest, death itself may be to *some* of you a certain, and to *all* a probable event. By putting you in mind of this, I would not mean to intimidate, but caution you to maintain an habitual fear of God, and a concern about death and eternity which may beget in you a readiness to meet the worst of events. True courage does not consist in proud contempt or thoughtless disregard of death; nay, he is possessed of true courage who allows the serious thought of death its proper weight, yet in a virtuous cause prefers his duty before his life. A man of true fortitude is one who sees the danger, yet from superior motives despises it.

"You may therefore observe from this, that there is no soldier so truly courageous as a pious man; no army so formidable as those who are superior to the fear of death, and consequently, that no one qualification is more necessary in a soldier than true religion. And now as you are about to go on this service, I would have you to apply this to yourselves. Many of you have been under my care, and as it may perhaps come to pass, that this may be the last time

I have in this manner to speak to you, suffer me with the greatest earnestness to beseech and exhort you to be watchful over your souls, to strive after acceptance with God; for, you must know that if you are not at peace with him and are strangers to the Lord Jesus, that however you fall, you must be wretched. Endeavour, therefore, to cultivate religion; and in good earnest care for your precious souls. Without this you cannot prosper. Especially be watchful that neither your thoughts, words, or actions be dishonourable to God. Avoid swearing, profaneness, lewdness, drunkenness, and every instance of cruelty. How awful is it to think that those who engage in war should be despisers of God, and abusers of the sacred name of the Lord of Hosts—that they should expect success while they are the enemies of Jehovah, and expose themselves to the imminent danger of being immediately sent from their profanity and wickedness on earth, to the blaspheming rage and despairing horrors of the infernal pit! It is too often the case, that soldiers claim a latitude to themselves in vice; and so armies have been observed to be almost sinks of wickedness. Let it not be said of any of you. Nor let anything which would bring a dishonour on the cause you serve, or the profession you have made, be remarked concerning you."

Such was the spirit of Dr. King in those perilous times of our country's history. And such was the spirit of patriotism in this congregation, that it contributed its full proportion of men and officers to advocate our cause and to defend our rights. I have no means of ascertaining the precise number of men and officers who were thus actually engaged in the war of Independence; but there were *many* of the best and noblest sons of this congregation who for the sake of their country, had "pledged their lives, their fortunes, and their sacred honour." I find, however, from the Church Register, that the number of those who were killed, and who died by oppression of the enemy, and in consequence of disease contracted while in service, amounts to *nine*.* How highly should we prize our liberties which were thus so dearly bought by toil and self-denial, by sufferings and death! How closely should we consider the connexion which exists between these liberties and our own beloved Church! And how solicitous should we be to transmit these liberties to the generations which are to succeed us, as pure as we received them from those who preceded us and bequeathed them to us. Never may the time come in the history of this

* Jonathan Smith, a ruling elder, died of camp fever, at Amboy, Oct. 13th, 1776.

John Campbell, by oppression of the enemy, Oct. 30th, 1776.

James McCoy, killed at Fort Washington, Nov. 16th, 1776.

Dugal Campbell, died of camp fever in New Jersey, January, 1777.

Patrick McClelland, by oppression of the enemy, 1777.

Joseph Watson, killed in battle, Dec., 1777.

Capt. Robert McCoy, killed at Crooked-billet, May 1st, 1778.

William Dean, " " " "

William Sterret, " " " "

Church, when the spirit of patriotism which dwelt in the bosoms of our friends and forefathers, shall lose its vigour, or become extinct in the hearts of those who are their descendants and successors!

In 1777, the following persons were added to the session: Messrs. Patrick Maxwell, Joseph Van Lear, Matthew Wilson, William Lowery, James McFarland, and Henry Helm. In 1786, the town of Mercersburg was laid out. Its population, and that of the adjacent neighbourhood increasing, it was deemed expedient to have preaching in town.* For this purpose an edifice was erected in 1794, and for a number of years was without a ceiling, floor, pews, or pulpit. The ground on which it stands, and that which surrounds it, was given to the congregation by the Hon. Robert Smith. In 1772, Messrs. William Waddell, Archibald Irwin, James Crawford, and John Holiday, were added to the session; in 1799, Messrs. John McMullin, John Johnston, Edward Welsh, William Reynolds, Robert McFarland, and John McCullough; and in 1800, Mr. John Scott, Robert McDowell, and James Dickey.

From the close of the war, after the state of public affairs had become more settled, until 1811, when Dr. King, in consequence of increasing bodily afflictions, resigned his pastoral charge, the state of the congregation was peaceful and prosperous. At every communion season, its numbers of professing dis-

* The original place of preaching is two and a half miles from town.

ciples were increased by new accessions. During the whole of Dr. King's ministry in this church, he *baptized* nine hundred and fifty persons; and there were admitted to the *Communion* four hundred and eighty. These numbers, however, are not strictly accurate, as the Doctor's infirmities during the latter part of his ministry were so great that the Church Register was but imperfectly kept. There were persons both baptized and admitted to the communion of the church, whose names are not recorded. Dr. King was a man of piety and of extensive acquirements. His labours were owned of God, and eminently blessed in building up this church. His memory still lives in the grateful remembrance and strong affections of not a few who are spared with us to the present time, some of whom bear the seal of baptism as administered by his own hand, and others of whom are his spiritual children, and will be "his joy and crown of rejoicing in the presence of Jesus Christ at his coming."

It may be interesting to know something more of the life and character of this divine, who was second to none in his day in the Presbyterian Church in this country. For this purpose we will avail ourselves of a brief memoir, penned by himself, and extending to the tenth year of his settlement as pastor of this church; and of a sermon which was preached by the Rev. John McKnight, D.D., his intimate friend and companion, at the request of the church.

Dr. King thus writes: "I am now nearly thirty-nine years of age, being born December 5th, 1740. The wonderful providence of God has so long spared my life!—a life dishonourable and unprofitable! Oh, that my soul may be deeply humbled in the review of such a vain and froward, such a slothful and inactive life as I have spent, while I here record my thankfulness for that goodness and mercy of God, that has educated and protected me, that has so long spared me notwithstanding my innumerable provocations of him, that has in any degree fitted me for some usefulness in the world, that has given me at least talents which might be profitable for the good of my fellow-creatures, and especially so if I had improved them as I ought; and let my soul be thankful that I have been made acquainted in any comfortable measure with that amazing way of salvation in the gospel of the Lord Jesus Christ, and that, through the providence, and, I hope, the grace, of God, I have been brought to be a preacher to others!

"It is impossible for me to recollect or record all the instances of the goodness of God to me, his unworthy creature and unprofitable servant. No more can I call to mind the innumerable instances in which I have dishonoured him, through my sinful life. But these I must remember, for I know and feel them; and oh that that gracious God, who has been so liberal in his goodness, would deeply impress my heart with a sense of them, and awaken in my soul that love and thankfulness and praise which becomes a creature so highly obliged! Let me from henceforth take a more particular notice of the goodness of God, and (not in that careless, unfeeling manner I was wont, but with all my heart) acknowledge it. Let me with care and exactness observe his dealings toward me, and that which may be most remarkable in my own temper and conduct toward him, and labour to improve in humility, heavenly-mindedness, and holy walk with God.

"My father, Robert King, whom I believe to have been a pious man, was careful to educate me in the principles of the religion of Christ, and inculcate the necessity of holiness and faith in order to salvation. When I grew up, I recollect that I was sometimes exercised very seriously with the consideration of eternity, and the necessity of preparing for it; with the thoughts of sin and my liableness to misery, which led me to the exercise of prayer, in which I fear I too much rested, though I had found my heart sometimes much softened, and thought I had some freedom in receiving and resting on Jesus Christ for salvation. The sins of my heart and frequent falls prevented me from forming any conclusive judgment that my state was good, though I had some hope that I had such a view of my sins as had led me to Jesus Christ, and that I had a prevailing love to God and holiness.

"When I was about thirteen years old, I was put to the grammar school, at which I continued till I had read the Greek and Latin classics, Logic, Metaphysics, and Moral Philosophy. After this, my father not judging that he could bear the expense of sending me to college immediately, I came to West Conococheague, in Cumberland (now Franklin) County, where I spent almost three years in teaching school, during which I initiated some young boys in the Latin language. During this time I was, in general, too careless about the exercise of religion in my own soul, and recollect not anything very remarkable about such exercises, until at the celebration of the sacrament of the Lord's Supper, at East Conococheague, by the Rev. Messrs. Steel and Roan, —the first time that I joined to partake in that solemn ordinance,—when I found myself unusually impressed with the concerns of religion, and in the exercise of prayer before and in the work of communion during the service, had much freedom in devoting myself to Christ and receiving him. Yet still, afterwards, I had reason to complain of my heart, as careless about religion, and too vain and prone to diversions and unprofitable and hurtful pastimes, as well as inclined to know sin too much.

"The Indian war increasing in 1763, my sister that lived here being killed by the Indians, and the school declining, I quitted this part and returned to Little Britain, in Lancaster County, the place of my birth and education. There I continued until the middle of the fall, 1764, in great perplexity about the manner of life I should engage in. I had often entertained a thought of the ministry, but for many winters had been prone to a hoarseness, and my voice weak at best, I concluded, after much exercise in prayer for light in the determination, to lay that aside and apply myself to the study of physic. I went to Philadelphia, and there agreed with Dr. John Boyd, as an apprentice. Returned home, and set off for Baltimore, where I continued near three months, when Dr. Boyd, who had been at Philadelphia for the recovery of his health, returned home. I found that the place did not suit me, as he, at that time, dealt as an apothecary and followed not the practice of medicine. I again came home, after much loss of time and money, and still intent on the practice of medicine, went to Philadelphia, applied to Dr. Kearsly, and had nearly agreed with him, which probably would have fixed my condition in that way; but in the mean time was led, by the advice of my first Latin master, Thomas McGee, to go and consult Dr. Allison, Vice-Provost of the College, on that head. The Doctor advised me warmly to desist in my attempts towards physic, and to enter College with a view to the ministry. I reflected on the various providences with which I had been exercised in the matter, and followed his advice. I entered College May 6th, 1765, and commenced, A. B., May 20th, 1766. Having returned home, I applied myself to the study of divinity till March 11th, 1767, when I entered upon trials for the ministry in the Second

Philadelphia Presbytery, and was licensed to preach on the 13th day of August following.

"The most of that fall and ensuing winter, I preached at New London, in the bounds of the New Castle Presbytery, having paid a visit to West Conococheague before the winter. Near the opening of the spring, I was invited to Conococheague, by the congregation of which I am now the pastor. After accepting their call, I was received on trials in the Donegal Presbytery. April 11th, 1769, I delivered my first trial discourses; and on the 30th day of August following, was ordained and installed as Pastor of the Church at Upper West Conococheague. During all these changes, my exercises about religion had been various, but a prevailing desire to glorify God in being useful to immortal souls, I trust, was my ruling motive in entering into this great and awful service; while the consideration of the pre-mentioned providential dispensations, the talents which God has given me (which however small in comparison of others) I thought might render me, through grace, of some use in the Christian Church, and the unanimous call of this people, led me to think it my duty to enter upon this work. O may God forgive my innumerable neglects and miscarriages in it, and strengthen my dependence on his all-sufficient grace, to enable me for the future more faithfully to discharge the important duties of it! Having settled in this congregation in June, 1768, I was married to Elizabeth McDowell, the third daughter of Mr.

John McDowell, of this place, on April 2d, 1771, and have continued in the enjoyment of agreeable circumstances until now. I had been always healthy and visited with no considerable sickness, until in September, 1775, when I fell into a dangerous fever."

Thus far we have given Dr. King's autobiography. We now follow the Rev. Dr. McKnight in his funeral sermon.

"Dr. King was Pastor of this Congregation for forty-two years. During the last six years of his life, he laboured under a rheumatic complaint, with which he was severely afflicted, and which baffled every medical application. For four years, however, of this time, he continued in the exercise of his ministry, in the latter part of which, his limbs were so enfeebled that he was not able to stand, and officiated in a chair fixed in the pulpit. Finding his complaint still increasing, and his prospects of usefulness, in a public capacity, at an end, he resigned his charge September, 1811. His complaint continued to increase, and his bodily strength to decline, until he became utterly helpless. Some time before his death, he was seized with a violent fever, which brought his natural life to a close. He died July 15th, 1813, in the seventy-third year of his age.

"Dr. King was a man of good natural parts, which he diligently cultivated. And in particular, from the time of his being settled in the ministry, being placed in favourable circumstances for study, he industriously improved what time he could redeem from the immediate duties of his office, in acquiring the knowledge of all those branches of literature and science which tended to respectability and usefulness. Besides being a good Latin and Greek scholar, he had a competent acquaintance with the Hebrew and the French. He had studied Natural and Moral Philosophy, Astronomy, the Mathematics, and Logic with attention, and had a considerable general knowledge of Chemistry. He had paid considerable attention to Ecclesiastical History. With Divinity and its several branches, he was well acquainted. Influenced by his well-known and established character, as a scholar and a divine, the Trustees of Dickinson College, at one of its first commencements in the College, viz., in the year 1792, conferred on him the degree of D.D. In the same year, he was elected Moderator of the General Assembly.

"Dr. King was the author of several small publications, particularly a Catechism for the instruction of youth in the principles of the Christian religion, and more especially calculated to fortify them against the spirit of scepticism and infidelity which, at the time of its publication, threatened to corrupt the principles and morals of many; of some pieces in the Assembly's Magazine, on the subject of a man's marrying his former wife's sister; of a Dissertation on the Prophecies, referring to the present times, &c. As a companion, Dr. King was sociable, cheerful, and instructing. As a friend, he was sincere, affectionate, uniform, and faithful. In his principles, Dr.

King was strictly orthodox—a uniform and warm friend of the great doctrines of grace. His piety was rational and warm. His life fully corresponded with his profession, and he has left behind him a character unsullied by a blot. He evinced an increasing concern for the interests of Zion; and, so far from being of a bigoted or contracted spirit, he held friendly intercourse with persons of different denominations, and was ready to countenance and encourage all who appeared desirous of promoting the cause of religion. He was ready to distribute, and willing to communicate to every real object of charity that presented itself, and to such literary institutions as promised to be useful. Though his afflictions were severe and of long continuance, and though he was considerably advanced in years, yet he retained, until very near the close of his life, his intellectual powers, very little impaired. His mind was still vigorous and active.

"Let us now take a view of the state of his mind under his affliction, and in prospect of his approaching dissolution. And here I shall introduce a communication on the subject from Mr. Elliott, your present worthy pastor:—'I visited Dr. King,' remarks Mr. Elliott, 'some weeks before his death, and during his last illness. He entered into an animated conversation with respect to his views of religion, and the peculiar experiences of his mind. He spoke in exalted terms of the doctrines of grace, as the only foundation of a sinner's hopes. He said he could see nothing in his past life which afforded him any ground of dependence, and that he had no hope from any other quarter, but from the glorious scheme of redemption, as revealed in the word of God. "*No other way!*" said he: "*Nothing will do but this!*" He observed that he frequently felt a desire to be more fully acquainted with the glorious character of God than what perhaps was justifiable. He believed Christians ought to be careful not to transcend the limits assigned them in the word of God, adding, 'that the word was our only standard and directory with respect to the great mysteries of religion, and that to it we ought to keep close.' During the intervals of fever, when his mind was capable of regular exertion, he said he was generally in prayer for himself and others. He was much afraid that he was too desirous to depart. He longed for the time when he should be delivered from his affliction. But he frequently observed, that he strove and prayed against an improper solicitude, wishing to wait the Lord's time.

" 'About two weeks after the above conversation, and about ten days before his death, I was present at his bedside, and upon his complaining that he suffered much, I observed that I hoped he received abundant support from above. "*O yes,*" said he, "*I am greatly supported.*" He then observed that he had been strongly tempted, some time before, to doubt with respect to the foundation of his hopes; and whether that system of truth on which he had built his faith was agreeable to the word of God. Convinced that he had, long ago, carefully examined into the ground of his belief, he sought comfort in prayer to God, and it was not long till he experienced it. "*I have now*," said he, with a tear of joy sparkling in his eye, "*I have now no doubt of my love to God. He is the most glorious of all objects. None other can be compared to him!*" Thus lived and thus died this servant of the Lord. Both in his life and by his death, he has borne honourable testimony to the religion of Jesus, of which he was a professor, and of which he was a minister. Having done much, and suffered much according to the will of God, he has "fallen asleep," and has been gathered to his fathers.' "

## PERIOD III.

FROM THE SETTLEMENT OF THE REV. DAVID ELLIOTT, D.D., AS PASTOR, A.D. 1812, TO THE CLOSE OF HIS MINISTRY IN THIS CHURCH, A. D. 1829.

AFTER an interval of about a year from the resignation of Dr. King, the congregation invited the Rev. David Elliott, a Licentiate of the Carlisle Presbytery, to become their Pastor. He having accepted the invitation, was ordained and installed, October 7th, A. D. 1812. The number of families belonging to the congregation at the time of his settlement was one hundred and thirty-seven.

In 1813, the Presbyterian Church in St. Thomas was organized; most of the families and members of which were connected with this Church. This new organization was found to be expedient on account of the increase of the population of that district of country, and their distance from our places of worship, which rendered it difficult for them to attend upon the public means of grace. By the organization of the Church at St. Thomas, the limits of this congregation became still more circumscribed: and yet in the end, it has resulted more in the furtherance of the Gospel, than if the parts separated had continued in connexion with us.

In 1814, the following persons were added to the Session: Messrs. Thomas M'Dowell, David Dunwoody, and John M'Coy (of John). In 1815, the Sabbath School was commenced. It was begun amidst great difficulties and discouragements. At this early period, it was a new thing in the Christian Church in this region. But by the perseverance of the few who had engaged in it, not only did they see it begin, but they were also permitted to see it subsequently in full and efficient operation. And from that time to the present, though attended with many fluctuations, its exercises have never been suspended for any length of time. How much good has been achieved by it, in its nearly forty years' existence, Eternity alone will disclose. Impressions have doubtless been made upon the minds of those who have been, and those who are now scholars, which can never be effaced. And though, for a time, the seed which has been sown may seem to be lost, yet under the life-giving influence of God's Spirit, it may still issue in a rich and glorious harvest.

The year 1818 is memorable in the history of this Church for the establishment of the Social Prayer-Meeting. The circumstances which led to its formation are thus related in a letter from Dr. Elliott. "The want of some meeting of this kind had been sensibly felt by me, from the time of my settlement, but the difficulty of getting suitable persons to lead, prevented an earlier attempt to organize one. After the removal of Mr. James M'Farland to town, it was a frequent subject of conversation between him, Major Brownson, and myself. Finally, one Sabbath afternoon, Mr. M'Farland, Mr. George King, Major Brownson and myself were together at Mr. M'Farland's. The prayer-meeting became the topic of conversation, and it was agreed that we would attempt its organization. This being agreed upon, I remarked to them, that it was the best time to begin immediately, and that we should date the commencement of the meeting from that afternoon. This was assented to, and after spending some time in social prayer, we adjourned to meet again on the next Sabbath afternoon, or perhaps that day two weeks. In the mean time we mentioned the subject as we had opportunity, to several of those who we supposed would favour the object. A few additional persons attended the next day; and in a few weeks the meetings were so large that we held them in Mr. Cowan's shop. In these meetings we had many delightful seasons." And thus from this small beginning, did one of the most important means of grace in this Church take its origin. And from that time onward has it been continued; sometimes flourishing and at other times depressed; but at all times a source of richest consolation, and a means of quickening and of encouragement to those who attend it in a becoming spirit.

In 1819, the congregation having so increased, it was found necessary to erect in the country a new house of worship. The old church had been twice enlarged, but was still insufficient to accommodate the congregation. The new church edifice was completed in 1820: it cost near six thousand dollars. About this time the congregation was in a condition the most flourishing and prosperous. It numbered upwards of one hundred and seventy families, and had connected with it two Bible classes; the female consisting of one hundred and seven members, and the male of seventy. This prosperous state of things, however, did not long continue. A change took place, which, carrying its influence through a series of years, so greatly diminished the congregation in numbers, that it has never fully recovered from it. The following causes may be mentioned as bringing about this change:

1. The organization of a church in Loudon. This took place in 1820, and was the means of taking off a number of families, which had been connected with this congregation. After it was organized, it enjoyed for several years the ministerial labours of the Rev. Isaac Kellar; and subsequently those of the Rev. Robert Kennedy; but it has since become extinct.

2. Another cause was a change in the *times*. Prior to this, everything appeared to be in the most prosperous condition. Providence had smiled upon the labours of the husbandman, and the earth had yielded her increase. Our commerce was whitening every sea; and our manufactories were accumulating vast wealth for their owners. The expansion of the credit system was never greater; and our citizens began to feel that they were in the full tide of prosperity. But a change ensued. The smiles of Providence were withdrawn. Judgment began to be mingled with mercies. And the *pressure* became universal throughout the whole extent of our country. It was felt here also. Not a few of our farmers, who had purchased their lands at enormous prices, and others who had made improvements at a great expense, were so affected by this 'change of times,' that to meet their liabilities their all was swept from them. It is supposed that by this reverse of fortune more than half a score of the best families and supporters of this congregation were almost entirely ruined in their temporal circumstances. O that men would profit by the history of the past! How vain

and fleeting are all earthly possessions! "Riches make to themselves wings." Why not then, from such considerations as these, give heed to our Saviour's counsel: "Lay not up for yourselves treasures upon earth, where moth and rust do corrupt, and where thieves break through and steal; but lay up for yourselves treasures in heaven, where neither moth nor rust doth corrupt, and where thieves do not break through nor steal." (Matt. vi. 19, 20.)

3. But there was still another cause, which was far more felt in this respect than either of the preceding. In the years 1821, '22, and '23, an epidemic sickness prevailed to so great an extent, that the whole neighbourhood resembled a vast hospital. The number of those in health were almost insufficient, in many places, to take care of the sick. The effect of this visitation was, that in the first mentioned year twenty-five persons died; and in the latter, forty-five —thus making an aggregate of *seventy-two* persons within two years. And of these seventy-two, many were members of the church in full communion; many were heads of families; and some of them among the most liberal contributors to the support of the Gospel. So extensive and so rapid was the work of death, that in a period of nine years, commencing in 1820, not less than *one hundred and thirty* communicating members became its victims,—a number equal to that which, under ordinary circumstances, would not occur in eighteen years. On these scenes of sadness and sorrow I will not dwell. They are deeply im-

pressed upon the minds and hearts of many among us. Many there are who in the rending of relationships the closest and most endearing on earth, will never forget the poignancy of that grief, which during that distressing season, was poured forth more than once, around the bed of their dying, or at the grave of their departed friends. With these impressions still vivid and deeply fixed in the mind, may they have the consciousness and the evidence, that they have been sanctified to them. "For the Lord will not cast off for ever: but though He cause grief, yet will He have compassion, according to the multitude of his mercies. For He doth not afflict willingly, nor grieve the children of men."

In 1822, the following persons were added to the Session: Messrs. John Brownson, John McCoy (of Robert), and William Crawford. In 1825, the Female Domestic Missionary Society was formed. At first, it was auxiliary to the Foreign Missionary Society, but subsequently changed its relation, and became auxiliary to our Domestic Board. At its first formation it numbered eighty-three members. The total amount of funds contributed since its organization is one thousand dollars. It is worthy of remark, that probably there is not another society of the kind within the bounds of our Synod, which has been in existence for so long a time, or which has operated more efficiently. What may be the fruits of these offerings of love, will not be known in time; although even here, the hearts of its members may be gladdened, as by the reports of our missionaries they hear of churches formed where before they did not exist; of feeble ones, strengthened and supplied with the ministry of reconciliation; of saints, built up in holiness and comforted; and of sinners converted to God. Long may it continue to prosper; may the list of its members increase; may its contributions be augmented a hundred fold; and may the blessing of the Most High descend upon the giver and the gift!

In 1826, Messrs. Alexander McCoy and James Culbertson were added to the Session.

The year 1828 is memorable in the history of this church for a revival of religion. The history of this interesting work of grace, I give in the words of Dr. Elliott. "It was in the fall of 1828 that God visited this church with a season of reviving grace. The work was chiefly confined to that branch of the church which was in town. It commenced rather suddenly, and to me, unexpectedly. I had been mourning over the low state of religion—particularly the worldly spirit which prevailed. On the Sabbath preceding the meeting of the Presbytery at Newville, I preached on the Parable of the Talents. I felt unusual liberty, and a deep and solemn concern for the salvation of sinners. The people appeared very solemn and tender. At the prayer-meeting in the afternoon there was great solemnity and some weeping. Having seen these things several times before, I attached no great importance to them. The next day I left for Presbytery;—reported to the Presbytery a low and formal state of religion; remained abroad the next Sabbath, assisting with a communion service; and returned home early the week following. No sooner had I reached home, than I was greeted with the intelligence, that their prayer-meetings in town seemed to be visited with the special tokens of God's presence; and that the solemnity and tenderness which appeared on the Sabbath before I left, had increased, and that many evinced great anxiety about their souls. I immediately proceeded to town, and found all to be as stated. Religion was the engrossing subject of conversation, and the people of God prayed in a manner very different from that in which they had done before. Things progressed in this way for some time. The work did not extend, as I expected it would, through other parts of the congregation; although there was some increase of attention on the part of the people generally." As the fruits of this work of grace, it may be stated, that twenty-four persons were added to the church on profession of their faith.

Dr. Elliott having received an invitation to become pastor of the church in Washington, Pennsylvania, and having accepted it, resigned the pastoral charge of this church, October 29th, 1829. During his ministry, he baptized six hundred and fifty-five persons; and there were admitted to the communion of the Church three hundred and forty: on profession, two hundred and sixty-one; and by certificate, seventy-nine. Dr. Elliott, as a man and as a minister of our Lord, needs no panegyric. His name is in all the churches. It has become identified with our Church at large. It forms part of its history. And so long as soundness in the faith is appreciated, and the Presbyterian form of Church Government and its discipline are respected, the name of Elliott will shine forth with resplendent lustre. During the seventeen years that he was pastor, he made full proof of his ministry. Many among us are the seals of his ministry, and will arise to call him "blessed." Long may he live to honour his Divine Master in the work in which he is engaged!

## PERIOD IV.

FROM THE CLOSE OF DR. ELLIOTT'S MINISTRY IN THIS CHURCH, A. D. 1829, TO THE PRESENT TIME, A. D. 1852.

On the 17th of November, 1831, two years after the close of Dr. Elliott's ministry, the Rev. Thomas Creigh—a licentiate of the Presbytery of Carlisle—was ordained, and installed Pastor of this church.

In the beginning of the year 1832, this church was again visited with a revival of religion, which commenced with great power during a Protracted Meeting held in the month of February; although there had been indications, before this, of a change for the better. As the fruits of this gracious outpouring of the Spirit, one hundred and seven persons were added to the church that year. Of these, forty-five were males; sixty-two were females; and thirty-five were heads of families. In regard to the character of this work, it may be remarked, that while there were some measures used of a very questionable tendency—although in accordance with the spirit of the times—yet, if there have ever been genuine revivals of religion, this deserves to be classified with them. Unworthy members will find admittance to the Communion of the church, even when the greatest vigilance has been used to guard its portals. Among our Saviour's own immediate followers—his chosen twelve—there was a Judas. And He has given us intimation in the "parable of the wheat and the tares," that the "visible church" will be a mixed society, until "the Day of Judgment," when He will separate the righteous from the wicked. Why, then, should we look for a different state of things from that which now exists? Ardently as we pray for, and earnestly as we desire it, we cannot expect it fully, while the Church is in an imperfect state. I would then briefly add, that after a period of nearly twenty years since these one hundred and seven persons were received into the Church, the following is the result. Seventeen have died; forty have received letters of dismission to other churches; six have removed without taking certificates, and of whose residence we are ignorant, but who, for aught we know, may be, at the present time, consistent members of other churches; three have been the subjects of church discipline; and one has been ordained to the ministry of the gospel; while all the rest are still in connexion with us, and are in good and regular standing. I simply ask, even when persons are received into the communion of the Church in the ordinary way—when there is no special interest on the subject of religion—whether any Church Register presents a more favourable result? To God alone be all the praise!

In this same year, 1832, the Female Sewing Society was organized, the object of which was to educate poor and pious young men for the Gospel ministry. After a short time, however, it changed its relation, and became auxiliary to the Foreign Missionary Society, and has educated a heathen youth in the Orphan Asylum at Futtehgurh, in North India, under the care of the Rev. Henry R. Wilson, and who bears the name of their former much-loved pastor, David Elliott. The amount of funds contributed since the formation of this society is six hundred dollars.

In 1833, the following persons were added to the Session: Messrs. John Witherspoon, John McCullough, and John Dorrance.

In the winter of 1842 and '43, this church was again visited with a revival of religion. During the nine months immediately following its commencement, thirty-four persons were received into the communion of the Church, on profession of their faith. Of those who were then received, seventeen have been dismissed, and two have entered the ministry. Not a case has occurred requiring the exercise of the discipline of the Church. The manner in which this revival was conducted; the truths which were presented, and the manner in which they were exhibited; the instructions which were given to the inquiring; and the care which was exercised in receiving applicants into the membership of the Church, afforded us every reasonable ground from which to expect the most favourable results.

In 1844, the church edifice in town was repaired, new-modelled, and a vestibule added to it. The expense of repairing and furnishing it was two thousand dollars. It was occupied for the first time, January 12th, 1845, on which occasion the pastor gave an historical sketch of the church, from the time of its organization. In 1849, the following persons were added to the Session:—Messrs. Andrew L. Coyle, John McDowell, James Roberts, and William Patterson.

In 1849, a lecture-room was commenced contiguous to the church. It was finished and furnished at an expense of six hundred dollars. The first time that divine worship was held in it, was August 7th, 1850, on which occasion the pastor delivered a dedication sermon from the words: "For where two or three are gathered together in my name, there am I in the midst of them." (Matt. xviii. 20.) Prior to this, our social meetings were held in the houses of the families belonging to the church in town. We had forty places of meeting, which required nine months to complete their circuit.

During a part of this period which has been claiming our attention, our Church at large was agitated by a difference of opinion, chiefly in reference to doctrines and polity, and which resulted in a division, in 1838, known by the names of *Old School* and *New School.* In all this controversy, which was deep and wide, spread throughout the whole length and breadth of the land, while *here*, too, intense interest was felt in relation to it, yet as a church we have stood fast in the faith of our fathers. Nor, at the present time, is there a church, composed of as many members, more harmonious, or more united, or more cordial in their adherence to the symbols of our faith, as taught in the Westminster Confession of Faith, Catechisms, and Form of Government. We record the fact as a matter of sincere and heartfelt thankfulness.

In November, 1851, the present pastor having completed the twentieth year of his ministry in this church, delivered a sermon commemorative of this interesting event, from the words: "Then Samuel took a stone, and set it between Mizpeh and Shen, and called the name of it, Ebenezer, saying, Hitherto hath the Lord helped us." (1 Sam. vii. 12.) It may not be out of place to give the concluding part of this discourse, which exhibits the results of this score of years in the pastoral office in this church:—

"And, 1st, The Families. When I settled among

you, there were connected with this congregation one hundred and forty families. There are at the present time one hundred and fifty-five. Twenty-two are families of colour. One hundred of them reside in the country, and fifty-five in the village. In all this number who compose this congregation at the present time, there are but sixty who were here when I became pastor—so many and so great have been the changes! And yet we still retain the original number, and have fifteen additional. 2. Baptisms.—Four hundred and fourteen were baptized in infancy, and ninety-six adults, making a total of five hundred and ten. 3. Members.—There have been added to the church, on profession of their faith, four hundred and eight members, and by certificate one hundred and thirty-two, making the whole number five hundred and forty, or an annual increase of twenty-seven. At the present time we have three hundred and sixty under our immediate oversight. Of this number two hundred and forty-two are females, one hundred and eighteen are males, forty-seven couples are husbands and wives, thirty-six are widows, and forty-five are coloured persons. Of those who were members twenty years ago, but seventy-six remain. 4. Ministers.—Seven young men have been either licensed or ordained to preach the Gospel, and two of them have gone forth as missionaries to preach Christ to the heathen. 5. Marriages.—Two hundred and twenty-one marriage ceremonies have been performed. 6. Contributions.—Five thousand eight hundred dollars have been contributed to different benevolent objects. 7. Visits.—The number which has been made amounts to seven thousand six hundred, or annually to three hundred and eighty-five. 8. Sermons, lectures, and addresses.—The number of times which I have preached, lectured, and given addresses within the bounds of the congregation, is twenty-three hundred; and I have in manuscript eleven hundred and thirty sermons and lectures, nearly all of which have been prepared during my connexion with this Church. 9. Deaths.—The number of deaths which have occurred within these twenty years is, two hundred and seventy-two. Of this number, one hundred and sixty-one were members in full communion. The ages of those who have died may be thus classified: Fifty have died in infancy; from infancy to their twenty-fifth year, thirty; from their twenty-fifth to their forty-fifth year, fifty; from their forty-fifth to their sixtieth year, forty-five; from their sixtieth to their seventieth year, thirty; from their seventieth to their eightieth year, thirty-three; and over their eightieth year, twenty. Among these dead, we have to reckon four members of Session,"—and another, since this discourse was delivered, leaving but one of the original members, who composed the Session when the present pastoral relation was formed.

## CONCLUDING REMARKS.

1. To God's care and kindness we are indebted for the permanency and prosperity of this church. It has had its trials and its changes, but the gates of hell have not prevailed against it. At one time in its early history it was entirely scattered; at another time it was nearly broken up; and a third time it was greatly diminished by death, in connexion with pecuniary embarrassments: and yet, in the midst of all these adverse circumstances, the Lord has kept it. And this day, after a period of *one hundred and fourteen years*, notwithstanding all the disasters which have befallen it, the number of its families and communicants has not only *not* diminished, but has been greatly augmented. It is an interesting fact connected with the history of this church, and which ought not to be passed over unnoticed, that for the space of eighty-three years, as far back as our records reach our Church has maintained its ground, as will be seen from the following statements:—In the year 1769, when Dr. King became its pastor, the number of families then connected with it was *one hundred and thirty*. In 1789, twenty years afterwards, he makes the following remark: "*The number of families connected with this congregation is about the same as when I settled.*" In 1812, the number was *one hundred and thirty-seven.* In 1820, upwards of *one*

*hundred and seventy.* In 1831, about *one hundred and forty*—having been greatly diminished by the causes already mentioned. And at the present time (1852), they number *one hundred and fifty-five.* Thus has it never sunk below the first-named number, but has always exceeded it. And rarely has there been a communion season at which, according to the Register, there has not been an addition to its membership. And thrice has it been visited with the special tokens of Divine grace. With devout gratitude we record these facts; and in recording them we give all the glory to Him who has brought them into being. Ministers and members of the Church may labour and pray for the building up of Zion, but unless God hears their prayers and blesses their efforts, Zion cannot prosper. "Not by might, nor by power, but by my Spirit, saith the Lord of Hosts." Or, in the expressive language of that most laborious of all Christ's Apostles, "I have planted, Apollos watered; but God gave the increase. So then neither is he that planteth anything, neither he that watereth, but God, that giveth the increase."

2. If God has thus prospered this Church for so long a time, let us never yield to despondency in regard to its future condition. If, in looking back upon its past history, we can discover that the Lord has led it, and kept it, and prospered it, we are warranted in drawing the conclusion, that if we remain *faithful* to Him, he will continue to dwell among us. These are the terms:—"The Lord is with you

while you be with him ; and if ye seek him, he will be found of you ; but if ye forsake him, he will forsake you." On this principle He has always acted towards the Church. Its entire history, from its commencement to the present time, warrants the remark. And what is thus true of the Church in general, is equally true in its application to particular churches. It is true in relation to *this* church. If this church has been preserved and prospered, it is because it has been *faithful* to its Head. If it would continue to prosper, it must continue in its fidelity to its King. Its *minister,* and its *officers,* and its *members,* must possess the Spirit of their Lord and Master ; must follow closely in His footsteps, must yield implicit obedience to his commands ; must maintain and disseminate the truth ; must be united to one another in sentiment and in affection ; and must labour and pray for its welfare. Thus living and thus acting, God will still bestow upon it the choicest riches of His grace ; its prosperity shall continue to increase, and its permanency shall be rendered sure.

And to secure these ends, may all who belong to this Church, in humble dependence upon the grace of our Divine Lord, adopt the language of the captive Israelites and ever live under its constraining influence: "If I forget thee, O Jerusalem, let my right hand forget her cunning. If I do not remember thee, let my tongue cleave to the roof of my mouth, if I prefer not Jerusalem above my chief joy ! Psalm cxxxvii, 5, 6.

# CHAPTER VI.

## WELSH RUN CHURCH.

This Church, formerly known as "Lower West Conococheague," was originally a part of "Upper West Conococheague," or what is now called Mercersburg." It was organized, A. D. 1741, and grew out of the controversy which about that time so deeply and so extensively agitated the Presbyterian Church at large, and ultimately led to a division which continued for seventeen years.* But though the effects of this division were felt here also, and brought about the formation of this new interest, it was what their situation as a congregation required. The territory covered by the mother church, was much too extensive to allow the people to meet weekly in the same place of worship. And yet when the separation was made, it was done with so much good feeling, that both churches, still adhering to the same Presbytery, were frequently represented in the same Judicatory by the same commissioner.

* See Appendix III.

This church, at a very early period in its history was supplied for a season with the preaching of the gospel by a Rev. Mr. Dunlap. The church edifice in which the congregation then worshipped, was burnt down by the Indians in their wars with the whites. A second building was afterwards erected, which, having undergone frequent repairs, still stands. The congregations which assembled at this place of worship on sacramental occasions were so numerous, that the church being insufficient to accommodate them, it was not an unusual thing for two ministers to be preaching at the same time; the one in the church, and the other in a temporary building, near at hand, called the Tent. From this circumstance, this place of worship was sometimes called the "Tent Meeting-House."

The Rev. Thomas M'Pherrin having become pastor of this church, August 17th, A. D. 1774, continued in this relation until October 2d, A. D. 1799, when he resigned his charge. He died February 3d, A. D. 1802, aged 51 years. Besides preaching to this congregation, he also preached a part of his time to a congregation near Greencastle, which worshipped in a tent that stood on the farm formerly belonging to Mr. Andrew Snively.

From the time of Mr. M'Pherrin's relinquishment of his charge, this church became connected with the Greencastle Church, and was supplied with the pastoral services of the Rev. Robert Kennedy. He commenced his labours among them in 1802, and continued in this connexion until April 9th, 1816, when he removed to Cumberland, Maryland. Having resided in Cumberland for nine years, he returned to this charge in the year 1825, from which time to his decease, he continued in the exercise of the pastoral office among them. Mr. Kennedy died in the fall of 1843.

This church has been subject to many changes. At an early period in its history, it was large and numerous, composed of the most respectable and influential families in the neighbourhood. In the year 1814, the number of families had diminished to seventeen. And at present, there are about seven. There are but two families connected with it now, who stood in this relation to it seventy years ago. At that early period, the entire population of the surrounding country were Scotch-Irish, and all of them belonging to the Presbyterian congregation. Now, the great mass of them are Germans, and belong to the Dunkers and River Brethren.

The materials for the foregoing sketch of the history of this Church, in relation to its early state, were furnished to the writer of it (Rev. Mr. Creigh), by Mr. David Dunwoody, now in his eighty-second year, who was born and reared within its bounds, and who for forty years has been a Ruling Elder in the Church at Mercersburg.

## CHAPTER VII.

### THE CHURCH AT CHAMBERSBURG.

As we have had occasion to state elsewhere, though the Land-office of Pennsylvania was not open for the sale of lands west of the Susquehanna, until they were purchased of the Indians, in October, 1736, yet the proprietary offices and agents were disposed to favour settlements west of that river, with the consent of the Indians, who were conciliated by the settlers. "These settlements were encouraged and recognised, though without official grants, in order to resist the encroachment of the Marylanders on what was considered part of the Province of Pennsylvania. This policy, and the fine country forming that part of the Kittatinny Valley, extending from the Susquehanna, at the mouth of the Conodoguinett, along the waters of the beautiful Conococheague to the Potomac, induced men of enterprise to seek and locate desirable situations for water-works and farms, in the valleys of those two streams, and of Yellow Breeches Creek."

Among the first to explore, and settle in this valley, were four adventurous brothers, James, Robert, Joseph, and Benjamin Chambers, who emigrated from the County of Antrim, in Ireland, to the Province of Pennsylvania, between the years 1726 and 1730. The last of these gentlemen, when about twenty-one years of age, settled where Chambersburg now stands, in 1730, and "The Falling Spring" was the name given by him to the place of his settlement, at the confluence of the large spring with the Conococheague Creek, over the bank of the latter.

The families that subsequently located themselves on and near the waters of this spring (which gave the name to the entire settlement, until 1764), were, with scarcely an exception, Presbyterians, and soon organized a congregation. Until the town of Chambersburg was laid out, in the year just mentioned, this congregation was known as the Congregation of Falling Spring, but after that it was called the Presbyterian Congregation of Chambersburg, and also that of Falling Spring.

Col. Benjamin Chambers, who was himself a Presbyterian, made an early appropriation of some suitable ground for a graveyard, school-house, and place of public worship. This was the romantic cedar grove on the bank of the creek, on which the present church stands. In this grove, and near the spot which the present edifice occupies, there was erected a small log building, which was used for the double purpose of a school-house and place of worship. This building, as would appear from the following extract from the Records of Presbytery, at their *sederunt* in 1739, was erected in that year.

"A Supplication from the people of Canigogig was presented by James Lindsay, commissioner, wherein they requested that Mr. Caven's ordination be hastened. The Presbytery inquired of said commissioner what provision they had made for Mr. Caven's sustenance among them; it was answered, that their subscriptions amounted to forty-six pounds, which they will make good, and what can be had over and above shall be allowed him; and further, they will do what they can to procure a plantation to live upon. The commissioner also learns in writing from that people, signifying that they have agreed about the bounds between them and the west side of Canigogig, west from Alexander Dunlop's to the fork of the creek, and thence the creek to be the line until it come to the line of the Province; and that they have agreed that their other Meeting-House shall be at the Falling Spring."

This old building, as already intimated, was small and exceedingly plain in its structure. It was formed of logs, entered by a door on the eastern side and another on the southern, and lighted by long, narrow windows, which were of the width of two small panes of glass, and reached from one end to the other of the building. When this building, as was frequently the case, was not of sufficient capacity to accommodate all who wished to worship in it, the congregation abandoned it for the time in favour of the saw-mill of Col. Chambers, which stood on the bank of the creek, on what is now known as "The Island," and which was surrounded by a lovely green plot. On that grassy space, when it was at all proper, the gathered crowd seated themselves, and received with interest and eagerness the messages of God from his commissioned ambassador.

In the year 1767 this rude log building was demolished. Its dimensions were entirely too contracted for the increasing community, and besides, something a little more tasteful was demanded by the advancing spirit of the times. Another edifice, therefore, was erected, in which the sacred services of the Sabbath might be performed. This was considerably larger than its predecessor, being about thirty-five by seventy feet, and was of better finished material. It stood where the present church does, though its position was somewhat different, as it presented a side-view to the street. One year after the erection of this church, Col. Chambers by deed conveyed to trustees the grounds that had before been dedicated to the use of the congregation and burial-ground. The form of this appropriation was as follows:

"Deed for ground of Falling Spring Church, dated January 1st, 1768, from Benjamin Chambers and Jane, his wife, to Patrick Vance, Matthew Wilson, Edward Cook, Robert Patterson, William Linsly, Jr., William Gass, and William Brotherton, in trust for the Presbyterian Congregation of Falling Spring, now professing and adhering to, and that shall hereafter adhere to and profess the Westminster Confession of Faith and the mode of Church Government therein contained, witnesseth, that the said Benjamin Chambers and Jane, his wife, as well for their regard to the true religion of the blessed Redeemer, Jesus, the Son of God, and for and in consideration of their regard to the interest and advantage of said congregation, and in consideration of the rents, convey to the Trustees, &c., yielding and paying therefor and thereout unto the said B. C., his heirs or assigns, at the said town of Chambersburg, on the first day of June next first after this date, the yearly rent or consideration of one Rose, if required."

In 1787, the congregation of Falling Spring was incorporated by Act of Assembly, and has ever since been governed in its property affairs by Trustees elected under this Charter. At that time "it would seem that the congregation was larger than in 1832, though at the latter period the population of Chambersburg was tenfold that of 1786. After the revolutionary war and peace, a German population supplanted the first settlers, and possessed themselves of most of their choice plantations by purchase, and the families and descendants of these settlers moved west of the mountains."

The present church edifice at Chambersburg, which was erected in 1803, is a handsome and comfortable building. It is of stone, and indicates by its external structure that it was the product of a past age, yet is it not on this account less, but rather more attractive in its appearance. We like many of the improvements which have of late been made, and the liberality which has generally been displayed in church architecture throughout our land. We undervalue not a due regard to external beauty and becoming decoration in the erection of a house of worship. We sympathize not with those whose penuriousness, though they give it a holier name, makes them content to dwell themselves in houses of cedar, whilst the ark of

God dwelleth within curtains. Rejecting, indeed, on the one hand, a religion of attitude and show, a religion of picturesque and imposing observances, "wherein the fine arts, and the power of genius, the chisel of the sculptor, the ode of the poet, the combinations of instrumental music, the trillings of various voices, the stated procession, the scattered flowers, the blaze of many lights, or the costly frankincense of Arabia, are directed to excite the fancy and the passions to a pitch which lulls the conscience and draws away attention from the conduct,"—on the other hand, we as much admire the taste, the liberality, the sincerity, and the spirit of devotion, which find somewhat of their expression in exercises at once simple and sublime, and in a building for the worship of God, which is convenient in its arrangements, chaste in its design, neat in its furniture, and attractive by its comeliness, rather than repulsive to the eye. To be satisfied that all this is true of the Church at Chambersburg, and that besides, its exterior has an impress of antiquity which throws around it a peculiar interest, it is but necessary to see it. It is at once simple, neat, and beautiful. Its elevated site, also, is a most desirable one, calling as it does, for those who worship within the sanctuary, to leave the associations and pursuits of a bustling yet fading world, and come up to the service of the Lord. The shadows which fall around it, likewise, from trees which were standing when the footstep of the white man first broke the silence of the wilderness, are not without their deep significance; neither is the ivy which covers its walls, as if to bear constant testimony to the truth, that with a steadiness and tenacity, which neither sunshine or storm or revolving seasons can impair, man's affections should rise above the earth, cleave to the risen Saviour, and cluster around the Church which He hath purchased with his precious blood.

There can be no doubt that the congregation at Falling Spring was for a time supplied by ministers sent from the Presbyteries of Donegal and Newcastle. But this arrangement was of short continuance, as the following extract from the minutes of a meeting of a committee of Presbytery, held at "Canigogig, 16th November, 1739, plainly shows.

"Mr. Boyd having published an edict at the door, in the hearing of both societies, Thomas Brown appeared, declared that if said societies are willing to have Mr. Caven ordained among them, he will make no objection against it; at the same time said Thomas Brown desired that the ground of the censure laid on him by the Presbytery be inquired into: the committee, after some discourse on said request, agree to defer the consideration of that affair until the work of ordination be over. Richard O'Cahan, Joseph Armstrong, Benjamin Chambers, and Patrick Jack, have publicly engaged to pay to Mr. Samuel Thompson the sum of one pound five shillings, at or before next meeting of Presbytery, as being the whole of arrears due him by the people at Canigogig."

From this record it is evident that, in all probability, Mr. Thompson preceded Mr. Caven as pastor of "the people of Conococheague," the name by which the congregations of Greencastle and Falling Spring were then known. Mr. Caven resigned his pastoral relation in 1741.

About the year 1767, the Rev. James Lang (or Long, as he was generally called) became the pastor of the church at Falling Spring for one-half his time, the other half being given to Greencastle, where he resided.

In 1792, in compliance with a "supplication" from the united congregations of Falling Spring and East Conococheague, the Rev. William Speer was "appointed for six months statedly to supply them, in rotation with their present pastor, Mr. Lang; to which arrangement Mr. Lang declared his hearty consent."

In 1794, the union between the congregations of Falling Spring and East Conococheague was dissolved, and the latter became the sole charge of Mr. Lang. At the same time Mr. Speer accepted the pastorate of Falling Spring. Mr. Speer was licensed by the Presbytery of Carlisle, June 22d, 1791, ordained and installed pastor of Falling Spring, Oct. 8th, 1794, and his pastoral relation was dissolved in April, 1797.

After being supplied for a time by appointments of Presbytery, the congregation at Chambersburg, in the year 1800, secured the services of the Rev. David Denny, who was set over them in the Lord, and continued to labour among them until 1838, when, on account of the infirmity of years, his resignation was tendered and accepted.

We transfer the following truthful sketch of the history and character of this excellent man, from the Presbytery's book of obituaries of deceased ministers.

"Died at his residence in Chambersburg, on Tuesday, the 16th of December, 1845, the Rev. David Denny, in the 78th year of his age, formerly pastor of the Falling Spring Church, in that place. To those whose sympathy or admiration is limited to terrestrial displays, the memorials of valour or political eminence address a grateful spectacle, but the mind that has learned to reverence religion, and contrast the triumphs of the Cross with the loftiest of mere human attainments, will turn with more delight to the sublime but less ostentatious records of Christian virtue. The modesty that distinguished the venerable servant of God who forms the subject of this notice, would have been sensibly shocked, had he known that a sketch of his retired life would be submitted to the public eye after his decease; and the feeble tribute that is now offered to his memory is not without the restraint imposed by that humble sentiment of self-approbation which he was always known to cherish.

"The Rev. David Denny was the third son of a revolutionary soldier who fell in battle, when his eldest son, contending at his side, was captured by the enemy. He graduated at Dickinson College, while Dr. Charles Nesbit was Principal of that Institution, and under that learned and classic divine began and completed his theological studies. He was a fond admirer of his distinguished preceptor, and the writer has often heard him narrate anecdotes illustrative of his wit, learning, and accomplishments. The sources of Philosophy and Divinity at that day were neither as copious nor accessible as at present, and the acquisitions of the student were consequently earned by severer toil and application, than the facilities of learning now exact. The lectures of Dr. Nesbit were delivered at a modulated rate and tone, that the members of his class might be able to reduce them to writing as they fell from his lips. The deceased has left in his library seven quarto volumes of these discourses, in his own handsome and legible handwriting, which form together a respectable body of metaphysics and divinity. Whatever the present intrinsic value of these lectures may be, when the bounds of sacred and profane learning have been so much enlarged, the diligent reader will find in many pages of them, strong marks of the erudition, original thought, and classic taste of the author.

"Mr. Denny was licensed to preach about the year 1792, by the Presbytery of Carlisle, within whose bounds he remained until the close of his pastoral office. He was first installed over two congregations in Path Valley, that had lately become vacant by the death of the Rev. Mr. Dougal, where he continued until the year 1800, in the enjoyment of the esteem and affections of a much-beloved people. In the year last mentioned, he was transferred to the pastoral charge of the Falling Spring Church, in Chambersburg, which he retained until the termination of his public ministrations,—a period of 38 years. That church, then in comparative infancy, was delivered over at his retirement to his estimable successor in the pastoral office, in the vigour and maturity of improving manhood. His means derived from the ministry being inadequate to the demands of a large and growing family, he was obliged to combine with it, for a series of years, the labours of a teacher of the learned languages in an academy, and being a master of economy he secured that enviable maintenance midway between poverty and wealth, so desirable to the good man, and that proves at once a defence against the inconveniences of penury, and the vices of profusion.

"In the year of Mr. Denny's retirement from the active duties of the sanctuary, death snatched from his side the fond partner of his pilgrimage, a lady of exalted worth, and by the same stroke broke his cheerful spirit and firm constitution. Companions also who shared his better years and pastoral intimacy, had then dropped away one by one around him, until he was left almost alone, like the gray oak of the forest, surrounded by generations of a younger growth. He continued to languish under increasing infirmity, until repeated attacks of paralysis accelerated his decline and deprived him of the power of articulate speech. It was not until several months after this trying visitation, that the mysterious hand which often chastens out of plenitude of love, called him, by a voice gentle and meek as the breathing of infant slumber, from the sorrows of his earthly state to the joyous assembly of the just. His person, cast in the finest mould for strength, activity, and proportion, was well adapted to the air of dignity which Nature herself had impressed upon it. His mind was of a strong and discerning order, always governed by candour and sincerity, and warmed by the love of truth. His views were expressed in the language of simplicity and earnestness, neither adorned nor obscured by the garnish of imagery or the flashes of rhetoric.

"In doctrine Mr. Denny was a decided Calvinist, and conscientiously attached to the standards of the Presbyterian Church. The tide of new measures that threatened, about the close of his ministerial career, the subversion of everything like rational religion in the church, was consonant neither to his judgment nor taste, but regarded rather as the offspring of Pelagian error than the fruit of evangelical repentance,—a decision which the overseers of the honour and purity of the Church are fast vindicating, by the substitution of a higher and more solemn test of spiritual improvement. Modesty and humility were interwoven with the very texture of his heart, and its liveliest sympathies were always in expansion for the sick, the suffering, and the desolate.

"Neither inclemency of weather nor transient illness were suffered to detain him from the exercises of the pulpit, and he enjoyed in no ordinary degree the esteem and affection of the people among whom he laboured. He was actuated in social intercourse by a manly, tolerant, and liberal spirit, and has left to all who stood in private or public relations to him, an example of many virtues with which humanity is not often adorned, which they may fail to imitate, but can never cease to admire and love."

As in addition to his active interest in other Christian enterprises, the Rev. Mr. Denny took a prominent part in the organization of "The Franklin County Bible Society." We give some account of the origin of this association.*

After Mr. Denny's withdrawment from his pulpit, the Rev. William Adam was chosen to fill it, in September, 1839, and did so until April, 1841, when impaired health demanded a temporary cessation of his ministerial labours.

The Rev. Daniel McKinley was Mr. Adam's successor, and continued to be pastor of the church for nine years. At the time of his resignation Dr. McKinley accepted a call to a congregation in the city of Pittsburg.

After being vacant for about twelve months, the congregation invited Mr. Joseph Clark, a Licentiate of the Presbytery of Carlisle, to be their stated supply for a year, and before the expiration of this time, he was unanimously called to be their pastor. Mr.

* See Appendix IV.

Clarke was ordained and installed in June, 1852,—the Rev. Messrs. D. D. Clarke, Creigh, Morris, and Dr. McKinley, officiating on the occasion.

The Session of the Church, at present, consists of the following members:—Samuel McIlroy, David Lytle, Robert Sharp, Holmes Crawford, John Cree, and Robert Black.

As Fayetteville lies within the ancient limits of the congregation of Chambersburg, this may be the proper place to notice the church there. This congregation was organized, July, 21st, 1833. For a number of years it was favoured with preaching by the pastors of the Chambersburg church, and for a brief season, was served by Mr. Thos. K. Davis, a licentiate, but for some time it has been under the care of the Rev. James F. Kennedy, who unites with his ministerial office the charge of a flourishing classical academy in Chambersburg. The congregation is not large, but is steadily increasing. It worships in a comfortable brick building, which stands near the centre of the village, and which is owned jointly by the Presbyterian and the German Reformed congregations of the place.

Let us now turn to the churchyard of the congregation of The Falling Spring.

"A churchyard! 'tis a homely word, yet full
Of feeling: and a sound which o'er the heart
Might shed religion. In the gloom of graves
I read the curse primeval, and the voice
That wreaked it seems to whisper by these tombs
Of village quiet, which around me lie
In green humility. Can Life, the dead

Among be musing, nor to God advance
The spirit of her thought? True Nature wears
No rustic mourning here: in golden play
Her sprightly grass—flowers wave, the random breeze
Hums in the noon, or with yon froward bough
A murm'ring quarrel wakes: and yet, how oft
In such a haunt, the insuppressive sigh
Is heard, while feelings which may pilot years
To glory, spring from out a minute's gloom."

The expression of admiration is universal on the part of those who visit the Cemetery at Chambersburg. And it is, unquestionably, one of the loveliest homes of the dead that is anywhere to be seen. Though within the precincts of the town, it is yet in a great measure hidden from the view, and pervaded by much of the solemn stillness of the country. A wanderer among its tombs might easily imagine himself in some lonely retreat, secluded from the world, and where none would be likely to disturb his meditations or see the falling tear. This beautiful place, which lies in the rear of the church, is skirted on the north by the Conococheague, whose waters flow noiselessly along beneath a steep and high descent. In the direction of its southern extremity, and but a short distance from it, are to be heard the murmurs of the Falling Spring, as it rolls onward, soon to lose itself in the deeper stream to which it pays its tribute. The time was when this spring flowed through the graveyard, in the deep ravine which yet divides it in a direction nearly north and south, but it was at an early day diverted from this channel to its present course, that its power might be employed for a useful and profitable purpose. That ravine is now occupied with a number of majestic trees, which have since grown up in its bosom, and its sides are thickly studded with smaller ones, and bushes of various kinds. This, indeed, is true of the entire yard : it is nearly altogether protected in this way from the rays of the sun. The visitor at once, and with interest, observes the rich shrubbery which adorns the undulating ground on which he treads, the numerous cedars scattered through the enclosure, as if to represent the unfading recollections of the departed which are cherished in many a heart, and the refreshing shade which is spread around him by stately trees which once sheltered the redman in his slumbers after the toils of the day, and which yet maintain their vigour and freshness amid the very ravages of death. Sacred spot! How many warm tears have gushed upon thee! How many crushed hearts have poured forth their wailings upon thy passing breeze! How many affections hast thou seen to bleed, and how many hopes to perish! How many loved treasures hast thou unveiled thy bosom to receive, which now rest beneath the grassy mounds which mark thy surface! How many sad memories continually linger about thee! How many, too, are there, among thy silent and shattered occupants, who, because they died in faith in Him who is the Resurrection and the Life, shall catch with triumph the last trumpet's stirring sound,

> "Then burst the chains in sweet surprise,
> And in the Saviour's image rise!"

## CHAPTER VIII.

### THE CHURCH AT SHIPPENSBURG.

SHIPPENSBURG is the oldest town, except York, west of the Susquehanna River. It was originally wholly settled by Irish. In it the courts were held when Cumberland was organized, 1750. During the French and Indian wars, two forts, Fort Morris and Fort Franklin, were erected there, the remains of one of which, were, until lately, still to be seen. Some idea of the size and condition of the place, a little more than a century ago, may be derived from the subjoined extracts from a letter, dated June 14th, 1755, to Governor Morris, from Charles Swaine, who, it appears, was on a visit to the place on public business.

"I judge there are sufficient buildings for storing the provisions, without erecting any."

"I find not above two pastures here, those but mean as to grass, from drought, but there is a fine range of forage for upwards of four miles, in the woods, quite to the foot of the South Mountain. "There are no bricks here, and little lime at present, so the making ovens would be difficult, and if made of clay, then there would be some iron-work wanting."

One of the earliest churches organized in Shippensburg was the *Associate Reformed Presbyterian.* Until this organization was effected, the Episcopal element was, perhaps, dominant in the borough, through the influence of Mr. Shippen, the proprietor, who was connected with that denomination. This church was under the care of the Second Presbytery of Philadelphia, in connexion with the Associate Reformed Synod. For a number of years the Rev. Mr. Walker was its pastor. After his separation from it, the pulpit was filled, for about eighteen months, by the Rev. Mr. Strong, now of New York. In 1823, the Rev. Henry R. Wilson was called, with the permission of the Presbytery, to take charge of the congregation. Mr. Wilson continued in connexion with that body until 1825, when it was dissolved, and he was received by the Presbytery of Carlisle. Mr. Wilson continued to be pastor of this church until 1839. The following sketch of the history and character of this useful servant of the Lord, is an abridgment of his obituary, as published in the "Presbyterian," June 14, 1849.

"The Rev. Henry R. Wilson, D.D., was born in the neighbourhood of Gettysburg, Adams County, Pa., on the 7th of August, 1780. He was graduated at Dickinson College, Carlisle, whilst the venerable Charles Nesbit presided over that Institution, in the days of its prosperity. He was licensed to preach the gospel by the Presbytery of Carlisle in 1801.

After labouring for some months in Virginia, as a supply, he removed with his family to Bellefonte, Centre County, Pa., where Presbyterians had neither organized church nor house of worship. He commenced preaching in the court-house. His labours were greatly blessed in gathering here a church, as also another at Lick Run, twelve miles distant. Over these congregations he was installed pastor by the Presbytery of Huntingdon, in 1802.

"In 1806, Mr. Wilson was chosen, at the early age of twenty-six, to fill the Professorship of Languages in Dickinson College. A part of the time, during his connexion with the College, he preached to the Presbyterian Church of Carlisle, as colleague with President Davidson. In 1814, a call was presented to him by the congregation of Silvers' Spring, which he accepted.

"In 1823, Dr. Wilson received a call from the church in Shippensburg. During his ministry there, the church enjoyed some precious seasons of refreshing, 'and many were added unto the Lord.' He was indefatigable and abundant in labours.

"In 1838, Dr. Wilson was chosen the first General Agent of the Board of Publication, in which station he laboured arduously until 1842, when he resigned his office in that Board, and accepted a call from the church at Neshaminy, at Hartsville, Bucks County, Pa. Here, with his accustomed fidelity, he continued to discharge the duties of pastor until the month of October, 1848, when, at his own request, the pastoral relation was dissolved.

"For some months previous his health had become so infirm, that he was seldom able to preach, except when carried from his bed to the church, and placed in a chair, in which posture he delivered his message, amidst much bodily weakness and suffering, but with his usual clearness of mind, and earnestness of manner.

"Dr. Wilson's health continued to decline, notwithstanding the cessation of his ministerial labours.

"After a sore conflict of forty-six hours, he died in Philadelphia, on the morning of Thursday, the 22d of March, 1849, and was interred the day following, at Hartsville, the scene of his closing labours in the ministry. An appropriate discourse was delivered on the occasion by the Rev. Dr. Steel, of Abington, and the sympathies and affections of the people of his recent charge were abundantly shown toward one whom, though absent, they had not ceased to regard and love as their pastor.

"The life of Dr. Wilson was an eventful one. More can be said of him, than that he passed through scenes of some interest, grew old, and then died. From his earliest labours in the Gospel there was demand for a steadiness of purpose, and an energy of execution, that not every man is equal to.

"The influence of such a man in the Church, we cannot duly estimate. He was a pioneer in the cause of the Gospel in Central Pennsylvania, and his labours essentially contributed to lay firm and deep the foundations of those churches that adorn and bless the region of his earliest toil. Ministers of Dr. Wilson's character stamp an impression upon the times in which they live. They give a fixedness to the order, the government, the instruction, and standard of piety in the church, by which, they being dead, yet speak.

"The ministerial labours of this venerable man were abundant. His preaching was in character with the man. It came down from a former generation, with all that seriousness of manner and weight of instruction, that are the fairest ornaments of the Christian Pulpit. His whole deportment and performance may truly be said to have been characterized by simplicity and godly sincerity. Eminently instructive, his preaching always made the impression, 'these things are so,' and religion is a serious and important matter.

"I never knew a man less influenced in his ministerial work by the changing circumstances around him. Whether the congregation was large or small, whether prosperity attended his steps, or disappointment was his portion, not in these was he to find the measure or the motive of his labours. He felt himself to be of that number to whom it has been commanded, 'Go and preach,' and whose the promise is, 'Lo, I am with you alway.' Not the increase, the *work* was his. Not the measure of his success, but the command of Christ, and the assurance that God would bless and prosper his own truth;—this was the rule and the measure of his toil.

"Thus he *lived*, a laborious and eminently useful preacher of the Gospel, the crown of his family, and an ornament to the ministry of reconciliation.

"Thus he *died*, amidst great bodily suffering, with the language of praise upon his lips. Not weary with his ministerial labours, and his conflicts as a sinner saved, but in obedience to the Master's call, 'It is enough, come up higher,' he bade the world adieu, with a full hope of immortality, most beloved by those who knew him best, and lamented by all pious men of every name."

The Rev. James Harper was the successor of Dr. Wilson at Shippensburg. The call was given to him and accepted, in 1840, and in that Pastorate he has ever since continued, with a sustaining evidence of the Divine blessing upon his labours, and a large and influential congregation committed to his care.

The first elders of the congregation of whom there is any record, were, John Means, who died September 1, 1823, and William Bard, who was ordained in May, 1805, declined in 1823, was re-elected and installed in 1825, and declined in 1826. The Session is at present composed of George M'Ginnis, installed April 11, 1824; John Reside, ordained and installed at the same time; Daniel Henderson, installed January 2, 1825; Alexander P. Kelso, ordained and installed Oct. 4, 1845; Dr. Wm. Rankin and Robert Mateer, ordained and installed, Feb. 6, 1848; and Benjamin

Snodgrass, John Mateer, and John Bridges, ordained and installed, Sept. 7, 1851.

A few years after Mr. Harper's settlement among that people, the church property was brought into litigation. It was claimed by the few Associate Reformed members still remaining in the town and neighbourhood, and suit was brought by them to establish their exclusive right to the building. Their effort was successful. The Presbyterian congregation then purchased a lot in a different part of the town, and erected the edifice in which they now worship. This is a neat brick building, constructed and furnished according to the modern style, with a gallery for a choir, and of sufficient capacity to accommodate about four hundred and fifty persons. Immediately in the rear of it is a lot, which has been set apart for a graveyard, and which already has received not a few who have, since the transfer of the place of worship, yielded to the doom that is appointed unto all men.

Though feeling a deep interest in all the Presbyterian congregations of Cumberland Valley, it would be strange if we did not cherish, and perhaps as strange if we did not here acknowledge, a special regard for the Congregation of Shippensburg. Within its boundaries we were first numbered among the living; to its sanctuary our infant feet were led by the hand of love; by the venerable servant of the Lord who presided over its interests during our childhood were we taught the holy truths of Christianity;

at its altar we first entered publicly into covenant with God; and in its cemetery there are those entombed, for whom an ardent affection must be felt whilst memory shall endure. It, therefore, naturally occupies a warm place in our heart. True, the years which have rolled away since we have been absent from it, in preparing for, and in the performance of, professional duty, have wrought in it, as in other churches, many changes, yet still is it ever remembered with an interest which advancing time increases rather than abates. Long may it exist in peace and prosperity, and long may the very large contribution which it has hitherto made of its pious young men to the holy ministry, continue.

# CHAPTER IX.

## GREENCASTLE CHURCH.

In the year 1738, the Congregation, which, previously to that time, seems to have been known as the Congregation of the "*Conococheague Settlement*," was divided. The following extract from the Records of Presbytery, will show their action in the case.

"The affair of Conegocheck reassumed, and several papers being read, and a pretty dale said by several persons on that affair, at last the Presbytery understanding that the people of the east and west sides of the creek, had agreed among themselves to divide into two societies, the one on the east and the other on the west side, and those on the east side having presented a call for Mr. Caven to be their minister, the Presbytery, taking these things into consideration, do, in the first place, considering circumstances, approve of the division, though we think they have acted somewhat precipitantly in separating without consent of the Presbytery, and have likewise presented the call of the east side to Mr. Caven, which he has taken under his consideration. N. B. That Alexander Dunlop is the highest that belongs to the society on the west side."

At the time the separation here referred to took place, the eastern part of the congregation thus set off, embraced the people of the region which is now known as the town of Greencastle and its vicinity, but which was then called "East Conococheague." At that time, also, the congregations of "East Conococheague" and "Falling Spring," were united as one charge, and were under the pastoral supervision of the Rev. Mr. Caven.

The connexion of Mr. Caven with this people as their shepherd was but of brief duration. A complaint was preferred against him before Presbytery, in 1741, by a part of the congregation of "Falling Spring," and although Presbytery "could not find any gross immorality proved against him, yet they thought he ought to be admonished for some expressions which appeared to them imprudent and unguarded, such as speaking of his sacred office under the notion of a trade, and his running to drive the devil; and accordingly they admonished him, and yielded to his request to be dismissed from his congregation."

The probability is, that Mr. Caven continued to be pastor of "East Conococheague" until 1747. His place was supplied in 1754 and '55, by the Rev. John Steel, who had charge of the congregation for this length of time in connexion with the congregation of "West Conococheague," but was then obliged by the Indian disturbances to abandon his post.

In the year 1769, the union between the congregations of East Conococheague and Falling Spring which had previously been dissolved, was re-formed, and the Rev. James Lang was called as Pastor of the charge. It seems scarcely credible that the former of these congregations should remain vacant for more than twenty years, with the exception of the two years' service rendered them by the Rev. Mr. Steel, yet such is the fact, for anything that appears to the contrary in the Presbyterial records; and the sessional records of the church, which might be expected to throw some light upon this point, if indeed they ever had an existence, have perished.

We here take occasion to express our regret, that there is generally so much indifference on the part of our church sessions, in regard to preserving a history of their respective congregations. We were not aware that this neglect was so common or extensive in the Presbytery of Carlisle, until we came to seek the information necessary for the satisfactory accomplishment of our present undertaking. In the case of the church now before us, we were sad to learn that "its sessional records, previous to the year A. D. 1837, are not to be found." The late pastor of another large congregation writes, that "In furnishing you with facts relative to our church, I will have to depend almost entirely on oral communications from some of our oldest and most intelligent church members." In several other instances, also, where we hoped to meet with full and accurate records, we were referred to floating, and sometimes vague, traditions.

In affirming that these things ought not so to be, we are sure we utter a sentiment in which no one, after due reflection, can fail to concur. In addition to the reasons which must suggest themselves to every mind, in favour of a measure which would enable children's children to trace back to its beginning the congregation in which their ancestors worshipped, we may be allowed to suggest that another is to be found in the fact, that in this vast country of ours, so rapidly rising to a magnitude and importance almost overwhelming to the mind, and in which Freedom's and Christianity's last battle seems destined to be fought, every revolving year is attaching augmented interest to the past, and especially to the primitive churches, which were organized for the diffusion of religion and morality, so essential to national greatness and perpetuity. So, too, we may add, is it constantly becoming of more and more importance, for those who believe that "God is in history," to look back upon the moulding power which the former years have exerted upon the present, and to study the Christianity of the first settlers of our land, in the light of the circumstances and peculiar influences under which it was developed.

It is also to be deplored, that something of the blame to which we have just adverted, attaches to the Presbytery to which these churches belong. Only in the year 1847 was it that a resolution was adopted by this body, requiring an obituary of its deceased clerical members to be prepared and preserved. Previously to this time, the simple entry upon their book of records, "The Rev. A. B. was removed by death since our last meeting," was all the notice that was taken of the demise of men, many of whom for long years preached the Gospel faithfully and successfully within their bounds, and whose history, consequently, has well-nigh faded away.

But, returning from this digression, we proceed to say that, in the year 1793, "in consequence of some late proceedings of the congregation of Falling Spring," the union between that congregation and the congregation of East Conococheague was severed. After this separation, the congregation of East Conococheague became the sole charge of the Rev. Mr. Lang, and enjoyed his whole labours. This gentleman, on a charge of intemperance, "was suspended from the exercise of the Gospel ministry *sine die*," in 1802.

In October of the same year, a call was presented to Mr. Robert Kennedy, from "the united congregations of East and Lower West Conococheague," or Welsh Run, which was accepted. In April, 1803, public notice having been given (according to the custom which then prevailed), that if any persons had any objections to the ordination of Mr. Kennedy, and his installation in the congregations to which he had been called, they should state them at a specified time, and no objections having been presented, Mr. Kennedy was ordained and installed. On this occasion the sermon, previous to the induction into the ministerial and pastoral offices, was preached by the Rev. Mr. Snowden, and Dr. Davidson "presided and gave a charge." In 1816, the pastoral relation between Mr. Kennedy and these congregations was, by his own request, dissolved.

In relation to this good man, the Rev. A. A. M'Ginley, D.D., for many years his co-presbyter and familiar friend, has thus written:

"In the year of our Lord 1803, the Rev. Robert Kennedy was ordained and installed Pastor of the Churches of Greencastle and Welsh Run. He had officiated as their stated supply for six previous months. Mr. Kennedy was born in the lower end of Lancaster County, Pa., in 1775. He graduated at Dickinson College, Carlisle. He was the best scholar in his collegiate class. Immediately after leaving College, he commenced the study of Theology, with a view to the Gospel ministry. He was licensed by the Presbytery of Newcastle in 1800. At that time there were a number of vacant churches in the bounds of the Presbytery of Carlisle, where Mr. K. laboured until he was settled as above stated. On the morning of the day of his ordination, he requested the Presbytery to dispense, in his case, with the ceremony of imposition of hands, alleging that it was not intended to be continued in the Church after the cessation of miraculous gifts. Presbytery was not disposed to listen to his objection, but gave him half an hour to decide whether he would remain unordained, or submit to be ordained in the usual way. With deep feeling, he at length submitted to the judgment of Presbytery.

"As a preacher, Mr. Kennedy had few superiors. The plan of his discourses was as clear as the sun. He could pour a flood of light on almost every subject he discussed. And although his voice was unmusical and his pronunciation somewhat peculiar, yet there was no difficulty, but great pleasure and profit, in attending to his sermons. They were always orthodox, always to the point, always instructive, and frequently very impressive. As a scholar, Mr. Kennedy was superior to most ministers of his day. Without the assistance of an instructor, by his own industry, he obtained a competent knowledge of the Hebrew language, and was master of Greek and Latin. As a friend, Mr. K. was most valuable. Firm and constant in his attachments, he would not suffer dangers or difficulties to alienate him from those for whom he professed friendship."

Two years after the pulpit was vacated by Mr. Kennedy's resignation, a call from the congregation of East Conococheague was given to the Rev. James Buchanan, in which they promised him nine hundred dollars annually, and agreed to allow the people of Waynesburg to enjoy the one-third of his pastoral labours. Mr. Buchanan, who had previously been settled at Harrisburg, accepted this call, and continued to serve the congregation, though never installed as its pastor, until 1839, when, in consequence of ill health, which disqualified him for the public duties of the ministry, his connexions with it was dissolved. It is, we need scarcely say, an anomalous thing, in the Presbyterian Church, for a minister to preach to a congregation so long a time without installation, but this irregularity was tolerated in this case by Presbytery, in view of Mr. Buchanan's feeble health, which from year to year, seemed to render such a solemnity unadvisable.

For the following notice of this excellent man, we are indebted to the Rev. David Elliott, D.D., of the Theological Seminary at Allegheny, who was long and intimately acquainted with him.

"The Rev. James Buchanan was a native of Chester County, Pennsylvania. He received his collegiate education in Dickinson College, Carlisle, where he was graduated Sept. 28th, 1803. He studied Theology with the Rev. Nathan Grier, D.D., of Brandywine, and was licensed by the Presbytery of Newcastle, when he was about twenty-three years of age. His first settlement was in the Presbyterian Church of Harrisburg, Pennsylvania, where he laboured some years with faithfulness and success. His health having become impaired, he resigned his pastoral charge, and spent several years in travelling, with a view to its restoration. At length, finding his health in some degree restored, and having received a call from the congregation of Greencastle, he accepted it, and became their pastor in the year 1816. In this pastoral charge he laboured with great fidelity and acceptance for about twenty years, when on account of declining health, and his inability to discharge his pastoral duties to his own satisfaction, he resigned his charge, to the very great regret of his congregation, who were devotedly attached to him. In hope of retaining him with them, they generously offered to accept a diminished amount of labour, such as his weak health would allow, without any diminution of salary. But a sense of duty and a regard to their highest interests, induced him to withdraw, and open the way for the settlement of another pastor, who would be able to give them the full amount of labour. By changing his location, also, he hoped that something might be gained in point of health, and that his life might be rendered more useful in the service of his Divine Master. He accordingly removed with his family to Logansport, Indiana, where, in charge of the Presbyterian church in that place, he laboured with encouraging success, until the Head of the Church dismissed him to the possession of his reward. As pleasing evidence that he did not labour in vain, we have been informed that during the short period of his ministry there, the church increased from about twenty to an hundred members. His death took place at Logansport, on the 16th of September, 1843, at the age of sixty years. His disease, which was congestion of the brain, and which at its first appearance on the Sabbath, obliged him to close abruptly the public services of the sanctuary in which he was engaged, terminated in death on the Saturday morning following, at five o'clock. The nature and violence of his disease incapacitated him for much satisfactory conversation. He gave ample evidence, however, of his resignation to the will of God, and that his hope of salvation was firmly fixed upon the atoning blood of Christ.

To strangers who did not know Mr. Buchanan, his appearance was rather harsh and repulsive. His delicate health and shattered nerves, often greatly affected his spirits, and gave to his countenance the appearance of severity and moroseness. But he was a man of a warm heart, and of a kind and generous disposition. In his friendships he was steadfast, as the writer's experience for upwards of twenty years enables him to attest. Although he was generally grave, yet in the midst of his intimate friends he often relaxed, and was highly cheerful and sociable. His piety was of a retiring and unostentatious character. It was, however, eminently practical, prompting him to the diligent discharge of all incumbent duties. He placed a very low estimate on his own piety, and although no one else doubted its reality, he himself often did. His bodily complaints gave a melancholy complexion to his religious experience, and interfered largely with his Christian comfort: occasionally, however, he was favoured with seasons of comfort, during which he greatly enjoyed the consolations of religion.

As a preacher, he held a very respectable rank. His sermons, in their structure, were neat, systematic, and short; in their matter, solid, evangelical, and practical; and in their manner, grave, solemn, and earnest. Although he could not be considered eloquent, he scarcely ever failed to interest and please those, who were capable of judging correctly and had a taste for good preaching. Indeed, we have known very few men who preached so uniformly well.

In the Judicatories of the Church, Mr. Buchanan rarely spoke. This was not owing to any want of interest in the affairs of the Church, or any want of readiness in communicating his thoughts, but to his nervous debility, which induced embarrassment, and rendered it exceedingly painful for him to make the effort. He was, however, a judicious counsellor, and did his part, in this way, in the disposal of the business of the Church.

In his doctrinal views, he adhered strictly to the standards of our Church, which he believed to be in conformity with the Word of God. He eschewed all novelties in doctrines and forms of worship, being content to walk in "the old paths," and the "good way" in which his fathers had trod. He was decidedly and from conviction Old School, and gave his hearty approval to the measures which were adopted by the Assemblies of 1837 and 1838, to purify the Church from error."

The Rev. J. T. Marshall Davie was the successor of Mr. Buchanan. Mr. Davie, in 1840, received a call from the congregations of Greencastle and Hagerstown. This call he accepted, at the same time resigning his connexion with the Church at Lancaster; and in this new relation he continued until 1845, when, by his desire, it was dissolved.

After Mr. Davie's resignation, the Rev. T. V. Moore, of Carlisle, was chosen pastor of the Church at Greencastle; and the Church at Waynesboro', which until that time was in connexion with it, then became separated, and attached, as it still is, to the charge of the Rev. D. D. Clarke, of Adams County. After Mr. Moore's acceptance of a call, in 1847, to the First Presbyterian Church of Richmond, Va., the Rev. W. M. Paxton became pastor at Greencastle, and continued in that relation about two years, when he took charge of the First Presbyterian Church of Pittsburg. The congregation, after having been vacant for a year or two, has recently had installed over it the Rev. Edwin Emerson, of New York, and a member of the last graduating class at the Theological Seminary of Princeton.

The following are the names of those who, fifty years ago and subsequently, were ruling elders in the East Conococheague congregation:—John M. Davidson, Robert Robison, Mr. Sellar, John Watson, John M'Lean, Dr. John Boggs, Dr. Andrew Heatherington, David Fullerton. All of these have gone the way of all flesh, except Robert Robison, who now, in the 85th year of his age, still continues a member of session, and a regular attendant on the public ministrations and ordinances of God's house. "In him," says a correspondent, "there is full illustration of the words of the Psalmist, 'The righteous shall flourish like the palm tree, he shall grow like a cedar in Lebanon.—They shall still bring forth fruit in old age: they shall be fat and flourishing.' "

The Session, as at present constituted, consists of Robert Robison, James Davison, John Waddel, and Dr. James K. Davidson.

The first building used as a place of public worship, within the bounds of the East Conococheague congregation, was erected near a spring, on the lands of Wm. Rankin, about three-quarters of a mile east of Greencastle. The plan of the edifice was one, which appears to have been very generally adopted throughout that section of the country, at that time. It was a frame building, 42½ by 28½ feet, one story high, weatherboarded, and painted red. The inside was ceiled and lined with boards. There was an aisle running the whole length of the building, and from this, running at right angles, were two aisles, leading to the front of the building, the former communicating at each end with a door, and the latter, each with a door in front. The pulpit, made in the style of those days, stood at the middle of the north side of the house. The pews were arranged on either side, and in front along the aisle. The precise number of pews, before and after the enlargement of the building, is not known. During the incumbency of the Rev. Robert Kennedy, for want of sufficient room to accommodate the congregation with seats, an addition twelve feet wide, was made to the front. From all the information, we can gain, it is about one hundred years since the "Old Red Meeting-House," as it was, and is still called, was built. This was about thirty years before the town of Greencastle was laid out by Col. John Allison. This house continued to be the place of worship, until the year 1828 or '29, when it was sold, and some of the material, we have been told, was used in the construction of a barn, which still stands on an adjacent farm. At that date the place of meeting was transferred to Greencastle.

The present church edifice, is situated on the south side of West Baltimore Street, and was built in the years 1829 and '30. It is a plain brick building, being 60 feet long by 50 feet wide, finished in a very neat and substantial manner, and having a basement under part of it. There are two aisles running its whole length, and communicating at each end with double doors. It contains sixty-eight pews, and can, under the present arrangement, very conveniently accommodate with seats, an audience of four hundred persons. The pulpit, constructed in a very plain and chaste style, somewhat on the modern plan, stands in the middle of the southern end, contrasting well with the rest of the building. The room in the basement being damp, and without means for its proper ventilation, the congregation, a few years since, built quite a neat and beautiful lecture-room, near to the church, in which the Sabbath School now assembles, and the weekly meetings are regularly held.

# CHAPTER X.

## ROCKY SPRING CHURCH.

[A series of articles, entitled "*Chambersburg and its Changes*," from the pen of William C. Lane, M.D., appeared in the "Cumberland Valley Sentinel," during the past year. To the politeness of this gentleman we are indebted, for the use which is now made of the following one of those well-written historical sketches. It was prepared with so much accuracy, as to render unnecessary on our part, a repetition of the labour of its author, in the collection and arrangement of the materials which it embodies. We have modified the article somewhat, to adapt it to our purpose, and made to it several considerable additions, but it is substantially the same as at its first publication.—A. N.]

So we descend; and winding round a rock,
Attain a point that showed the valley—stretched
In length before us; and, not distant far,
Upon a rising ground a gray church towers,
Whose battlements were screened by tufted trees.
And, towards a crystal mere, that lay beyond,
Among steep hills and woods embosomed, flowed
A copious stream with boldly-winding course;
Here traceable, there hidden—there again
To sight restored, and glittering in the sun.
Green is the churchyard, beautiful and green,
Ridge rising gently by the side of ridge,
A heaving surface—almost wholly free
From interruption of sepulchral stones,
And mantled o'er with aboriginal turf
And everlasting flowers.

WORDSWORTH.

WE are acquainted with no spot in our County,

around which cluster more hallowed and interesting associations, than the Church at Rocky Spring.

After a ride of four miles from Chambersburg, over the tortuous road which runs over the Slate Hills, towards Strasburg, we approach the venerable edifice. It stands near the brow of a hill, which slopes gradually away in the distance, towards the east. The hill seems to be composed almost entirely of limestone rocks, and, at the foot, near the Spring, where some excavating has been done, are to be seen large masses of rock, rising to some distance above the level of the water, and indicating that the whole hill is composed of the same material. The country for miles around is all slate land, through which a vein of limestone runs, upon which the church is situated. At the foot of the hill, below the church, on the west, the Rocky Spring gushes from the hill, and spreads out into a broad sheet of cold and clear water in the vale; and after forming a pretty cascade by falling over an embankment, soon becomes lost among the luxuriant meadows, and quietly wends its way to Back Creek, into which it empties. As we approach the Spring from Chambersburg, we pass a beautiful woods upon a high hill, opposite to which, in the valley, is an old orchard, thickly filled with ancient fruit trees. There are several roads leading to the church from different directions, which make it easy of access from all points. From the hill-top, the view is one which is not often excelled for picturesque and lovely scenery. The hills and valleys spotted over with farm-houses, the thick woods and green fields, the beautiful stream meandering through the rich meadows, the old building and its graveyard with its ancient tombs and fragments of broken fences about the graves, make the prospect one of more than ordinary beauty and interest.

The church is an ancient and time-worn structure, which stands upon the hill-side, without any ornament near it, except a single large hickory tree, which grows near the north end, and a small cluster of trees a few rods distant towards the southwest. Its form is nearly square, and is in size, about 60 by 48 feet. It is built of brick, upon a stone foundation which is several feet in height. On the southern side is the front of the church. There are two doors by which it is entered, and, as the floor is some feet above the level of the ground, some kind of steps are requisite. One door is reached by five rude steps, similar to those used in cellars, formed out of heavy boards, and which are not cased on either side. At the other door lie two rough logs, which answer the purpose of steps. The west side is also provided with steps, precisely like those just described, and has one door only. A single door is found on the eastern end, where we find old steps also of similar description. These steps look as if they had stood there for many years, probably ever since the church was built, and are now in a state of rapid decay. On the northern side, there is no entrance, but there are four windows, between two of which is a small square one, which is immediately behind the pulpit. The window-shutters are made of plain boards, without any panel-work, and, together with the doors, were formerly painted red. Time has, however, nearly removed the paint, and leaves them of a dark rust-colour. The doors are somewhat more elaborately made, and like the window-shutters, exhibit the same evidences of age. The arches of brickwork above the windows and doors were painted red, and form a contrast with the rest of the building. There is no enclosure around the building, which stands alone upon the barren and dreary hill. The inside is in correspondence with the exterior of the edifice. As we enter, we observe the pews formed very much like those of modern times, with high straight backs, and without any paint. Their arrangement is like that in our modern churches. The aisles are paved with bricks, and in some places, these having crumbled away, limestones have been substituted. The broad space in front of the pulpit, and between it and the pews, is also paved with brick. The floors of the pews are boarded. The pulpit is old-fashioned and rough. It is of a circular form, and extends some feet from the wall. Above, there is an oval-shaped sounding-board, or canopy, on which is a rude representation of a star. A plain wooden casement extends on either side of the pulpit, which, together with the pulpit, is painted a deep blue colour. The pulpit is entered by a staircase, towards which a passage, with railing on each side, leads. In front of, and below the pulpit, is the chancel. It is a square enclosure with board walls, and contains an old-fashioned walnut table, a bench formed of heavy timber with rough supports, a hickory chair, and a couple of benches attached to the sides of the enclosure. The ceiling is arched, and at the place where the walls and the ceiling meet, there is placed all around the room, a narrow strip of board, which, together with the edges of the window cases, is painted blue, similar to the pulpit. There are standing in the church, a couple of old ten-plate stoves, which have a rough, ancient appearance, and were doubtless among the first of the kind cast in the country. The pipes extend directly upwards, and two holes are cut into the ceiling, through which they are admitted into the garret above. There are no chimneys on the church, and we presume the pipes are extended through the openings which are near the upper portion of the end walls, and which are now covered with rough boards, that are some distance apart.—At one end of the ceiling, near the entrance at the south side, is a square opening, which serves as an admittance to the loft. This is reached by means of a rude ladder, which is permitted to remain in the church, and which makes the ascent steep and dangerous.—The numbers of the pews are marked upon the doors with red chalk. In several of the back pews, is a quantity of wood, and the utensils necessary for digging graves.

Strange feelings occupy the mind, while wandering through this ancient House of God. Those pews once held the venerable forms of our forefathers, who, in imagination, resume their places, but who have long since been laid in their tombs. Not one member of those who worshipped there in olden times, now exists. In yonder pulpit, for more than half a century, the men of God delivered their exhortations, and in powerful and eloquent strains pointed their hearers to the "Lamb of God which taketh away the sins of the world." There, upon yonder platform stood the clerk, who raised the song of praise from Sabbath to Sabbath, for a lifetime of years. We can almost yet hear those songs as they ascend from the worshippers, and are borne upon the breeze towards the throne of the Almighty Being, in whose praise they are sung. Those places are now all filled by strangers, and among the congregation can only be found, a few of the old men, who were children when the church was built. Those ancient walls have resounded with countless songs of praise; and thousands of eloquent sermons have been delivered from the old pulpit, and who can tell how many immortal spirits have found admittance within the gates of heaven, through their instrumentality?

While we gaze on the old building, and reflect upon the memories of those who worshipped there long ago, we are forcibly reminded of our own mortality. The persons engaged in constructing the venerable edifice, and those connected with it as members at the time of its erection, are all gone. So too with us—a few short years will fly swiftly away, and, as with eagle wings, we will soon be in the eternal future. Soon we will meet, face to face, in another world, the old worshippers whose place we are now contemplating in the lonely church.

The original church, which was built about the time the ancient congregation was organized, stood between the present building and the graveyard. It stood pretty much in the relation to the points of the compass, which the new church sustains,—the front being towards the south, and smaller ends facing the east and west. It was erected about one hundred and ten years ago, and was a rough log building, a story and a half high; and was built in the rude style of architecture peculiar to that early day. It had one row of windows on the lower story, the lights of which were small and few in number. It was entered by two doors, which were placed in the eastern and western ends of the house. The doors were small and single; they were made of plain boards, without any panel-work.

We find the following reference to this church, on the minutes of a meeting of a committee of Presbytery, assembled at "Canigogig, 16th Nov., 1739," for the settlement of certain difficulties which had arisen:—"A supplication being presented and read, requesting the committee's concurrence that the meeting-house be erected at the Rocky-Spring, and hearing a great deal on both sides of the question, the Committee observing that proper methods were fallen into some time ago to regulate this affaire, and that a report of the good issue thereof being made by Bro. Craighead and a Commissioner from that people, together with several other circumstances too tedious here to insert, doe agree and conclude that the house for publick worship be erected as nigh to the Falling Spring as conveniently as may be."

The present building was erected in the year 1794, by Mr. Walter Beatty, the gentleman by whom the old Court House was erected, soon after the formation of Franklin County. The old building, although rude and uncomfortable in many respects, answered the purpose of a place of worship very well, for some years after the organization of the congregation. But, as this increased, it was found necessary to build an addition to the house. This was formed by constructing a small square building, which was attached to the south side of the church, and which extended only one-half the length of the main structure. The roof was then continued over it from the original edifice. When completed, the wall between it and the church was sawn away. There were no windows in this addition, and it was consequently poorly supplied with light. In a few years after this alteration, the increasing size of the congregation demanded still more room, and another similar addition was built by its side. These alterations gave the house a singular, slanting appearance towards the south end. The logs with which the former building was erected, were used in constructing the dwelling-house now occupied by Mr. George Sprecher, who resides some two miles from Rocky Spring.

About the time the original church was erected, there was also built a small, rough log structure, about fifteen feet square, with a wide fire-place, and a large, wooden chimney, covered with mortar, and extending nearly along the whole end of the house. This structure stood close beside the church at the northeastern end, and was called the "Study House." We are told by an aged member of the congregation, that it was originally built as a receptacle for the saddles of the members in rainy weather, as, in those early days, they generally came to church on horseback—carriages and other vehicles being rarely used. In later years, the minister was accustomed to use it, in preparing for the services, when he chanced to arrive before the hour at which they began. The church session also met here, and arranged the business of the church, and examined candidates for admission to membership. After service, the minister would resort to it to prepare for any afternoon service which was to be held. The necessity of such a place will be obvious, when it is remembered that the church officers, from the distance at which they lived from the church, were obliged to hold their meetings on Sabbath, when they had collected for the exercises of the day; and, as the church would then be occupied by the congregation, private business could not be transacted there. The "Study House" stood for nearly a hundred years, and only a few years have elapsed since its removal.

It was in the old log church that its first pastor, the Rev. Mr. Craighead, preached for many years. There it was that the minister, in glowing terms, preached Jesus Christ, the only hope of salvation, and after the delivery of his sacred message, in eloquent and patriotic strains, exhorted the youth of the congregation to rise up, and join the noble band, then engaged under the immortal Washington, in struggling to free our beloved country from British oppression. It is related that, upon one occasion, from the pulpit, the patriotic preacher declaimed in such burning and powerful terms against the wrongs we then were suffering, that after one glowing description of the duty of the men, the whole congregation rose from their seats, and declared their willingness to march to the conflict.

There was but one, tradition says, in the entire assembly, who was not overcome by the stirring appeal that was made, and that was an aged female, in whom maternal affection, recently caused to bleed, completely mastered both a sense of propriety and the love of liberty. "Stop, Mr. Craighead," she exclaimed; "I jist want to tell ye, agin you loss such a purty boy as I have, in the war, ye will na be so keen for fighting; quit talking, and gang yersel to the war. Yer always preaching to the boys about it, but I dinna think ye'd be very likely to gang yersel. Jist go and try it."

As we walk reverentially over the hill, we feel as if we were treading upon sacred ground—dedicated to God and American Liberty. We can almost fancy we see the man of God standing where we now stand, telling to the assembled multitude the story of their country's wrongs, and urging them to hesitate no longer which to choose, cowardly inactivity or the noble part of brave defenders of their country's rights. We hear him call on them as he stands before his old church, and requests those who desire to march with him to battle, to hesitate no longer, but place themselves by his side, and acknowledge him their commander, who will lead them to the field of battle, where they will save America, or perish in the cause of Freedom. One by one they approach their pastor, and soon a long line of dauntless spirits stretches across the green to the neighbouring wood. The wives, mothers, and sisters, stand gazing on the exciting scene, and with sweet, encouraging words, urge them to stand by their pastor and captain, and trust in the arm of the Lord of Hosts for the result. At length the line is completed, and they are dismissed, to meet on the following Monday. Soon after the dawn of day, might be seen the sturdy husbandman, with gray hairs scattered over his brow, and the youth of few years, reaching down their old fire-arms, hitherto used only for beasts of prey, or the wild game, but now to be used for other purposes. They fling around their necks their rude powder-horns and bullet-pouches, and shouldering their guns, march to the place of rendezvous. As the eye wanders over the neighbourhood, in the distance they may be seen, one by one, drawing near the hill. Soon they are all assembled, and their company is organized, and after an eloquent appeal to the Almighty, the Reverend Captain places himself at their head, and the noble band marches off to battle. As they march away over the hills, ever and anon they cast a lingering look back upon their beloved friends, who stand weeping upon the hill, and upon their old and loved place of worship, which many of them will never enter again. The company joined the army of Washington, and gave undoubted evidence that their courage was of no mean order, but was based upon the hallowed principles of Christianity; which, although discountenancing bloodshed and war, does not forbid the oppressed to make an effort to throw off the yoke of the oppressor.

Their Captain engaged vigorously in the war, and during the hours spent in camp, habitually acted as chaplain to the soldiers. After the war was over, he returned to his charge, and faithfully watched over the congregation until the period of his death, which occurred in 1799.

We will now enter the graveyard, and describe

the appearance of the tombs which mark the places where many of the old members of the congregation sleep. The graveyard is large, and is enclosed by a rough post-and-rail fence. Over the gateway is a yoke, extending from one post to the opposite one. Along the fence, on the outside of the yard, near the gate, stand three or four oak trees. These, with two poplar and wild cherrytrees in the southern end, and a single cedar near the centre of the yard, are the only trees about the enclosure. The ground is covered with thick and high grass, and wild thyme grows luxuriantly over the greater portion of the graveyard. We are sorry to say that this destitution of trees is not natural, but is owing to the destructive propensities of uncultivated man. In looking over the yard, we may see many trunks of noble trees which fell before the axe. One stood near the tomb of the Rev. Mr. Craighead, and the beams of the beating sun were obstructed by its wide-spreading branches. It has been removed; and now the spot is bare and cheerless, and the tomb lies exposed to the rays of the scorching summer sun. Previously, it was shaded and cool, and was a lovely spot for the visitor to linger and meditate upon the life and character of the departed; and, also upon the interesting scenes which were long years ago enacted on the hillside near by. What think you, reader, was the cause which was deemed sufficient to justify such wanton destruction? We are told they shaded the tombs and made them and the yard too damp! This very fact would have appealed urgently to a cultivated heart in their behalf, but the bold destroyers deemed it a sufficient reason for their destruction. We envy not the feelings of a man who would thus ruthlessly enter the place where rest the dead, and rob their graves of their proudest ornaments. They had stood there perhaps, ever since the old log church was erected, now more than a century ago, and had sheltered the ancient congregation from the oppressive heat of many a summer's day. For many long years, under those trees, the Reverend Pastor and his flock assembled, and exchanged the courteous salutations of friendly intercourse, upon each successive Sabbath day. Here, the venerable sires and matrons of the congregation met before the hour for service, or during the intermission at noon, and talked over the exciting events of the Revolution, and expressed their kind interest in the welfare of those of their brethren and neighbours, who were then fighting for our independence, under the illustrious Washington. There they recounted each gallant deed of the patriot band, until their youthful auditors burned with patriotic enthusiasm, and bravely declared their determination to march off to the tented field, and join their comrades in the fight. Amongst those lofty boughs, the gentle dove built her nest and reared her young, whose mournful notes, as the shades of evening drew near, seemed a fitting requiem for the spirits of the dead. Upon the topmost branches of those venerable trees, the lark alighted, as the morning dawned from behind the eastern horizon, and in sweet, harmonious strains, sung her matin song, as if offering her tribute of praise to the Great Creator of the lovely scenes amidst which she lived. From some ancient walnut, the timid squirrel looked out from his nest, with curious eye, upon the assembly below, until, at length becoming accustomed to their presence, he skipped playfully among the branches, and gathered the ripened fruit to provide against the approaching winter.

We will now enter the old churchyard, and endeavour to trace out the inscriptions on its ancient and moss-covered tombs. A feeling of awe pervades our mind as we wander over the resting-places of those who lived, many of them, almost a century ago. Here sleep many brave spirits who freely ventured their all to secure the precious freedom which we now enjoy. Here are they who settled among the hills and dales which surround us on every side, and the stroke of whose axe first broke the stillness of the forest, and who cleared the fruitful fields, now covered with the luxuriant harvest, which are in the possession of those who were then unborn. Here lies the beloved Pastor of the old congregation, and all around him repose the remains of the persons who listened for many long years to his eloquent teachings, and who, in time of danger, marched with him to share the perils of the protracted struggles which released our land from the tyranny of a foreign foe. Here rest the honoured remains of the ancestors of many of our community, who have long since ceased the struggle incident to human life. All around us lie the brave men of other nations who came to our land, and among the wilds of a savage and uninhabited region, built the House of God, and disseminated through our remote settlements, the hallowed principles of the religion of Jesus Christ. The graves of many of these bear no inscriptions, by means of which the name and station of the occupant can be ascertained. Many of them are only marked by rude stones, or boards, which have almost crumbled into dust after the long lapse of years since they were erected.

As we enter the graveyard, from the gate, at the distance of a few feet from the fence, we meet the resting-place of the first regular minister of the Rocky Spring Church. When the tomb was first built, it consisted of a brick wall, upon which a large flat slab of gray stone was placed. Through the effects of time, the walls have sunk, and the slab now lies upon the ground—we are sorry to say, broken into several pieces. These again, are broken into numerous smaller portions, and are so scattered about, that it is somewhat difficult to make out the inscription. In a short time more, these numerous fragments, bearing parts of the letters of the inscription, must necessarily become scattered and lost, and the visitor will vainly endeavour to read the remaining characters.

It shows little respect for the memory of the great and good man who lies beneath, for the children of his old congregation—the co-labourers in his efforts in disseminating the precious messages of the Book of Life—thus to permit his tomb to be destroyed, without making an effort to save it. The recollections of the past should induce them to protect it, and not permit even this last memento of departed worth to be broken into fragments, and cast uselessly away. After collecting the broken pieces, and placing them in their proper position, we were enabled to read the following inscription:

"In memory of the Rev. John Craighead, who departed this life the 20th day of April, A. D. 1799, aged 57 years. Ordained to preach the Gospel and installed pastor of the congregation of Rocky Spring, on the 13th of April, A. D. 1768. He was a faithful and zealous servant of Jesus Christ."

To the right of the grave, stands the stump of a large forest tree: and a beautiful cedar, the only one in the yard, grows near its foot. The space all around the tomb is beautifully covered with thyme, which somewhat relieves the barrenness of the spot. Near the tomb of the Minister are three graves, marked by stones of a very ancient appearance, one of which contains the following inscription:

"In memory of James Robertson, who departed this life August 13, 1793, aged 4 years and ten months."

Another stands by its side, and bears the inscription:

"In memory of Elizabeth, wife of Alexander Robertson, who departed this life 8th April, 1780, aged 30 years."

Near by is a third stone, from which we copy the following words:

"In memory of William Robertson, who departed this life April, 1796, aged 44 years.

"In the same grave lieth their infant daughter Elizabeth."

These three stones are of gray slate, of a much harder quality than the ordinary slate, and which seems to be little influenced by the hand of time. They are all near the grave of the Pastor, a little to the east of his tomb, and partly under the shade of the cedar tree which stands near by. To the left, as we enter the gate, is an old stone, formed of slate, upon which we find the following words, cut in very old-fashioned letters:

"In memory of Mary Cummins, who departed this life Nov. 9th, 1790, aged 17 years."

By its side is another stone, of the same character, of which the following epitaph is a representation:

"In memory of John Boyd, who departed this life in the year 1770."

"In memory of Elizabeth, wife of Charles Cummins, who departed this life 9th Sept., 1802, aged 54 years."

These three last-mentioned graves stand side by side, and contain members of the same family.

Near the latter is another old stone, of the same kind, and upon which the following words appear:

"In memory of Mary, wife of John Boyd, who died June 30th, 1778."

"In memory of Elizabeth Cummins, who died Decr. 30, 1792, aged 12 years."

To the right of these graves, and near the entrance to the yard, is the oldest tombstone in the burying-ground. It is roughly carved on a hard slate stone, similar to those already described, and which differs considerably from the slate found in the neighbourhood. We are ignorant of the source from which it was derived. It has a venerable and antique appearance, and in the form of the letters, and the mode of spelling, differs materially from the custom of later times. The stone is nearly round on the top, and contains a rim cut into it in a rough manner. Above the inscription appears a representation of an angel's face and wings. The stone is covered with moss, which sticks tenaciously to it, and renders its deciphering a task somewhat difficult. The following is a copy of the inscription:

"Here lys the body of John Burns, who departed this life December y[e] 23, 1760, aged; 79 years."

The occupant of this tomb lived at a period before any settlement was made in this part of the State, and when nearly all of Pennsylvania was a howling wilderness. He was born in 1681—one year before William Penn came to America. His remains have lain here for nearly one hundred years. At the period of his death, he lived where Mr. Tobias Crider now resides. In the neighbourhood, near this grave, is another, marked by a couple of moss-covered limestones, bearing no letters, but covered with grass, and about which fragments of a fence yet remain. This is doubtless amongst the oldest graves in the burying-ground.

In the southwestern corner of the yard, is an old tomb, the walls of which are of rough, unhewn limestone, and which is covered by two marble slabs of large size. Beneath this tomb sleep an aged couple and several of their children. The venerable pair far transcended the usual limits of human life, and lived to an extreme old age. The wall is falling away on one side, and the rough stones, together with the old marble slabs, coloured almost black by age, give the tomb an ancient and interesting appearance. One slab of mottled marble gives us the following memorial of those who rest beneath it.

"In memory of James M'Calmont, who departed this life July the 2d, 1780, aged 96 years."

"Also, Jane, his wife, who departed this life, May the 4th, 1794, aged 100 years."

"Also of Charles, Elizabeth, and Isabella, their children."

The other stone is the memento of their son, James M'Calmont, of whom we shall speak somewhat at length.

"In memory of James M'Calmont, Esqr., who departed this life July the 19th, 1809, aged 72 years."

The occupant of this tomb lived near Strasburg, on the farm now occupied by Mr. John Dice. He was a Major in the Revolutionary War, and became distinguished as a brave and accomplished soldier. When the British had possession of Philadelphia, Major M'Calmont commanded a company of Rangers, whose duty it was to intercept the supplies of provisions which the Tories might be disposed to send to the city. Upon one occasion, while on duty in New Jersey, opposite the city, he captured about a dozen Hessian soldiers. Having no convenient way of disposing of them, he marched them to Strasburg, near which he owned a large tract of land, and induced them to settle there, by presenting one with a few acres of land, another with a tannery, a third with a tavern stand, and providing for the residue in a manner suitable to their several capacities.

During the war, the inhabitants of the Cumberland Valley were much annoyed by the inroads of the Indians, who murdered the people, burned their houses and barns, destroyed their crops, and committed the usual atrocities characteristic of savage warfare. The inhabitants were obliged to work in their fields after night, for fear of being surprised and murdered by their subtle foes. The farmer would drop his corn, as he ran through the fields, and cover it with his foot, while he held his rifle in his hand, and feared to stoop, lest he might be attacked by the lurking Indian. In this manner a farmer would plant his field in a single night, as he did not pretend to raise more grain than was absolutely necessary for the subsistence of himself and his stock, and considered himself fortunate if he did even thus much. In the neighbourhood of Strasburg and Roxbury, the Indians were particularly troublesome. We have been told by an old and highly respected citizen of this vicinity, that, on one occasion, the Indians captured a number of persons in the neighbourhood of, and not far from, Rocky Spring, and proceeded with their prisoners towards Bedford. About the same time another party burned the fort (which then stood near Bossart's Mill), after shooting the only man who happened to be in it at the time, and then followed in the same direction taken by the preceding gang. A company of the inhabitants of the neighbourhood, under the command of Captain Alexander Culbertson, went in pursuit of the Indians, and overtook them near Sideling Hill. A desperate fight ensued, in which the company of Capt. C. was defeated, and himself killed. A number of the men were made prisoners, and carried off by the Indians. The stream known as Bloody Run, is said to have derived its name from this battle, which is represented to have occurred in its vicinity. We wish it clearly understood, that we do not give this statement as historically correct; but we think it is as plausible an explanation of the naming of Bloody Run, as any we have yet seen. A short time before the battle, a man, named McConnell, was ploughing near the Spring, and was surprised by a couple of Indians, who shot at, but fortunately missed him, and lodged a ball in the handle of his plough. He ran into a house near by, where the Indians did not follow him. His remains now repose in the churchyard at Rocky Spring. His brother, not yet arrived at manhood, was taken, but managed to make his escape at the slaughter at Bloody Run. There were a number of forts in the neighbourhood, to which the people fled upon the approach of the enemy. One stood at the mill on Mr. Bossart's farm, near the foot of the mountain; another (called Reed's Fort) on the farm now owned by William Etter, about one mile and a half from Rocky Spring; another at Strasburg; and a strong fortress stood on the hill, in the town of Shippensburg.

The above remarks may appear to be somewhat of a digression, but we deem them essential to a clear understanding of what follows, respecting the adventures of Major McCalmont. This gentleman was generally selected as the leader of the parties sent in pursuit of the savages, after the perpetration of their numerous hostile acts; and, from his success in discovering their haunts, and inflicting summary vengeance upon them for their atrocities, he became quite celebrated as an Indian-hunter; and was considered by the savages as a daring and formidable foe. As a bush-fighter he was quite equal to the most wily Indian. One day he met unexpectedly a tall, desperate-looking savage, while alone in the woods, near his residence at Strasburg. Both happening to see each other simultaneously, took to trees, and each endeavoured to get a shot at his antagonist; after evading each other for some time, the savage incautiously peeped from behind the tree, and instantly received a ball from the rifle of his dexterous enemy. Upon another occasion, while returning home from Chambersburg, he was pursued by a party of Indians, who were bent on securing the scalp of their old and hated enemy. After running for a considerable distance, he darted into a barn which stood near by, and escaped out of the other side, and secreted himself in a thicket, unobserved by his pursuers. The savages supposing he was yet in the barn, set it on fire, and stood around it, yelling in exultation at their supposed success in capturing their foe. When they discovered that they were baffled, they commenced the search after the Major, and soon found his trail, and again joined hotly in the pursuit. The Major was remarkable for his swiftness of foot, and succeeded in outrunning the Indians, who pursued him to the fort at Shippensburg. They often chased him to this fort, we are told; and, on several occasions, he selected men from the garrison, and, in turn, pursued the Indians, and avenged himself by returning with their scalps. During the war, he was working one day in the field with several other persons, at harvest-time. The guns of the party were in a distant part of the field. A gang of several prowling savages suddenly sprang from the thicket, and one, more bold than the rest, ran for the guns. McCalmont also started off on the same errand; and, although the Indian had the advantage of the ground, reached the guns first, one of which he snatched from the stack, and with it shot the savage dead. The settlers coming up soon after the Major, the Indians retreated. He was considered by the Indians as quite as swift a runner as they, and fully equal to themselves in all the wiles and strategy of their peculiar warfare. In consequence of his extraordinary fleetness and agility, they bestowed on him the appellation of "Supple McCalmont." On the southwestern side of the town of Strasburg, there is a cave, called "McCalmont's Cave," in which he was accustomed to hide, when closely pursued by the Indians. It was in the midst of a thicket, and so covered by thick vines and bushes, that it afforded an admirable retreat in times of danger.

The Major was a tall, muscular man, of modest and unpretending manners. In private life, his quiet, diffident deportment gave no indication of the dauntless spirit of the man, of which he presented so many evidences in his encounters with the Indians, as well as with the British army during his campaign under General Washington. After the conclusion of the war, he was appointed one of the Associate Judges of Franklin County, soon after its formation. He died at Strasburg in 1809.

Near the fence, in the western end of the yard, is a tomb, formed in the usual square, or rather oblong shape, with a brick wall and marble slab, which is nearly blackened by age and exposure. The wall is falling away, and the bricks are scattered about the tomb, which was formerly surrounded by a paling fence; a few posts of which, with two or three decaying rails, yet remain. On the stone is the simple, modest inscription:

"Joseph Armstrong; born 1739, and died 29th Augt., 1811."

The tenant of this tomb lived on Mr. Wise's place, near the mountain. During the Revolution he was a major in the Pennsylvania militia.

In the eastern end of the enclosure, we find two graves, which strike the eye on account of their ancient appearance, which results rather from the gray colour of the stones, than any peculiarity in the wording or carving on them. The inscription on one of them reads thus:

"In memory of Mary Machen, who departed this life August 2d, 1803, aged 75 years."

Close beside this gravestone is the other, which we are told is

"In memory of Elizabeth, wife of John Machen, died 24th September, 1804, aged 54 years."

In the extreme southwestern corner of the burial-ground, beneath the poplar trees, are a number of pieces which form a very beautiful monument. They are scattered about in confusion over the ground; and some of the handsome slabs were so covered with clay, that it was difficult to read the engraving which they contained. The sides of the tomb, and many of the columns were deeply sunk into the ground, in consequence of having lain there for so many years. There are more than a dozen of pieces, many of which are now partially injured by carelessness, and the confused manner in which they are strewn over the ground. Some pieces lean against the trees, and others are so much covered by grass as to be hidden from view. The side stones are handsomely made in the form of panel-work, and the columns are beautifully fluted. They are all of fine, white marble, which, however, is now blackened by exposure to the elements, for more than half a century. The whole monument was a beautiful structure, much handsomer we presume than any now there. We are told that these pieces were brought to the graveyard, from Philadelphia, more than fifty years ago; but owing to some cause, with which our informant is unacquainted, they were never erected into a tomb, but have remained as separate pieces ever since. After cleaning the letters of the topmost slab, we have copied the inscription and the verses accompanying it, without any alteration as regards arrangement and punctuation.

"Jane Cooper, was born, 1st of July, 1768, and (J. N.) died, on the 26th evening of June, 1796.

"JANE NICHOLSON'S respected dust, now here,
Once liv'd esteem'd, and shar'd health's warmest cheer
Her life seem'd fix'd, as but with age to cease
Till fated accident produced disease
Young, wise and good! she was her children's guide
Bliss to her partner, joy to all alli'd.

"From tender youth, sh' obey'd, with love and awe
Reasons, religion, and her parents, law;
So grew, her dignifying strength of mind;
Tho' firm, yet soft, and happily refin'd
No affectation, pride, or passion, stain'd
Nor harbour'd ills her candid breast prophan'd.

"Her face expressive, spoke each thought sincere
Truth and its friends, to her, were ever dear.
Eager she priz'd each social, virtuous joy;
But prudent shunn'd the haunts, which peace destroy.

"For other's woes, her keenest sorrows flow'd
Or for th' impious wandering from their God
Is she perhaps, your guardian Angel, still?
O children! live as would obey her will,
So shall you join her on that happy shore
Where death or grief, will visit you no more."

On one of the side pieces of the monument, which had sunk deeply into the earth, and which was removed with difficulty from its bed, we read as follows:

"William Cooper Nicholson died on the 16th morning of April, 1798.—Before the end of his third year."

On the other side piece we find the following verses:

"Oh! when will spring visit the mould'ring urn
And celestial dawn bless the night of the Grave?
Blest Angels rejoicing, will all hail the great Morn,
When Saints bright descending, their bodies receive."

A few feet from the above, are three square tombs, with walls of hewn limestone, and slabs of white marble, which are erected over the remains of the departed members of the Wilson family. Upon one are the names of John Wilson, Sr., who died in 1826—aged 76 years; and Sarah, consort of John Wilson, who died in July, 1848, at the advanced age of 96 years. The one next to this is dedicated to the memory of John Wilson, Jr., who died in 1818, aged 27 years. Upon the third is the name of Alexander Wilson, who died on the 24th September, 1828, aged 24 years; it also contains the name of James Wilson, who died in July, 1847, aged 56 years. Upon these monuments are several verses of poetry, which we will not copy, on account of their length. To the right of these and somewhat nearer the lower fence, are two handsome marble monuments, erected over the remains of the McClellan family, from which we copy the names of those who sleep beneath them; omitting also several verses, for the reason given above. Upon the first is the name of George McClellan, Esq., who departed this life July 15th, 1823, in the 62d year of his age. The next is dedicated to the memory of Lydia McClellan, who died in 1840, aged 68 years. In the rear of the McClellans are the graves of David McKinney, who died in 1835, aged 68 years; and Eleanor McKinney, whose death occurred in 1825, in her 53d year. Near the spot where repose the ashes of the McKinneys, are two plain marble stones, which are erected in commemoration of Grizida, consort of Robert McConnel, who died in 1832, in the 36th year of her age; and of Captain John McConnel, who died in August,

1819, aged 73 years. At the distance of a few rods, towards the northern end of the yard, are a number of neat tombstones which mark the last resting-place of several members of the Davis family. Mr. Davis died in October, 1823, in his 62d year. Sarah, wife of William Davis, died in 1825, aged 64 years. Close by is the tomb of Col. Stephen Wilson, who died in 1823, aged 46 years. Near this point are three beautiful marble tombstones which indicate the place where repose the Grier family. The deceased are Thomas Grier, whose death occurred in 1818, in his 17th year; Margaret Grier, who departed this life in 1822, in the 20th year of her age; and Michael Grier, who died in 1844, aged eleven years. Near by is the tomb of John Durborow, whose decease occurred in 1825, when he was sixteen years old. In the southern part of the yard, near the monuments of the Wilsons, is an old grave, covered over with thyme, and marked by a headstone of gray-coloured sandstone, upon which is carved, in very old-fashioned, rude characters, the following inscription.

"Here lies the body of John Wade, who departed this life, January 17th, A. D. 1799, aged 80 years."

On the footstone, in the same style, is chiselled the following exhortation:

"Remember, man, as you pass by, as you are now so once was I; as I am now so must you be; remember, man, that thou must die."

Close by the above is another stone, of the same kind, upon which we decipher the following words, with some difficulty, owing to the rough manner in which they are cut.

"Here lyes the body of McDonell McConnell who departed this life, July 29, 1776, 75 years."

The next grave is the resting-place of Rosannah McConnell. Upon the gray sandstone, at the head of her grave, we are told that

"Here lyes the body of Rosannah McConnell, wife of Robert McConnell, who departed this life—1770."

The stone is broken into two pieces, and part of the inscription remains below the ground, and cannot be read.

In the northwestern portion of the yard, are two white stones, which are placed at the graves of Mary Jane and Samuel, son and daughter of Charles and Elizabeth Culbertson, who died at early ages in the years 1815 and 1816.

Near the centre of the yard are two monuments, which we will next describe. The first is composed of a marble slab which rests upon a brick wall, part of which has sunk into the ground, and the whole of which appears to be in a decaying condition. On the slab we are informed that it was erected

"In memory of Hugh Beard, who departed this life, December 3d, 1771, aged 14 years; also Sarah Beard who departed this life, March 16th, 1794, aged 20 years."

Adjoining this tomb stands one which was originally much handsomer, but is now much impaired by time. The sides are formed of broad stones, of a yellowish colour, fastened at the angles by iron clasps, and supporting a slab, which is moved partly from its position, on which we find the following inscription:

"In memory of Martha Beard, wife of John Beard, Junr., who departed this life, December 17th, 1795, aged 40 years; also Agnes Beard, mother of the above, departed this life, Feb. 20th, 1810, aged 80 years."

Beside these two graves is another, marked by a head and foot of blue slate, which was erected

"In memory of Jane Jamison, daughter of John and Agnes Baird, Senr's, departed this life, December 9th, 1799, aged 24 years."

Around these graves a paling fence once stood. This has now partially fallen down, and parts of it lie scattered about the tomb. Two sides yet remain, which meet at a right angle. The whole appearance of the fence and graves, indicates exposure to the destroying hand of time for many years. In the south-eastern portion of the yard are two substantial limestone tombs, supporting marble slabs, one of which is dedicated to the memory of "Mrs. Mary Culbertson, consort of Joseph Culbertson, and daughter of James Finley, Esq.," who died in 1817. The other "is dedicated to the memory of James Finley, Esq., and Jane his wife. James died the 27th day of September, 1812, in the 73d year of his age. Jane departed this life on the 21st of July, 1814, aged 69 years." Not far from this is a grave, thickly covered with thyme, and marked by a couple of rough limestones, on one of which we read, "G. Vance, 1793." Near this, are three other graves, similar in appearance, all covered with thyme and marked by pieces of limestone, upon the respective headstones of which, the following initials are rudely chiselled:

"P × L
N × L
M × L."

A few paces from these is a marble stone, which is erected,

"In memory of Mary, the wife of James Gibson, who departed this life, April 25th, 17—, in the 71 year of her age.

"All you that come my grave to see
Prepare for Déath and follow me
Prepare for Death make no delay
For suddenly I was snatched away."

We copy the above just as we find it. It will be perceived that the year of her death is not given.

There are many other graves in the yard, a description of which would be tedious to the reader, and require more space than we can appropriate to it. We have given those which are the most prominent, and strike the visitor as interesting, either on account of their venerable appearance, or the quaintness of the inscriptions which they bear. Those about which we shall say nothing, are of recent date; and differ in no respect from those seen in any modern churchyard. We may also state that the inscriptions which we have given above, are copied from the stones without any alteration in regard to spelling.

Of the early history of the Congregation of Rocky Spring, we know little. We do not know precisely how many years have elapsed since it was organized, but we do know that divine services were held in the old church, one hundred and nine years ago. In the year 1742, we learn from the minute-book of the Session of the Middle Spring Church, near Shippensburg, that a meeting was held by the congregation, for the purpose of making some arrangement in relation to the distribution of the pastoral labours of the Rev. Mr. Blair, who, it appears, was the minister of the Middle Spring, Big Spring, and Rocky Spring congregations. It was then determined that the reverend gentleman should preach on every third Sabbath, at each of these places, alternately. These congregations were established about the same time, by the Donegal Presbytery, in Lancaster County, in this State. The Presbytery was accustomed to send out missionaries to preach for the different churches, in their infancy, before they were large enough to support a settled minister. This appears to have been the manner in which the church at Rocky Spring was supplied, for some years after its establishment.

At the time the old church was built, the land upon which it stood belonged to the government, and had never been surveyed by the congregation. When the present building was about being erected, a warrant was taken out by the Trustees, and the land occupied by the congregation was then, for the first time, surveyed. The following is a transcript of the original warrant, copied from the official draught filed in the office of the Deputy Surveyor, and politely handed to us by Samuel M. Armstrong, Esq. "Warrant for 5 acres, granted to George Matthews, Esq., James M'Calmont, Esq., James Ferguson, Esq., Joseph Culbertson, Esq., and Samuel Culbertson, Trustees for the congregation including the Rocky Spring Church.—November 6th, 1792." A draught of the land is attached to the above, which, of course, we cannot transfer to paper, without unnecessary labour and expense.

We shall now speak of the several ministers who have officiated at Rocky Spring as its regularly ordained pastors. The period embraced by the labours of these gentlemen, is about eighty-three years.

The first regular minister of the church, was the Rev. John Craighead, of whom we have already spoken. Mr. C. was the son of Mr. John Craighead, who settled at an early date on Yellow Breeches Creek, near Carlisle, and who was a cousin of the Rev. Thomas Craighead, pastor of Big Spring. He received his education at Princeton College, of which Institution he was a graduate. He was installed as pastor at Rocky Spring, in 1768, but we presume he had been accustomed to preach there before that time. At the commencement of the Revolutionary War, as previously stated, he raised a company from the members of his charge, and joined the army of General

Washington, in New Jersey. Of his valour there can be no question. "He fought and preached alternately," says a friend, in noticing his character, "breasted all danger, relying on his God and the justice of his cause for protection."

His company was present at the battle on Long Island, and acquitted themselves with much gallantry. Mr. C. was also with the army, when Fort Washington was evacuated, and fell into the hands of the British. His friend, the Rev. Dr. Cooper, for many years pastor of the Middle Spring Church, was also present on this occasion, and was, we believe, also captain of a company. He and Mr. C. were very intimate, and were in the same mess, as they were congenial spirits. Mr. Craighead was somewhat celebrated as a humourist, and many good jokes are told of him by many aged persons, by whom he is well remembered. One day, it is said, going into battle, a cannon-ball struck a tree near him, a splinter of which nearly knocked him down. "God bless me!" exclaimed Mr. Cooper, "you were nearly knocked to staves." "Oh yes," was his reply, "and though you are a *Cooper*, you could not have set me up."

Mr. Craighead was a tall, handsome man, with dark chestnut-coloured hair, and possessed a strong, clear, and musical voice. His disposition was mild, affable, and peculiarly winning; which, together with his agreeable social qualities, rare conversational powers, and fine humour, made him the favourite of all who chanced to know him; and from his prominent position, there were few persons in the neighbourhood who did not know him. His ministry was at one time interrupted for a few months, by mental alienation, and we are told by intelligent persons, that, after his recovery, his zeal and efforts in the cause of his divine Master, as well as his strong intellect, seemed to have been greatly increased in energy by his temporary insanity. His sermons were well prepared, forcible, and persuasive; and were delivered with a power and eloquence peculiarly his own. His public as well as his private life, was pure and unexceptionable. He lived on the farm recently occupied by Mr. Byers, which is a couple of miles from the church. In 1799, the year in which his pastoral relation had been dissolved, this good man gave up his spirit to his Creator, and entered upon the reward which, through divine grace, his long life zealously spent in the cause of Religion, so well prepared him to enjoy.

After the existence of a vacancy in the congregation for about one year,—Mr. Francis Herron, now the Rev. Dr. Herron, was elected to preside over the spiritual interests of the flock. He was ordained and installed April 9th, 1800, on which occasion "Dr. King preached a sermon from Matt. v. 14, and Mr. Linn presided, and gave a charge." Dr. H. continued faithfully to discharge the duties of his station for about ten years, at the expiration of which time he was chosen the pastor of the First Presbyterian Church in the city of Pittsburg. He continued to fill this station, with great credit to himself and benefit to his people, until about one year since, when, in consequence of advanced age, he resigned the charge, after having carefully watched over its welfare for about forty years. Dr. Herron's ministerial connexion with the Church at Rocky Spring was eminently successful, and through his zealous efforts, he added many converts to its numbers. Dr. H. ranks among the first ministers in the Church, as a pious and faithful shepherd, an accomplished scholar, an able and convincing preacher, and above all, as an humble and conscientious follower of the Lord Jesus Christ.

When Dr. Herron resigned his place at Rocky Spring, it was supplied by the Rev. John M'Knight, D.D., who ministered to the people for several years. The relation existing between him and the congregation was interrupted by an invitation to preside over Dickinson College, when the presidency of that Institution was made vacant by the death of its incumbent. The Doctor was well known to our older citizens, as he resided in Chambersburg; and for us to speak of his many virtues, his talents, his fervour in discharging the duties of his divine mission, would be a work of supererogation. He lived a useful and holy life, and at an advanced age was called to his reward. His death occurred in 1823, and his ashes now repose beneath a handsome monument in the lovely cemetery attached to the Presbyterian Church in Chambersburg.

The vacancy occasioned by the removal of Dr. M'K., was supplied by his son, the Rev. Dr. John M'Knight, for many years a resident of our town. The labours of this gentleman were abundantly successful: and all the members of the church yet living, will testify to the able and affectionate manner in which he discharged the duty imposed upon him. Mr. M'K., after preaching at Rocky Spring for several years, removed to Philadelphia, where he is yet engaged in the ministry, in connexion with the New School Presbyterian Church. His successor is the Rev. A. K. Nelson. Mr. N. accepted the call from "Campbellstown and Rocky Spring," in 1840, with the understanding that the half of his time was to be given to each of these congregations; but he has, for some years, at least, been preaching also occasionally on the Sabbath at Strasburg, where many of his charge reside.—These are all the ministers, who have been regularly ordained to preach in this ancient temple of the Lord.

In latter days the congregation is gradually decreasing, and seems to be in a fair way soon to become entirely extinct. We learn this fact with much regret, and feel pained that the hallowed spot, around which so many endearing recollections cling, should cease to occupy a place among churches, or at least, should fall into other hands than those of the same denomination, who worshipped in it for more than a century.

At the time of its erection, it was attended by a few of the early settlers only, some of whom had come from the mother country to seek a home in the new world, where they might enjoy, unmolested, their cherished religious opinions. As the country became more thickly settled, the congregation also became large, and occupied an important position among the churches in the Cumberland Valley. People resorted to Rocky Spring, from Loudon, Mercersburg, Greencastle, Chambersburg, Culbertson's Row, Greenvillage, Roxbury, Orrstown, Strasburg, and from the whole valley along the mountain foot, extending nearly to Shippensburg. When there chanced to be no preaching at Middle Spring, the people of that congregation were accustomed to worship here.

But the original settlers have long since died, and their descendants, to a considerable extent, have moved to other regions; and persons from other places (particularly Germans) have taken their places. These, generally, belong to other denominations, and have deserted this ancient temple of the Most High. Then, again, other churches have sprung up in the neighbouring towns, and many of those who formerly attended at Rocky Spring, can now enter the sanctuary nearer their homes, without the inconvenience of riding several miles, as was formerly necessary. All these circumstances have conspired to diminish the congregation, and its doom seems inevitable. Services, we are told, are only held about once in four weeks, and we very much fear, that before very long, the interval will be indefinitely prolonged.

Patriotism has ever been a predominant feature in the character of the Presbyterians in the Cumberland Valley. It pervaded especially the old congregation of Rocky Spring; and when their bleeding country called for the services of her sons, none were more ready than they to respond to the call, and freely offer themselves, if need be, upon the altars of Freedom. Many of the people, as we have shown, marched with their minister; others had participated in the war previously, some of whom sealed their devotion to their country with their lives, on the battlefield. In 1774, a meeting of the Presbyterian Church was convened at Carlisle, in Cumberland County, of which our county then formed a part, and passed a series of patriotic resolutions, expressing their sympathy with the cause of oppressed America; and in the name of the Lord of Hosts, declaring their willingness to participate in the dangers of the struggle, whenever the government might demand their services. Considering the near connexion existing between the inhabitants of the two counties at that period, and the fact that the assembly was formed by the Presbyterians of the Cumberland Valley, it will readily be conceived that our churches acted a prominent part in making these patriotic declarations. Patriotism then pervaded all classes, from the minister down to the humblest member of his flock, and was something more than that wild, roving spirit of adventure, which so often prompts men, particularly in these latter days), to engage in warfare; it was a higher and nobler feeling—a principle of resistance to oppression, and a firm, unconquerable desire to establish the liberty of America, and secondarily, that of the whole world.

We may here also add, that this steadfast and self-sacrificing devotion to their country, was eminently characteristic of the Presbyterian ministry and membership, as a body, throughout the land, during the Revolution.

"That man," it has been remarked, with truthfulness that history attests,* "will go on a desperate adventure, who shall proceed to hunt out the Presbyterian tories of that day. Our ministers were Whigs, patriots, haters of tyranny, known abettors of the very earliest resistance, and often soldiers in the field. It was not they, nor any of them, who acted as guides for invading generals, or who wrote pasquinades for New York Journals, or who insulted Washington by scurrile letters. On these points we ask no better task than that of printing a few documents, when the truths suggested shall be denied. The name of a Presbyterian Whig stank in the nostrils of truckling courtiers, renegade Scots, and nonjuring semi-papists, as much in the Colonies as at home; and the revolutionary struggle was carried on,

* Review of "Davidson's Presbyterian Church in Kentucky," Princeton Repertory, October, 1847.

in a large part of the Middle and Southern States, by the sinew, sweat, and blood, of Presbyterians."

We have thus, hurriedly, given a general sketch of the venerable and romantic spot long known as Rocky Spring. The neglected condition, and general decaying appearance of the church, portend a speedy ruin. A few short years will only have elapsed, before the stranger will stand by the tottering walls on the hilltop, and sadly meditate upon the past history of the sacred pile. Then the descendants of the old congregation will have gone, and no one will be able to recount the many stirring events connected with it in former years, or reverentially commemorate its departing glory.

# CHAPTER XI.

## PATH VALLEY CHURCHES.

At an early day in the history of Pennsylvania, the people were forbidden by laws, "repeatedly signified by proclamations," to take possession of the lands beyond the Kittochtinny Mountains, not purchased of the Indians. This prohibition was grounded in a fear, on the part of the existing authorities, that if such a course should be pursued, "a breach might ensue between the Six Nations of Indians and this Province." Notwithstanding this precautionary enactment, however, the wave of emigration soon rolled beyond the limit designated for the residence of the daring pioneers. Neither the prospect of peril, nor the apprehension of the privations and toils incident to a settlement in the wilderness, could repress the adventurous spirit which swelled their bosoms, or restrain them from the occupancy of the vast and inviting tracts of land, which spread out beyond the Blue Mountains.

The following extract from a letter, dated July 2d,

1750, from Richard Peters, who had received orders from Governor Hamilton, to give information to the proper magistrates, against all such as had presumed to violate the law which he had published by proclamation, and to bring them to a legal conviction, will shed some light upon this subject, in regard to Path Valley:

"On Wednesday, the 30th of May, the magistrates and company, being detained two days by rain, proceeded over the Kittochtinny Mountains, and entered into the Tuscara Path, or Path Valley, through which the road to Alleghany lies. Many settlements were formed in this valley, and all the people were sent for, and the following persons appeared, viz.: Abraham Slack, James Blair, Moses Moore, Arthur Dunlap, Alexander McCartie, Felix Doyle, Andrew Dunlap, Robert Wilson, Jacob Pyatt, Jacob Pyatt, Jr., William Ramage, Reynold Alexander, Samuel Patterson, Robert Baker, John Armstrong, and John Potts, who were all convicted by their own confession to the magistrates, of the like trespasses with those at Shearman's Creek, and were bound in the like recognizances to appear at court, and bonds to the proprietaries, to remove with all their families, servants, cattle, and effects, and having all voluntarily given possession of their houses to me, some ordinary log houses, to the number of eleven, were burnt to the ground; the trespassers, most of them cheerfully, and a very few of them with reluctance, carrying out all their goods. Some had deserted before, and lay waste."

It is not possible, of course, to justify the conduct of these primitive settlers in this portion of Franklin County, in taking possession of it contrary to law, yet much apology is found for them in the circumstances of the country at the time, and in their willingness to risk any conflict into which they might thus be brought, with the aboriginal inhabitants. It is also gratifying to know, that they promptly and peaceably submitted to the requirements of the law, as carried into effect by the officers of government.

The first preaching by a Presbyterian minister, among the almost exclusively Irish or Scotch-Irish population of this region, of which we have any knowledge, was in 1767. In that year "verbal applications in behalf of a few in Path Valley," were made to Presbytery. The appointment, under this request, was given to the Rev. Robert Cooper, who was directed to preach to that people a Sabbath, "at discretion." After this, supplies were occasionally sent to that region, and not without success, as would appear from the fact, that in 1769, "application was made by a commissioner, for the Presbytery to endeavour to accommodate some differences subsisting among the congregation, concerning the situation of their meeting-house or meeting-houses."

The people, as we learn from the Presbyterial records, were divided into two parties. One party insisted for a meeting-house near James Montgomery's, where they had found a warrant for a piece of ground, for the sole purpose of a meeting-house and grave-yard, and where they had already put up logs for a place of worship. The other party insisted for two meeting-houses, and that neither of them should be at James Montgomery's; or, if one house only should be allowed, that it should be placed lower down, so as to be near the centre of the congregation. To harmonize these conflicting views and feelings, Presbytery appointed a committee of five Ministers and five Elders. This committee, however, after hearing the statements of commissioners from each of the parties, were not able to adjust the existing difficulty, as is evident from the following minute of their proceedings:

"The committee, finding that the majority of the people are for the house which is begun at James Montgomery's, and that they had never applied to the Presbytery to interpose in this matter, nor are now willing to leave it to the decision of this committee, judge that they can not proceed to do anything in this matter, except by way of advice, which was done by the Moderator."

In the year 1773, the congregations of "Upper Tuscarora" and "Path Valley," which were united as a charge, placed themselves under the pastoral care of the Reverend Samuel Dougall. In 1779, Mr. Dougall resigned his relation to the former of these congregations, and the other applied for, and obtained, the whole of his labours, "promising to contribute and pay annually to him, the sum of £100, and the quantity of one hundred bushels of wheat, during the present circumstances of the times." Mr. Dougall departed this life, October 4th, 1790.

After this event, the Rev. David Denny was called to the Upper and Lower Churches of Path Valley, and continued to serve them in the Gospel, from 1793 until 1800, when he accepted the pastorate of the Church at Chambersburg.

Mr. Denny was succeeded by the Rev. Amos A. M'Ginley, a native of Adams County, Pennsylvania, who became pastor of the congregations in 1802, and continued to be so until April, 1851, when he resigned his charge, though he officiated as their stated supply till October following. The Rev. William A. Graham is now the pastor of the Upper Church of Path Valley, and the Rev. L. W. Williams is the pastor of the Lower Church, in connexion with the Church of the "Burnt Cabins," which is a colony from the Lower Church.

Dr. M'Ginley, though he has retired, by reason of the infirmities of old age, from the active duties of the ministry, still lives in the midst of the people whom he has long and faithfully served, and is universally beloved. For nearly fifty years, has he proclaimed the glorious Gospel of the blessed God to the same community, and now at length, he has, under the burden of advanced years, forsaken his pulpit, that others may occupy it, and hold up, as he has done, Jesus crucified, as the hope of a guilty and perishing world. Thus we pass away; thus the day for activity in God's service hastens to its close;—and never perhaps is a sense of this rapid transientness or fugacity of life more vividly flashed upon the soul, than when turning over the records of an ecclesiastical body, we read, in almost the same book, of the licensure of a man in all the vigour of youth, to fight the battles of the Lord, and then, of permission given him as a veteran tottering with age, to lay down the weapons of his warfare. Certain it is, however, that if there is any vocation in which old age has nothing to be dreaded or deplored, it is that of serving God in the ministry of reconciliation. The life of a man invested with this high office, may have been spent in comparative quietness. It may, too, have presented but little to the world, to interest or attract. Yet has that man's life been devoted to the highest and holiest purposes. He has been striving to stem the current of human corruption; he has been labouring for God; he has been endeavouring to elevate and heal fallen and diseased humanity; he has been casting the seeds of life into a dying world; he has been battling for the right and the true against enemies seen and invisible; he has been watching for souls,—

> "For souls, which must for ever live—
> In raptures, or in woe,"—

and therefore, in his case emphatically, "the hoary head found in the way of righteousness is a crown of glory." How worthless, oh, how hollow and vain, do the honours lavished by the world upon the conquering hero, seem, in comparison with those to which HE is entitled as an ambassador for Christ, and which he shall receive and enjoy, when earth with all its pæans and plaudits shall have for ever passed away!

Toward the close of such a life Doctor M'Ginley has now far advanced. He has reached the seventy-fifth year. A long shadow stretches before him on the plain. All the days of his appointed time is he waiting until his change come. For a period longer than many are permitted to live, he has been enabled by grace, to exhibit to the world a happy exemplification of the wisdom from above, which "is first pure, then peaceable, gentle, and easy to be entreated, full of mercy and good fruits, without partiality, and without hypocrisy," and to preach the word with tenderness, and ability, and cheering success; and when the time of his departure shall come, we doubt not that he will enter heaven, to meet with many there, who, though casting their crowns at the Saviour's feet, will not forget the Saviour's instrument for their conversion. "For what is our hope, or joy, or crown of rejoicing? Are not even ye in the presence of our Lord Jesus Christ at his coming? For ye are our glory and joy."

The following statement, which has been furnished by Dr. M'Ginley, will be read with interest, especially by those living, or who have lived, within the limits of his recent field of labour.

"I can give no information with regard to the

prosperity of these churches, before A. D., 1802. During the time intervening between 1802 and 1831, there was a regular yearly increase of members. In 1831 there was an addition to the communion of 127 members; and, in the year following, sixty members were added. Those who were, at one time, in communion with us, are numerously scattered over the western country, from Pittsburg to New Orleans. Two western churches, which are now comparatively flourishing, never would have been organized, had it not been for the number and influence of our people who emigrated thither.

"By removal to the West, we lost in one year, thirty-five communicating members, and five were removed by death the same year. Notwithstanding our severe losses, we have nearly as many members now as we ever had.

"In the Lower Church, John Cunningham, Robert Walker, Francis Elliott, Samuel Walker, and Archibald Elliott, were the first elders of whom I can gain any information. Since their decease the following persons have been elders in the Lower Church:—David Walker, William Maclay, Paul Geddes, John Campbell, James Walker, and Joseph Brown, all of whom are now dead. The elders now living, and in connexion either with the Lower Church, or the Burnt Cabins' Church, are Alexander Walker, George Elliott, William Elliott, James Campbell, James Cree, Sen., James Cree, Jr., William Campbell, and Daniel Brown.

"The elders who have been in the Upper Church since 1808, were James Alexander, William Alexander, John Elder, John Holliday, Andrew Morrow, David Riddle, Stephen Skinner, James McCurdy, Sen., and James McCurdy, Jr., all of whom are dead. Those now acting as elders in the Upper Church, are James Dougall, John Alexander, James Stark, Jaçob Shearer, Peter Shearer, John W. Still, William A. Mackey, William Herron, and James McCurdy. The Trustees are James McCartney, John Alexander, and Stephen M. Skinner.

"The oldest elders in the Upper Church, whose names have been handed down to us, are John Holliday, James Ardery, David Elder, Samuel Mains, and Richard Morrow."

# CHAPTER XII.

## DICKINSON CHURCH.

"In rival haste, the wished-for temples rise!
I hear their Sabbath-bells' harmonious chime
Float on the breeze—the heavenliest of all sounds,
That hill or vale prolongs or multiplies!"

WORDSWORTH.

As the population of Cumberland Valley rapidly increased, at the beginning of the present century, there was necessity for additional churches. Villages springing up in various directions, and numerous families settling around them, a house was required in the several localities, in which the people could conveniently assemble for public worship, and especially such as had not means of conveyance to a distant point. Nor was there, at that time, any objection, that could legitimately be urged against yielding to such a demand, inasmuch as that region was then constantly receiving accessions to its numbers from abroad, instead of sending out, as it has done for the last score of years, family after family, and sometimes colonies, to the distant West. It was, it would seem, in part, at least, under the force of such a necessity, that the church in Dickinson Township, Cumberland County, came into existence.

The first notice of this congregation by Presbytery, is to be found in their records for the year 1810, and is as follows:—

"An application was made, subscribed by James Moore and Joseph Galbraith, in behalf of a number of persons, calling themselves the Presbyterian Congregation of Walnut Bottom, in the County of Cumberland, that the Rev. Henry R. Wilson should be appointed to supply them, any portion of time which he may be able and willing to give them. Presbytery thought proper to comply with their request." Mr. Wilson preached to this people a part of the time during his connexion with Dickinson College as Professor of Languages, and, we believe, until he accepted the call given to him from Silvers' Spring.

It was not, however, until 1823, that a congregation was organized in Dickinson Township. At that time an application, for this purpose, was made to Presbytery, by a number of persons residing near the "Stone Meeting-House;" and it was resolved that their request be granted. The Rev. Messrs. Williams, Duffield, and McClelland, carried this resolution into effect; and the congregation organized was reported by them as, "The Congregation of Dickinson."

There was no regular public worship among this people, until July, 1826, when Mr. McKnight Williamson, a Licentiate of the Presbytery of Carlisle, consented to act as a missionary within their bounds, one-half of his time, for the term of nine months. At the expiration of that time, Mr. W. was unanimously elected pastor of the congregation. The call given him he accepted, and he continued to labour successfully in this field until October, 1834; when, at his own request, he was dismissed, to connect himself with the Presbytery of Huntingdon.

Just one year after Mr. Williamson's resignation, the congregation, through Presbytery, presented a call to the Rev. Charles P. Cummins, which was accepted. Mr. Cummins faithfully discharged the duties of the pastoral relation, until April, 1844, when he relinquished his post, and was dismissed by Presbytery to connect himself with the Presbytery of Iowa.

Mr. Cummins's successor was the Rev. Oliver O. McClean, who was installed as pastor of the congregation, November 4th, 1844, and is still labouring among his attached people with gratifying tokens of the divine favour.

At the organization of Dickinson Church, John Ross and Samuel Woods were the only ruling elders.

At the close of Mr. Williamson's labours as pastor, the Session consisted of Samuel Woods, John Ross, William Woods, Jr., George Davidson, and David W. McCulloch.

At the time of Mr. Cummins's resignation, the acting elders were, William Woods, Jr., Robert Donaldson, William G. Davidson, and Lewis H. Williams.

The Session, as at present constituted, consists of William Woods, Jr., Robert Donaldson, William G. Davidson, William Mateer, and John T. Green.

When the church at Dickinson was organized, there were not, as far as can be ascertained, more than from seventeen to twenty members in full communion. The number at present is one hundred and sixty. The temporal condition of the church is prosperous. There is no debt resting on the people. The pastor receives a salary of six hundred dollars. The Board of Foreign and Domestic Missions and the Board of Education, have each separate and distinct appropriations made, in aid of them, annually. Other benevolent enterprises, of an incidental character, are regarded with a spirit of liberality. There are two Sabbath schools in the congregation in a flourishing condition.

At the first stated administration of the word and ordinances among them, the congregation worshipped alternately in the stone church belonging to the Covenanters, and in the log church of the German Reformed and Lutheran Congregations, both of which are in Dickinson Township. The building in which they now worship was erected in 1829, at an expense of nearly two thousand dollars, and stands on a slight eminence, at the point where the road leading from Mount Rock to Spring Mills crosses the Walnut Bottom Road, eight miles west of Carlisle. The lot of ground on which it is erected, was given for the purpose by William L. Weakley, Esq. The situation is in all respects a beautiful one. The building, which is of brick, is 45 by 56 feet, and is capable of accommodating with its seventy pews, five hundred persons. Its interior is neatly and comfortably finished, and does credit to the taste and liberality of the congregation.

# CHAPTER XIII.

## THE CHURCH AT CARLISLE.

ABOUT the year 1736, the Presbyterians erected a log church on the Conodoguinett Creek, about two miles north of Carlisle, or West Pennsborough, as it was then called, at a place known ever since as the "Meeting-House Spring." No vestige of this building now remains, nor are there any of the oldest surviving residents of the neighbourhood, who are able to give anything like a satisfactory account of it. The members of the large congregation which worshipped within its walls, have all long ago disappeared, and with them the memory of the venerable edifice and the interesting incidents which were doubtless associated with its history, have well-nigh perished.

The first pastor of this church was the Rev. Samuel Thompson, from Ireland. Mr. Thompson was ordained and installed November 14th, 1739. Of this there is the following notice taken on the minutes of a meeting of Presbytery, of that date, at "Pennsboro."

"Mr. Anderson at the meeting-house door gave

public advertisement that if any could advance any lawful objection against Mr. Samuel Thompson being set apart to the work of the holy ministry to both societies in this place, and no objection appearing, Mr. Craighead delivered a sermon from Ezekiel xxxiii. 6, and presided in the work of ordination. Accordingly, Mr. Samuel Thompson was set apart to the work of the sacred ministry by the imposition of hands."

It is probable, however, though Mr. Thompson was the first settled pastor at "Pennsborough," that the Rev. Messrs. Craighead and Caven laboured there for some time previously, in the character of stated supplies. This, at least, seems to be indicated by this record, made at the meeting of Presbytery just referred to:

"It being inquired whether the upper settlement of Pennsborough had paid the arrears due by them to the estate of the deceased Mr. Craighead, Daniel Williams appeared and publicly engaged to pay said arrears speedily, viz.: the sum of £5 6*s.* 8*d.* Said Daniel Williams likewise agreed to pay the arrears due by said society to Mr. Caven."

Mr. Thompson resigned his pastoral relation in 1748. To this step he was led "by several reasons, but chiefly by the fact, that he doubted he could not be farther useful in this congregation." He had withdrawn from Lower Pennsboro' in 1744. After his release from this charge, he settled at "Great Conawago," where he remained until the infirmities of age disqualified him for the active duties of the ministerial office. His son, the Rev. William Thompson, was an itinerant missionary, as late as 1766, for several years, in the counties of York and Cumberland, after these counties were founded, under the direction of the "Society for the Propagation of the Gospel in Foreign Parts."

Before taking leave of the Old Log Church, on the bank of the creek, it may be well to state that the congregation that worshipped in it, had some difficulty with the people of Hopewell, about the erection of a meeting-house at Great Spring. This the following extracts from the Presbyterial Records will serve to show.

"Aug. 31, 1737.—Mr. Black reports that he supplied at Pensborrow, and convened the people and those of Hopewell on the Monday following, and heard them confer about the meeting-house proposed to be built at the Great Spring; but the parties did not agree about the same."

"16th Nov., 1737.—The affair of perambulation being taken into consideration, and after much discourse upon it, the Presbytery agree to defer a further consideration of said affaire until Spring; the report made by the perambulators is, that, in their judgment, the distance between Pennsborough Meeting-House and that at the Great Spring, is 8 miles, and that another road is found to be 12 miles."

Shortly after Carlisle was laid out, a Presbyterian congregation was organized in it, and a church was built. In relation to this latter movement, John Armstrong wrote to Richard Peters as follows:—

"Carlisle, 30 June, 1757.

"To-morrow we begin to haul stones for the building of a meeting-house, on the north side of the square;—there was no other convenient place. I have avoided the place you once pitched for a church. The stones are raised out of Col. Stanwix's entrenchments: we will want help in this political as well as religious work."

"About the year 1760, a license was obtained from Governor Hamilton, authorizing the congregation to raise by lottery, 'a small sum of money to enable them to build a decent house for the worship of God;' and, in 1766, the ministers and others petitioned the Assembly, for the passage of an act to compel the 'managers to settle,' and the 'adventurers to pay,' the settlement of the lottery having been for a 'considerable time deferred,' by reason of the 'confusion occasioned by the Indian wars.' The act prayed for was passed." It is unnecessary for us, perhaps, here to state, that the method of raising money by lottery, for church purposes or any other, was not at that time regarded as it is now.

In the year 1759, the Rev. George Duffield was called to the congregations of Carlisle and Big

Spring, and installed as their pastor, with the understanding that two-thirds of his labours were to be given to the former. Two years after his settlement, an effort was made by the people of Big Spring, to obtain one-half of Mr. Duffield's time, but this effort was not successful, because the Carlisle congregation were unwilling to agree to such an arrangement, and because Presbytery apprehended that Mr. Duffield's constitution would not be able to endure, any length of time, the fatigue of being the one-half of his time at Big Spring.

As we find in the Records of Presbytery, of April 16th, 1760, a resolution to "meet the third Tuesday of October, at Mr. Steel's meeting-house in Carlisle," there would seem to have been two Presbyterian Churches at that time in this borough. There were, at least, two congregations, which had a separate existence, in virtue of the division of the church, which then prevailed throughout the Synod.* On this subject, Mr. Rupp, in his History of Cumberland County, says: "A short time afterwards (1761), the congregation in the country, then under the care of the Rev. Mr. Steel, constructed a two-story house of worship in town; and, some time before the Revolution, erected the present First Presbyterian Church, on the northwest corner of the centre square. Mr. Duffield's congregation erected a gallery in Mr. Steel's church, and the two parties worshipped separately."

* See Appendix III.

In the year 1764, Carlisle and East Pennsborough congregations agreed to unite, and to enjoy each an equal proportion of the Rev. John Steel's labours.*

After the removal of Mr. Duffield to Philadelphia, and the death of Mr. Steel, the two congregations, which had been known as the "Old Lights" and "New Lights," united, and called, in 1785, the Rev. Robert Davidson. The following year, the congregation thus united was incorporated. Dr. Davidson was removed by death, December 13th, 1812. In connexion with him, and as his colleague, the Rev. Henry R. Wilson preached some time to the congregation, whilst professor in Dickinson College.

In 1816, the Rev. George Duffield, a licentiate of the Philadelphia Presbytery, was called to be pastor of the congregation of Carlisle. Mr. Duffield's labours among this people were greatly blessed for a number of years. In 1832, a book was published by him, which was entitled "Duffield on Regeneration," and which as the embodiment of some new views introduced by him into his pulpit, produced a distracted state of his congregation. We have not the space to give a minute statement of the proceedings of Presbytery in relation to this book and its author. As, however, the case is interwoven with the history of Presbyterianism in Carlisle, we are warranted, at least, in presenting the following synoptical view of it.

* See call given to Mr. S., Appendix II.

At a meeting of Presbytery in June, 1832, a committee, previously appointed to examine the abovementioned book, submitted a report, in which they specified "a number of objectionable doctrines" which it contained, "doctrines in opposition to those contained in the Confession of Faith, and on subjects which are essential in the Gospel scheme of salvation."*

The report concludes in this wise:

"Finally, the committee would only add, that in many parts of the work the language is exceedingly obscure, or equivocal; many theological terms and phrases, long in use and well understood, are set aside, and a new phraseology is introduced unnecessary, and often unintelligible to most readers; which things are calculated greatly to embarrass and mislead even honest inquirers after truth, who are not accustomed to very elaborate investigation; that although the work sometimes professes to set all philosophy aside, and to adhere simply to Scripture and to facts, yet does the author range through every department of natural science; and it is evident his philosophy respecting the nature of life, runs through the greater part of the work and gives character to it."

The following resolutions were adopted by Presbytery in regard to this report. "Resolved, That we adopt the concluding part of the report, as expressive of our view of the whole matter of it.

* These doctrines are included in the "charges" to be found on a subsequent page.

"Resolved, That after deliberate consideration, having declared the foregoing doctrines contained in the book entitled 'Duffield on Regeneration,' as presented in the report of the committee, to be erroneous, and contrary to the doctrines of the Bible and the standards of our Church, we do most solemnly and affectionately warn all our ministers, and elders, and people, to guard against such distracting and dangerous errors, and this we feel constrained to do, under a deep conviction of our responsibility to the great Head of the Church, to guard against everything which will corrupt the purity or disturb the peace of the Church."

At a meeting of Presbytery in October of the same year, a committee was appointed to take into consideration the entire proceedings of Presbytery in regard to Mr. Duffield's book, in order to bring in, if possible, some minute which might be satisfactory to all, and arrest further proceedings. The report of this committee not having been adopted, a committee was appointed at the next meeting of Presbytery, to prepare charges against the Rev. George Duffield, and report to Presbytery.

We give the report of this committee, and the action of Presbytery in regard to it:—

"After due deliberation on the several articles of the report of the committee in the case of the Rev. George Duffield, the Presbytery adopted them as relevant charges, and they are as follows:

"The committee appointed to prepare charges of error, to be preferred against the Rev. George Duffield, are unanimously of opinion, that he may be fairly charged on the ground of 'common fame,' with maintaining and industriously propagating, both from the pulpit and through the press, the following doctrines or opinions, either absurd in themselves, or directly at variance with some of the most important and vital doctrines and truths taught in the standards of the Presbyterian Church and the word of God, namely:—

"1. That life consists in the regular series of relative, appropriate, characteristic actions in an individual being, and that the life of God himself is not distinguishable from his own holy volitions and actions.

"2. That the human soul equally with the body is derived from the parents by traduction or natural generation; that the soul and body are alike developed in their actions respectively, and the soul as created by God and brought into connexion with the body, whether in conception, quickening, or the first inspiration, is wholly destitute of all capacities whatever.

"3. That the image of God, in which man or Adam was originally created, principally consisted in a threefold life, with which he was endowed by his Maker, viz., *vegetable*, *animal*, and *spiritual life*.

"4. That Adam was not the federal covenant head of the human race; that he sustained no other relation to his posterity than that of a natural parent; and that there did not exist anything which could properly be denominated a covenant relation between God and Adam, as the representative of his natural offspring.

"5. That Adam's sin is in no proper sense imputed to his posterity to their legal condemnation, and that the temporal or natural death of infants is the natural result or consequence of Adam's sin, solely by virtue of their connexion with him as a parent.

"6. That all holiness and sin consists exclusively in voluntary acts and exercises of the soul; that there is no principle of holiness or sin inherent in the soul, which exerts any power or causal influence in producing holy or sinful acts and exercises; and that there is no innate, hereditary, derived depravity or corruption in our nature.

"7. That no moral character can be appropriately predicated of, or possessed by infants; that they are neither sinful nor holy, are not actually under the government of law, nor above the level of the mere animals; and that even our Lord Jesus Christ, in his infant state, possessed no holiness of character, other than what might be affirmed of the Mosaic tabernacle or inmost chamber of the temple, and other consecrated instruments of Jewish worship; and that our first parents themselves were not created in a state of moral rectitude, that is, they possessed no holiness or moral character, anterior to, and independent of, their own volitions and exercises, or, in other words, they had no spiritual life till they acquired it by their own voluntary acts and exercises.

"8. That man in his fallen state is possessed of entire ability to repent, believe, and perform other holy exercises, independently of any new power or ability imparted to him by the regenerating or new-creating influences of the Holy Ghost,—consequently,

"9. That regeneration is essentially a voluntary change or act of the soul, is exclusively the effect of man's own unassisted powers and efforts, independently of any divine influence whatever, except what is of a mere objective moral kind, or, in other language, the moral suasion of the spirit, or the suasive influence of the truth, in connexion with an arrangement of providential circumstances.

"10. That by election, in the Sacred Scriptures, is meant nothing else than the actual selection of a certain number from the great mass, by their being made the subjects of spiritual life, which is not possessed by the rest; that it is the actual display of God's sovereignty in making believers alive from the dead, or quickening them (believers), from the death of trespasses and of sins, in which they (believers), with all mankind were lying."

This report having been "considered and sustained" by Presbytery, they resolved to institute judicial process against Mr. Duffield, on the grounds of the specifications contained in it, and to cite him to appear before Presbytery at its next meeting, to answer the same.

When Mr. Duffield appeared, in obedience to the citation issued, the prosecuting committee which had been appointed, having submitted to Presbytery all the testimony in support of the charges preferred against him, he was heard at some length in his defence, and then the vote "whether Mr. Duffield is guilty or not guilty," was taken, with the following result:—

1st Charge,—guilty; seven votes affirmative, four negative, six non liquet. 2d Charge,—guilty; six affirmative, five negative, and seven non liquet. 3d Charge,—five affirmative and five negative; not guilty, by the casting vote of the Moderator. 4th Charge,—guilty; twelve affirmative, four negative, and two non liquet. 5th Charge, same vote. 6th Charge, same vote. 7th Charge, same vote. 8th Charge, same vote. 9th Charge,—guilty; ten affirmative, four negative, and four non liquet. 10th Charge,—not guilty; two affirmative, nine negative, and seven non liquet.

The trial being over, a motion was made to adopt the following minute as expressive of the sense of Presbytery in the case, and it was carried:

"As to the counts in which Mr. Duffield has been found guilty, Presbytery judge, that Mr. Duffield's Book and Sermons on Regeneration do contain the specified errors: yet as Mr. Duffield alleges that Presbytery have misinterpreted some of his expressions, and says he does in fact hold all the doctrines of our standards, and that he wishes to live at amity with his brethren, and labour without interruption for the glory of God and the salvation of souls, therefore, Resolved, that Presbytery, at present, do not censure him any further, than warn him to guard against such speculations as may impugn the doctrines of our Church, and that he study to maintain 'the unity of the spirit in the bond of peace.'"

It is proper to add, that this decision was not approved by Synod, as the annexed extract from the adopted report of Synod's committee to examine the Records of the Presbytery of Carlisle, will show:

"The committee cannot recommend an approval of this decision; because it compromises essential truths, defeats the ends of discipline, and, under the circumstances of the case, presents a result never contemplated by our constitution, after a judicial conviction upon points involving material departures from the doctrines of our standards."

In this brief statement of the trial of Mr. Duffield, we have omitted most of the interlocutory proceedings, such as protests, complaints, and exceptions, emanating from himself and those who sympathized with him, in relation to the alleged injustice and informality of the action of Presbytery. This, however, we have felt constrained to do by a regard to the limitedness of our space. And this course we have been the less reluctant to pursue, as our avowed object is not to argue the case, or act as reporter of it, but merely to state in the most compendious way possible, what Presbytery did in relation to the book and its author, and what was the ground of their action.

Contemporaneously with Dr. Duffield's difficulties in Presbytery, there existed also difficulties in the congregation of which he was pastor. The first intimation of these which we have in the Presbyterial records, is in "a memorial and a communication from part of the congregation of Carlisle, requesting Presbytery to redress certain grievances complained of in them." This was soon followed by a petition, which was presented by Mr. Andrew Blair, and signed by seventy-seven members of the congregation, praying to be set off and formed into a separate congregation. Presbytery having granted this prayer, "in view of the things now existing in that congregation and known to Presbytery," the Second Presbyterian Church of Carlisle was organized, by a committee appointed for the purpose, in the town hall of that place, on the 12th January, 1833. Of this new congregation, Messrs. Andrew Blair, John M'Clure, and Robert Clark, were unanimously chosen elders, and Peter B. Smith, Robert Irvine, John Proctor, and Robert Giffin, deacons,—all of whom had been elders and deacons, respectively, in the old church.

At a meeting of Presbytery in March, 1835, Dr. Duffield's pastoral relation with the First Church of Carlisle was, at his own request, dissolved, and he was regularly dismissed to connect himself with the General Assembly's Second Presbytery of Philadelphia.

For some time, the pulpit thus vacated was filled by supplies, among whom were the Rev. Mr. Granger, and the Rev. Mr. Burrowes, each of whom served for a number of months.

In July, 1837, the Rev. W. T. Sprole, a member of the Classis of Philadelphia, in connexion with the German Reformed Church, was called to the pastorate of the First Church of Carlisle. It is not necessary to notice, in detail, the difficulties which sprang up between the Session of this church and Presbytery, in connexion with the prosecution of this call, and subsequently, and therefore we only give the record of the final disposition of the case, as it is contained in the concluding part of the report of a committee of Presbytery, adopted April 13th, 1839. It is as follows:

"Therefore seeing that this Session has been twice duly cited to appear before the Presbytery, to answer for certain alleged improprieties and irregularities, to which citation they have not responded, nor have they in a single instance sent a representative to the Presbytery since our meeting at Newville, Oct. 3d, 1837, although we have had no less than seven meetings of the Presbytery since that time, and the present meeting and a preceding one in the town of Carlisle: from every view which the Presbytery can take of this subject, the conduct of this Session appears to us to have been disrespectful and rebellious against their authority. Therefore, Resolved, That the First Presbyterian Church of Carlisle be considered no longer a constituent part of this Presbytery, nor as belonging to the Presbyterian Church of the

United States of America, and that its name be stricken from the Roll of Presbytery."

The Rev. Daniel M'Kinley was installed as pastor of the Second Presbyterian Church of Carlisle, Aug. 7th, 1833, and continued to be so until July, 1838, when, on his own application to Presbytery, the pastoral relation was dissolved, that he might accept an invitation which he had received, to become an Agent for the Board of Foreign Missions of the Presbyterian Church. To this measure, the congregation, though warmly attached to Mr. M'Kinley, consented, under a sense of duty.

Mr. M'Kinley was succeeded, in October of the same year, by the Rev. Alexander T. M'Gill. The following papers which relate to Mr. M'Gill's transfer to the Presbyterian Church, and which were laid before Presbytery, will be read with interest:

"To the Associate Presbytery of Philadelphia.

"Rev. and dear Brethren,—

"It is the duty of all believers, and especially ministers of the Gospel, 'to prove all things,' not only before they make a solemn and particular profession of the faith, but afterwards and always till we cease to 'see through a glass darkly.' No process of time, nor investment of office, nor pressure of circumstances, can exonerate from the obligation to 'search and see whether these things be so', so long as we are fallible. Perhaps I have erred in not searching more thoroughly when I first made a profession of the peculiarities of the Associate Church. But it is now my painful situation to doubt the propriety and truth of such a profession. 1st. I cannot sustain the discipline of our Church, which makes it censurable for any member to attend the preaching of the word in any Church that we acknowledge to be a Church of Christ. 2d. I cannot see a warrant for excluding from the Table of the Lord, all who are not in full standing in our own particular communion. I cannot see that communion in the ordinance of the Supper, should not be as free to believers, as the ordinance of preaching the word is to sinners. As all men have the privilege of hearing the word from us wherever we labour, so all believers should have the privilege of receiving at our hands the symbols of Christ's dying love. To define believers, we need only inquire, 'Are they unblemished members of the Church to which they belong, and is that Church, according to our admission, a Church of Christ?' 3d. Although the Psalms of David should always be used in the worship of God, although they are doubtless intended for worship in New Testament, as well as Old Testament times, I cannot see that they were exclusively used in the days of Christ and his Apostles on earth. I believe that the warrant for singing praises to God comprehends human compositions, or the doctrines of the Gospel and the exercise of faith, couched in human language, as well as in the very words of a literal human version of the Scriptures.

"These views, Brethren, have been gaining on my

conviction for the last two years. It would have injured the peace of the Church, and my own usefulness, to have avowed them from time to time. Till now, I have concealed them wherever I have laboured, believing it wrong to broach anything contrary to our profession, while I remained in its connexion. But to pursue such a course any longer, is disingenuous, and ruinous to my own peace. I now, therefore, frankly disclose to you my belief, where it varies from the peculiarity of our communion. Believing that with such views, I would not be permitted to remain in connexion with you, I respectfully ask you for a dismission to join the Presbytery of Carlisle, in subordination to the General Assembly of the Presbyterian Church in the United States; or, if such dismission be not granted, I ask a certificate of my standing among you as a minister of Christ.

"Yours, affectionately,

"In the bonds of the Gospel,

"ALEXANDER T. M'GILL.

"October 24th, 1838."

"Whereas, the Rev. Alexander T. M'Gill has appeared before Presbytery, professing that he entertains doubts in regard to certain points of the public profession of the Associate Church, and has signified his intention to withdraw from the communion of this Church, and has to this end applied for a dismission; therefore,

"Resolved, That Mr. M'Gill be required to acknowledge his sin, and return to his duty. Further,

"Resolved, That in default thereof, he be suspended from the exercise of the ministry and the communion of this Church.

"A true extract from the minutes of the Associate Presbytery of Philadelphia.

"Attest, JOHN G. SMART,
"Clerk, pro tem.

"Mercersburg, October 24th, 1838."

"TO THE MODERATOR AND MEMBERS OF THE PRESBYTERY OF CARLISLE.

"Rev. and dear Brethren,—

"Believing that your confession embodies the doctrines of the Gospel, and that your practice is scriptural, and more accordant with my own views than that of any other branch of the visible church, I respectfully ask admission to your communion, and to the exercise of the ministry among you. My standing in the Associate (Presbyterian) Church was unblemished. But on disclosing to them doubts respecting sundry peculiarities in their public profession, the Presbytery of Philadelphia immediately suspended me, 'from the exercise of the ministry and the communion of the Church.' A paper containing a true copy of my letter to that Presbytery, and a paper containing a true extract from the minutes of their proceedings thereon, are herewith laid before you.

"Yours, with much respect and affection,
"ALEXANDER T. M'GILL."

After these communications were read before Presbytery, the following action was taken:

"Resolved, That the reasons contained in the above-named papers, for which the Associate Presbytery suspended Mr. M'Gill, namely: 1. Occasional hearing; 2. Catholic communion; and 3, the rejection of the exclusive use of Rouse's Psalms, are, in our opinion, insufficient grounds for any ecclesiastical censure, much less for suspension from the ministry of the Gospel; and, therefore, the act of the Associate Presbytery, suspending Mr. M'Gill from the exercise of the functions of his ministerial office, forms no bar in our way to his reception as a member of this Presbytery."

Mr. M'Gill was examined on his views of the doctrines, government, and discipline of the Presbyterian Church, and his examination was sustained: after which the Moderator proposed to him the constitutional questions contained in the Confession of Faith, Form of Government, Chap. XV., which he answered in the affirmative: whereupon it was

"Resolved, that Mr. M'Gill be received as a member of this Presbytery, and his name be entered upon our roll."

Dr. M'Gill's pastoral relation to the Second Presbyterian Church of Carlisle, which was formed in April, 1839, continued until December, 1841, when, at the earnest solicitation of the President and Secretary of the Board of Directors of the Western Theological Seminary, at Allegheny City, it was dissolved, that he might occupy the chair of Ecclesiastical History in that Institution. He has since accepted a professorship in the Theological Seminary at Columbia, South Carolina.

The Rev. T. V. Moore, a licentiate under the care of the Presbytery of West Jersey, was installed as Dr. M'Gill's successor at Carlisle, in the spring of 1842, and continued to be so until his acceptance of a call from the congregation of Greencastle, in the autumn of the year 1845.

After Mr. Moore's resignation, the Rev. James Lillie, of the Classis of Ulster, became pastor of the congregation, and served it for several years. The present pastor, the Rev. Mervin E. Johnston, was ordained and installed August 22d, 1849, and has since been favoured with gratifying evidence of the Divine blessing upon his labours. The Session, as now constituted, consists of Andrew Blair, Robert Clark, Samuel Hepburn, and Matthew Davidson. The church, which stands on the corner of South Hanover and Pomfret Streets, is a very neat and capacious building; and the congregation, according to the last report made to Presbytery, numbers two hundred and eighty-five communicating members.

It gives us great pleasure to add, that whilst the Second Presbyterian Congregation of Carlisle is in a flourishing condition, so likewise is that from which it seceded. Its esteemed pastor, the Rev. Mr. Wing, is cultivating, with success, the field in which God has placed him. Equally pleased are we to record, that any asperity of feeling, with which the history of these dissociated churches may have been attended, has largely yielded, as it ought entirely to do, to the harmonizing spirit of the Gospel of their common Lord.

# SUPPLEMENT.

# SUPPLEMENT.

## PAXTON AND DERRY CHURCHES.

PAXTON CHURCH is situated about three miles east of Harrisburg, and about one-fourth of a mile north of the Reading Turnpike. As this congregation is one of the oldest in the State, it doubtless had a house of worship before that which is now in use, but of this no knowledge can be derived, either from the recollections of the living, or the records of the dead. The Rev. A. D. Mitchell, the present pastor, in a letter in which he expresses his regret, that by reason of the loss of the records of the churches under his care, with the exception of those of comparatively recent date, he is unable to furnish more extensive and accurate information respecting them, says:—"When the present building was erected is not certainly known. From evidence that I have in my possession, I know that it has been standing for at least ninety-eight years. This is, perhaps, as near an approximation to the time of its erection, as can be made."

"Derry," Mr. Mitchell adds, "is located about

ten miles farther east, and but a short distance north of the turnpike leading from Harrisburg to Reading. The present building was erected about ninety years ago. The congregation, though at one time among the largest in the Presbytery, is now almost entirely broken up by emigration."

We could not, perhaps, make our brief sketch of Paxton and Derry more interesting, than by presenting, at some length, what is to be found concerning them, on the Presbyterial Records.

"Oct. 11th, 1732.—This day appeared Geo. Renick, and others, from Paxton and Derry, requiring an answer to their call, given to the Rev. Mr. Bertram, at Philadelphia, where the Presbytery of New Castle met, producing their subscription for his support; whereupon the Presbytery asking Mr. Bertram if he had considered said call, and requiring his answer in relation thereunto, he declared his acceptance thereof, and that he would take the people's subscriptions, without any other obligations for his support."

"Nov. 15th, 1732.—The Presbytery order the congregations of Derry and Paxton to pay up the arrears due to Mr. Anderson. Mr. Bertram gave in a list of more nominations by the congregations of Paxton and Derry, to be set apart for Ruling Elders: the Presbytery appoints that they be again published, and intimation given that if any objection be made against any of them, that said objections shall be given in in due time."

"The congregation of Paxton and Derry, with the concurrence of the Presbytery, appoints Thomas Foster, George Renick, William Kuningham, Thomas Mays, for Paxton side; and, for the other side of the creek, Rowland Chambers, Hugh Black, Robert Campbell, John Wilson, William Wilson, James Quigly, William M'Cord, and Jon. Sloan, to take care that the subscriptions for Mr. Bertram's maintenance be paid, and to collect the same until the congregation be better regulated."

"Paxton, Aug. 28th, 1734.—A visitation having been appointed here, Mr. Bertram, after previous intimation to the congregation, preached upon 2 Cor. iv. 5, with approbation. It being interrogated whether Mr. Bertram had performed his duty as a Gospel minister, and the several branches thereof, and had a conduct and behaviour suitable to his station; it was answered by the representatives of both societies in the affirmative, to their great satisfaction and spiritual edification. The said representatives being asked about the elders in both societies, replied that they had no objection, nor much time to make trial of their behaviour, said elders being but lately invested with that office. It was likewise proposed whether any proper modes were taken to collect Mr. Bertram's salary: they answered that suitable modes were laid down, and they hoped would be duly prosecuted. The elders of both societies being called in, were asked concerning the general behaviour of their minister in the congregation, and his particular conduct in managing sessional affairs; they replied that his conduct was exemplary and agreeable; and, because of the late formation of the session, they had not opportunity of much experience that way. Mr. Bertram was called in, and asked whether the people had performed their duty to him in all the branches of it: he answered that he had no general complaints, but was not fully satisfied in reference to his house; and, for the payment of his subscriptions, he had not computed his book accounts, but expected to be capable to give a particular account thereof against our next."

"Oct. 7th, 1735.—Mr. Bertram and his elder represented to the Presbytery, that inasmuch as Mr. Bertram is under an intolerable burden of labour and fatigue, in the discharge of the work of the ministry to both parts of the congregation to which he stands related, it is their desire that some of the ministers might be appointed, at a convenient time, to go unto and convene the people of said congregation, and inquire into their circumstances, as to their ability to be separated into two distinct congregations, and subsist by themselves, in order to Mr. Bertram's being eased of part of his burden, that he may be able, with more comfort, to go on in the discharge of his duty, unto whatever part of said people he shall be determined to continue with."

"Nov. 18th, 1735.—A supplication was presented from the Session of the congregation of Derry, desiring that if they should be separated from Paxton, as a distinct congregation, their bounds may be fixed so as that they may be able to take steps for their being supplied."

At this meeting of Presbytery, "Lazarus Stuart appeared to prosecute the supplication of *Monada Creek*, for a new erection." In answer to this supplication, Mr. Anderson, Andrew Galbraith, and one of the elders from Paxton—William Maxwell by name—were ordered to perambulate the bounds between the people of Derry and those of Monada. This committee discharged the duty assigned them, and the Presbytery approved their judgment, viz.: "That the people of Monada be erected into a distinct congregation, and that the place where now they have begun to build a house is the most commodious place for a meeting-house for that people."

In 1736, in the prospect of Mr. Bertram's release from one part of his charge, the people of Paxton declared that they could afford yearly for the support of their minister, £60, one-half in money, the other half in hemp, flour, linen yarn or linen cloth, at market price. The people of Derry, likewise, promised the sum of £55, to be paid in like manner, and both societies engaged to allow their minister the benefit of overplus subscriptions. It was farther agreed to by the people of Monada and Derry, and ordered by the Presbytery, that those living upon the borders of those two congregations, that is, between the two meeting-houses, and beyond the creek of Swatara, should, on or before the first of the ensuing November, declare, in an orderly way, whether they would connect themselves with the congregation of Derry or Monada.

About the same time, Mr. Bertram being asked by Presbytery which of the congregations, Paxton or Derry, he was willing to adhere to, expressed his desire to remain connected with Derry. Of the continuance of this connexion Presbytery approved, and declared the congregation of Paxton vacant. This approval was accompanied with a recommendation to the people of Derry, "speedily to improve upon the glebe-land that was talked of, in order to make it inhabitable for Mr. Bertram, that his easement of travel may be obtained."

In 1737, a supplication together with a call to the Rev. Mr. Sanckey, was presented by John Cunningham and Robert Grier, commissioners from the congregation of Hanover, by which said commissioners were empowered to promise toward Mr. Sanckey's outward support, among that people, as their orderly pastor, the annual sum of sixty pounds, that is, one-half in cash and the other in particular commodities, as flax, hemp, linen yarn and cloth, together with several gratuities mentioned in said supplication.

In 1738, Mr. Elder, of the Presbytery of New Castle, accepted a call, which was presented to him a second time, from the congregation of Paxton, with the promise for "a stipend," of £60 in money. His ordination took place in November of the same year, and was followed with an order of Presbytery, that "he and the Session take care, that none of those who are deficient, as to what they were to pay to Mr. Bertram, by note or otherwise, be admitted to any church privileges till they satisfy Mr. Bertram."

At a meeting of Presbytery at Derry, December 9th, 1741, "Mr. Bertram having given his reason for suing for a dismission from his congregation, viz.: bodily weakness and inability, the congregation answered by their representatives, Rowland Chambers and James Carothers, that they had enjoyed Mr. Bertram's labours when he was more able, and they were willing now to sympathize with him in his weakness, which so engaged Mr. Bertram to them, that he desisted from his suit at that time."

In 1762, the Rev. Mr. M'Mordie received a call from Hanover, which he accepted, with "the promise of £80, for his temporal support, to be secured by bond."

In 1764, on account of some difficulty which had arisen, several supplications from Hanover were brought into Presbytery and read, requesting a dismission for the petitioners, from the Rev. Robert M'Mordie's congregation, with liberty to join some neighbouring congregation under the care of Presbytery, till their way should be clear to return and join Hanover congregation again. This request was not granted, so far as to dissolve the relation of membership, but the petitioners were allowed, for the time, to put themselves under the care of any neighbouring minister belonging to the Presbytery, so as to enjoy any privileges or administration of ordinances they should desire, until something farther should be done in said affair.

Paxton and Derry, it would seem, were united to the congregation of Donegal in the year 1768, for in the Presbyterial Records of that date, reference is made to an authentic account produced by a commissioner for the congregations of Paxton, Derry, and Donegal, from which it appeared they were in arrears to the Rev. John Sloan, their pastor.

The Rev. Mr. Woods received and accepted a call from Hanover congregation, in June, 1781.

In 1787, the petition of a number of the inhabitants of Harrisburg and others in the township of Paxton, having been presented to Presbytery, in which they expressed a desire to be erected into a congregation, and to have the place of worship in that town, and this movement disturbing the peace and harmony which had existed between that people and Paxton congregation, a committee was appointed by Presbytery to visit that region, the result of whose interposition to adjust the difficulty, was an agreement to the following articles by Mr. Elder, his congregation, and Harrisburg.

1. The congregation shall have two stated places of public worship, the one where the Rev. Mr. Elder now officiates, the other in Harrisburg. 2. The Rev. John Elder shall continue to have and receive, during his life or incumbency, all the salary or stipends that he now enjoys, to be paid by his present subscribers,

as he and they may agree, and continue his labours in Derry as usual. 3. For the present, the congregation may apply to the Presbytery for supplies, which, when obtained, the expenses shall be defrayed by those who do not now belong to Mr. Elder's congregation and such as may think proper to join with them, and should such supplies be appointed when Mr. Elder is to be in Paxton, then he and the persons to supply shall preach in rotation, the one in the country and the other in the town; but should Mr. Elder be in Derry, then the supplies shall officiate in town. 4. The congregation, when able, or they think proper, may invite and settle any regular Presbyterian minister they or a majority of them may choose, and can obtain, as a co-pastor with Mr. Elder, who shall officiate as to preaching in the manner specified in the third proposal.

In 1791, the Rev. Mr. Elder resigned the pastoral charge of the congregations of Paxton and Derry, with which he had been intrusted for 60 years, on account of the infirmities of age, and in July of the following year he died, at the advanced age of 86 years, on his farm adjoining Harrisburg, beloved in life, and in death lamented.

The following extracts, which relate to the bloody outrage which was perpetrated on the Indians at Conestoga, on the night of the 14th December, 1763, and in which many of the people of Paxton acted a prominent part, are from a series of historical numbers in the Lancaster Intelligencer and Journal,

1843, by Redmond Conyngham, Esq., and may be of interest in this connexion.

"Imagination cannot conceive the perils with which the settlement of Paxton was surrounded, from 1754 to 1765. To portray each scene of horror would be impossible—the heart shrinks from the attempt. The settlers were goaded on to desperation; murder followed murder. Scouts brought in the intelligence that the murderers were traced to Conestogue. Rifles were loaded, horses were in readiness. They mounted; they called on their pastor to lead them. He was then in the 57th year of his age. Had you seen him then, you would have beheld a superior being. He had mounted, not to lead them on to the destruction of Conestogue but to deter them from the attempt; he implored them to return; he urged them to reflect. 'Pause, pause before you proceed.' It was in vain. 'The blood of the murdered cries aloud for vengeance; we have waited long enough on government. The murderers are within our reach, and they must not escape.' Mr. Elder reminded them that the 'guilty and innocent could not be distinguished.' 'Innocent! can they be called innocent who foster murderers?' Mr. Elder rode up in front, and said, 'As your pastor, I command you to relinquish your design.' 'Give way, then,' said Smith, 'or your horse dies,' at the same time presenting a rifle. To save his horse, to which he was much attached, Mr. E. drew him aside, and the rangers were off on their fatal errand.

"Mr. Elder frequently visited the Indians at Conestogue, Pequehan, and the Big Island, and was much respected by them. He had frequently represented to the Christian Indians the wrong they were doing to the whites by admitting stranger Indians among them,—conduct which made them suspected of treachery."

Extract from a letter of Mr. Elder to Governor Penn, January 27th, 1764.

"The storm which had been so long gathering, has at length exploded. Had government removed the Indians from Conestogue, which had frequently been urged without success, this painful catastrophe might have been avoided. What could I do with men heated to madness? All that I could do, was done. I expostulated, but *life* and *reason* were set at defiance. And yet the men in private life are virtuous and respectable; not cruel, but mild and merciful."

In the year 1788, Mr. James Snodgrass, after his ordination by Presbytery, was installed pastor of the congregation of Hanover. Mr. Snodgrass departed this life, July 2d, 1846, aged 84 years, after having long and faithfully served his Master in the ministry of reconciliation, and exhibited the power of godliness in his walk and conversation. The church in Hanover, where he preached for nearly sixty years, is now, as a Presbyterian church, nearly extinct.

In 1793, a call was received and accepted by Mr. Nathaniel R. Snowden, from the congregations of Harrisburg, Paxton, and Derry, in which each congregation engaged to pay him the sum of fifty pounds annually for his pastoral services. Three years afterwards, the relation between the Rev. Mr. Snowden and the congregation of Derry was dissolved, and the congregation of Paxton having by a considerable majority declared their determination to " hold a connexion with Derry," this arrangement was approved by Presbytery, and Mr. Elder was subsequently pastor of Harrisburg only.

In 1799, Mr. Joshua Williams was installed pastor of the united congregations of Derry and Paxton, with the agreement, that for two-thirds of his labours the congregation of Derry was to pay him one hundred and twenty pounds, and that for one-third of his labours he was to receive from the congregation of Paxton sixty pounds annually. This pastoral relation was dissolved in June, 1801, at the request of Mr. Williams. After this (1803), a call from these congregations was given to Mr. James Adair, but before the meeting of Presbytery after that at which this call was put into his hands, Mr. Adair was removed by death.

The next pastor of Paxton and Derry was the Rev. James Sharon. Mr. Sharon died, April 18th, 1843. We regret that the obituary of this excellent man, as well as that of Mr. Snodgrass, has not yet been reported to Presbytery so as to be entered in their book and be available for our purpose; but he was, as all know who ever came within the range of his influence, a sound divine, an exemplary Christian, and diligent in the great work to which his life was consecrated.

In April, 1809, the Rev. James Buchanan was installed pastor of the united congregations of Harrisburg and Middle Paxton. Two years afterwards Mr. Buchanan resigned the pastoral charge of the congregation of Middle Paxton, in which he had spent one-fourth part of his time. In 1815, the relation between the congregation of Harrisburg and Mr. Buchanan was dissolved at his request. Mr. Buchanan was succeeded at Harrisburg, in 1819, by the Rev. William R. Dewitt, who still continues to serve the congregation with every indication of attachment on the part of the people, and gratifying evidence that the long pastoral supervision of a flock, is not necessarily attended with a diminution of usefulness in their midst. At the request of Doctor Dewitt, in 1832, the re-organization of the Church of Middle Paxton was noticed on the Minutes of Presbytery.

In 1843, the congregation of Paxton obtained leave of Presbytery to procure the services of Mr. John M. Boggs for six months. In 1844, a call from the congregation of Paxton and Derry was received and accepted by Mr. Boggs. At Mr. Boggs's ordination and installation, the Rev. Doctor J. C. Watson was appointed to preach the sermon, Doctor Moody to preside, and Doctor M'Ginley to deliver the charge. The present pastor of these congregations, the Rev. A. D. Mitchell, has had the charge of them for several years.

The Session of Paxton, at present, consists of Benjamin Jordan, Robert W. M'Clure, and John B. Rutherford. Of Derry, the only Elder is, James Clark, Esq., of Hummelstown.

---

## MONAGHAN AND PETERSBURG CHURCHES.

THE Presbyterian Church at Dillsburg, York County, Pennsylvania, ecclesiastically known as "Monaghan," takes its name from the township in which it was formerly embraced. It is often called "Old Monaghan," because of its unquestionable antiquity. It was organized more than a century ago, although at this late period nothing certain is known as to the very year of its origin. At first it belonged to the old Presbytery of Donegal, for the Presbytery of Carlisle, with which it is now connected, was not erected until 1786. Tradition says, that for some years after its organization, the savages were numerous in the region round about, and daring in their movements of hostility towards the white settlers, so much so, indeed, that a part of the congregation, for the sake of protection, and to guard against surprise, found it necessary to carry their fire-arms with them to church.

We find the following reference to this congregation in the minutes of a meeting of Presbytery at East Pennsborough, September 3d, 1745. "Commissioners from a small settlement in Bermudin acquainted the Presbytery that, in order to have the ordinances dispensed among them, they desired to be adjoined to, and looked on as a part of, the Lower Congregation of Pennsborough, and that they might be allowed to build a meeting-house convenient for them." From this record, it is evident, we think, that the congregation had an anterior existence, and then only sought such a connexion as would secure to them the regular enjoyment of the public means of grace. In relation to the latter part of the above request presented to Presbytery, the following action was had at their meeting in April, 1760.

"Pursuant to Monaghan's application, the Presbytery orders Mr. Thomson, John M'Knight, Esquire, and John Davies, to meet at Mr. John Dill's, on Monday, the 28th inst., to judge respecting the situation of the place where Monaghan people design to build their meeting-house, and fix the bounds of that and East Pennsborough congregations, if they have sufficient clearness." The report which this committee made, two years afterward, was, "that Yellow Breeches should be the line between East Pennsborough and Monaghan, and that Monaghan meeting-house should be near John Dill's."

We are indebted, for the subsequent particulars in relation to this church, to the Rev. Joseph A. Murray, at present the pastor of Monaghan and Petersburg.

"The first place in which the early settlers worshipped, was a log house, which stood at the 'old grave-yard,'* about a quarter of a mile northwest of the present town,—for at that time there was not so much as a town commenced here. Where precisely this church was built, and how long it was used, cannot now be ascertained. In the year 1782, a stone edifice was erected at what is now the edge of the town. It was about 50 feet long, 40 feet wide, and 15 feet high to the square of the walls. The pulpit, small and elevated, was at the north side; and a door was at the south side, as well as at each end. A small stone building, about 15 feet square and 8 feet high, was attached to the north side, having two entrances, one communicating with the yard, and the other with the church, near the pulpit. In olden times this was called '*The Study*;' it was also used as a school-room. Here the Session met; here were prayer-meetings held; and here at last was the winter fuel kept. In 1813 this church was burnt, the fire originating in the small building attached, then used for a school. The year following it was repaired. The stonework was not taken down, and it was soon found necessary to support the south wall by huge props, in the form of logs, one end placed against the wall and the other in the ground. It was supposed that the wall had been injured by the fire, or else was not strong enough to sustain the new roof, which, with its frame-

* So called on account of its antiquity, and to distinguish it from another grave-yard, of more recent origin, adjoining the present church edifice.

work, was thought much heavier than the first roof; hence the wall began to bulge, and called for the props in question. Subsequently the interior was remodelled. Four supports, in the form of long columns, were placed within the church, near the south wall, reaching from the ground-floor to the rafters above, and the outside props were removed. The ceiling was gently arched, and lined with boards. The door at the west end was closed, and the pulpit placed there, leaving three entrances, one at the east end, another at the south side, and the other at the north side, communicating with the session-room. The pews had narrow seats, with a very narrow ledge to support the backs of the occupants; and uncomfortable as these would be to those accustomed to something better, yet doubtless they were considered a decided improvement where something worse had been enjoyed! This edifice had become so dilapidated, so unsafe and uncomfortable, that, in the spring of 1849, it was taken down, and gave place to another—built of brick, and occupying in part the same ground. The new church has many of the improvements of modern times, is as chaste and attractive as it is commodious and comfortable, and is capable of holding 400 persons,—a greater number than the previous building could conveniently seat. It was opened for divine worship on Friday, the 30th of November 1849, on which occasion the pastor gave a history of the church. On the day following, the congregation unanimously agreed to introduce and use the book of

Psalms and Hymns approved and authorized by the General Assembly.

"The Rev. George Duffield—grandfather of Dr. Duffield, of Detroit, Michigan—and the Rev. John Steel, members of the Presbytery of Donegal, preached at different times, to the congregation worshipping in the log church. Mr. Duffield was installed as their pastor, 'to give them one-third part of his stated labours,' November 15, 1769. The Rev. Samuel Waugh, a member of the same Presbytery, having accepted a call, was installed pastor of the united congregations of East Pennsborough and Monaghan, in the year 1782, and continued their pastor till the time of his death, which occurred in 1807. The late venerable Dr. Cathcart describes him as 'a most worthy, excellent man;' and there are those here who can bear similar testimony to his character. In March, 1809, the Rev. John Hayes—antecedently Professor of Languages in Dickinson College—became their pastor, and continued as such till the spring of 1815. He was not only a linguist, but a poet of no mean reputation, and in 1807 had published a volume entitled, 'Rural Poems, Moral and Descriptive.' His talents were consecrated to useful purposes; and, though 'dead,' he 'yet speaketh.' For a number of years after he resigned the charge—an event occasioned in consequence of his health failing—the church, which had become detached from East Pennsborough, or Silvers' Spring, was dependent upon supplies, stated and occasional. The Rev. Dr. A.

M'Clelland, now of New Brunswick, New Jersey, preached to the congregation during his connexion, as Professor, with Dickinson College. His character and services, his genius and wit, are well and favourably remembered. The Rev. N. R. Snowden, father of the late State Treasurer, was also a frequent supply.* The Rev. N. Todd, then a probationer under the care of the Philadelphia Presbytery, and now a venerable minister and teacher in Western Pennsylvania, supplied the congregation for some time; and during his services Watts's book of Psalms and Hymns was introduced, in the place of the old version of Psalmody by Rouse.

"In the spring of 1830, the Rev. A. B. Quay commenced his labours among the people; and in the spring of 1832 he was installed pastor of the united congregations of Monaghan and Petersburg,—on which occasion the Rev. Samuel B. Howe, D.D., then President of Dickinson College, preached the sermon, and the Rev. George Duffield, then of Carlisle, gave the charge to the pastor and people. The pastoral relation then constituted continued till the autumn of 1839; Mr. Quay then resigned the charge, having accepted of an appointment to act as an agent of the Board of Education. For about the space of two years afterwards, the united congregations were supplied by the Rev. E. M'Kinney, now a missionary

* He died at the residence of his son, Dr. C. G. Snowden, Freeport, Armstrong County, Pennsylvania, November 3d, 1850, in the 81st, year of his age.

of our Board among the Ottoe and Omahaw Indians. In October, 1841, Mr. Joseph A. Murray received and accepted a call from the united congregations of Monaghan and Petersburg, and in April following the Presbytery ordained and installed him pastor of the same,—on which occasion the Rev. George Morris preached the sermon, the Rev. Dr. Amos A. M'Ginley presided, the Rev. Dr. Daniel M'Kinley delivered the charge to the pastor, and the Rev. J. T. Marshall Davie gave the charge to the congregation. The pastoral relation then constituted still continues.

"Among the first elders of the church—of whom any recollection exists, and whose descendants are still with us—were Messrs. Lewis Williams,* Matthew Dill, John Williams, William Porter,† Alexander Ross,‡ William Mitchell, John Nisbet, and Alexander Sanderson. In 1802, Messrs. Edward O'Hail, Henry Logan, John M'Clellan, Allen Torbet, and George Robinette§ were appointed elders. These all repose with the dead. During the suppletory services of Mr. Snowden, Messrs. William Ross, Alexander M'Curdy, George Crocket, George Smith, and William M'Mullen were appointed elders. Most of these

* Father of the late Rev. Joshua Williams, D.D., and grandfather of Mr. Lewis H. Williams, an elder in Dickinson Church.

† Father of James Porter, Esq., one of our present elders.

‡ Father of William Ross, Esq., one of our present Session.

§ Father of George Robinette, an elder in the Petersburg church.

have finished their work on earth and entered upon their reward. When Mr. Quay assumed the pastoral care of the church, the Session consisted of Messrs. George Crocket, George Dare, G. W. Howard, James Porter, William Ross, and James Black. Mr. Crocket died in 1835. Messrs. W. W. Jones, Jacob Ritner,* and J. B. Hursh were chosen elders in the same year. In June, of 1837, Mr. Jones was dismissed to connect himself with the Second Presbyterian Church in Carlisle; and some time afterwards Mr. Ritner was dismissed for the same purpose. Mr. James Clark was chosen an elder in September, of 1842. In a letter received from the late Dr. Cathcart, he says:—'Monaghan Church was always well represented in Presbytery by her eldership, one of the three, either Messrs. Dill, Ross, or O'Hail, being always in attendance. Mr. O'Hail,' he adds, 'was once a delegate to the General Assembly, and attended its sessions with great punctuality.'

"The original settlers were chiefly, if not exclusively, from Ireland and Scotland; rigid Presbyterians, ardently attached to the Church—a sober, industrious, moral, intelligent people. At an early period the congregation was very large, comprising nearly all the inhabitants of the settlement, whose religious predilections were thoroughly Calvinistic, and it was not unusual to see the church crowded to overflowing. It is not so now, owing to the operation of manifest

* Son of Ex-Governor Ritner.

causes. Death has done its work, in removing many who had been pillars in the Church, and useful members of society. Another cause may be found in the spirit of adventure, and the hopeful prospects of emigration. And still another cause may be found in the establishment of other denominational organizations throughout the region. Here, as in many other places, the original race of settlers is becoming gradually displaced by another race. Still, the Presbyterian element is comparatively strong and influential.

"The year 1831 was rendered remarkable for the outpouring of the Holy Spirit in many parts of our land. It was a season of refreshing to the churches belonging to the Carlisle Presbytery. Here the means of grace were well attended and properly appreciated. On one occasion the concourse of people was so great, that, while Mr. Williamson was proclaiming the Gospel to those who found room within the church, Mr. Duffield was preaching it to those outside. And there were those then added to the Church who are still exemplary members, and doubtless look back to that period with tender emotions. In the winter of '42 and '43, there was an unusual degree of interest here on the subject of religion; there was a great longing for the means of grace; much and deep feeling existed; and some permanent good, we trust, was the result.

"The persons who were organized into the Petersburg Church—Adams County, Pennsylvania—previously worshipped at Monaghan, having to travel from 8 to 12 miles to church, and the same distance returning home, and it was on the ground of convenience that the little church was formed. For several years they had no church edifice. At first a *barn* in the summer, and a *bar-room** in the winter, served as the place of religious service. When the Academy was built in Petersburg, it became the usual place of worship. The present brick edifice was erected in 1830, on a lot of ground presented by Mr. James M'Cosh.

"The first Communion was held at the 'York Springs,' in 1826, when about a dozen of persons participated in the memorial of their Saviour's love.

"The Rev. McKnight Williamson, now in Ohio, spent a part of his early ministerial career among the little flock. The Rev. H. R. Wilson, now deceased, preached for them several times; and occasionally they would be supplied by others, till Mr. Quay was installed pastor of the united congregations of Monaghan and Petersburg.

"The first elders appointed were, Captain George Smith—previously an elder of Monaghan,—Major John Bonner, and James Robinette, Esq., son of George Robinette, one of the early elders of Monaghan. Captain Smith afterwards moved to the West, where he died. Major Bonner died several years ago; his son, Colonel William F. Bonner, is a trustee of the church. And within the current year 'Squire Robinette has been called to his reward in

* A public house, then kept by the two sisters, Agnes and Margaret Bigham—firm Presbyterians, well and favourably known, the latter of whom is still living, a steadfast and consistent follower of the Saviour.

heaven. During Mr. Quay's ministry, Mr. George Robinette, brother of 'Squire Robinette, and Mr. William B. Brandon, grandson of Captain Smith, were chosen elders; and since the present pastoral relation was constituted, Mr. John Mateer was elected an elder;—these form the present Session.

"Although the church has grown, yet it continues somewhat small, but contains a commendable amount of intelligent piety and active benevolence."

---

## LOWER MARSH CREEK CHURCH.

About the years 1734–6, a band of emigrants from Scotland and the north of Ireland, more usually known in Pennsylvania as Scotch-Irish, settled on the "red lands" in the southeastern part of York County. Not long afterwards, and probably about the year 1740, a number of the same race made the first settlement in what is now Adams County, among the hills near the sources of Marsh Creek. These settlers were of the better order of peasantry, and brought with them the characteristics of their native land. They were moral, industrious, and intelligent, and for the most part were rigid Presbyterians, or "Seceders." They were frugal, as the Scotch always are—plain in their mode of living, but cordial and hospitable. They were universally men of undaunted courage, and high patriotic feeling, and when the alarm of the Revolution first rung through the land, it called no truer or more willing hearts than those of the Scotch-Irish Presbyterians. The manners and character of the early settlers have been very generally inherited by their descendants,—many of whom still cultivate the same farms, worship in the same old churches, and hold fast to the rigid and venerated "form of sound words" of the Presbyterian Church. (Pennsylvania Historical Collections, p. 56.)

We make the following extracts, touching the history of Presbyterianism in the region of Marsh Creek, from the Presbyterial Records.

"In 1740, Mr. Sankey was appointed to preach at Great Conewago and Marsh Creek, the second Sabbath of August, and Mr. Samuel Thompson the fourth Sabbath.

"1742. Upon reading of the minute of our last, relating to the Committee appointed to fix the site of a Meeting-House at Marsh Creek, appeared Commissioners from both those places with supplications, signifying their acquiescence in the judgment of said Committee, viz.: that it is expedient that there be two Meeting-Houses, and that the people of Marsh Creek are agreed that their Meeting-House be at a certain spring near Robert McFerson's, which the Presbytery approve of."

Some time after this, the Rev. Andrew Bay was called to take charge of the congregation of Marsh Creek, and was, in all probability, its first minister Whether he was installed or not, is not known. Mr. Bay was succeeded by the Rev. Mr. M'Mordie, whose pastoral relation was dissolved in 1761.

In 1765, "A paper was brought in from Marsh Creek, Thom's, and Piney Creeks, respecting their having fixed the bounds between said congregations, which the Presbytery ordered to be entered on record, and which is as follows:

"We the subscribers, commissioners of the Marsh Creek, Thom's Creek, and Piney Creek congregations, being met this 25th day of April, 1765, in order to treat respecting the division lines between said congregations, have agreed, that a line being drawn straight from Marsh Creek Meeting-house to that of Thom's Creek, a line crossing that line at right angles, at the end of four miles and a half from Marsh Creek Meeting-house, and extended on the one side to Thom's Creek, and on the other till it intersect Piney Creek congregation, shall be the division line between said congregations, and that the division line between Marsh Creek congregation and that of Piney Creek, shall be midway between the meeting-houses of said congregations. Witness our hands this day and year above written."

(Et sic subscribitur.)

John Alexander,
Saml. McFarran,
Wm. Shields,
Andrew Hart,
Wm. Cochran,
Jno. McKinly,
James McGinley,
Wm. Porter.

The Rev. John Slemmons was ordained and installed pastor of Lower Marsh Creek congregation in 1765, and dismissed in 1774. He was removed by death, July 10th, 1814, and his remains lie in the graveyard at Piney Creek Church.

In 1779, "the congregation of Lower Marsh Creek entered into an agreement with Mr. Martin for one year of his labours, to which agreement Presbytery acceded."

In 1781, a supplication having been brought in by William Finley and James Ferguson, commissioners from Lower Marsh Creek congregation, that they might have leave to join with Thom's Creek, this request was granted by Presbytery.

The Reverend John M'Knight (afterwards Dr. M'Knight), became pastor of this charge in 1783, and continued to be so until 1789, when he accepted a call from the united congregations of New York City. Dr. M'Knight was a very popular preacher, and greatly beloved by his people.

In 1792, the Rev. Wm. Paxton accepted a call from Lower Marsh Creek and Thom's Creek congregations, and on the 3d of October in the same year (Dr. Davidson and Mr. Lang officiating on the occasion), he was ordained and installed in the woods near to the church, where a temporary pulpit and seats were placed for the use of the congregation which the house could not accommodate, and where the services, on communion occasions, were for many years afterwards held.

In 1794, the pastoral relation which the Rev. Mr. Black had sustained for some time to the congregation of Upper Marsh Creek, was dissolved by his request. We acknowledge our obligation to the present esteemed pastor of Lower Marsh Creek, for the following particulars:

"To me it seems that Lower Marsh Creek Church was formed by the division of the Presbyterian Church into *Old* and *New Side*. Lower Marsh Creek was *New Side*. I have seen no mention, on the minutes of Presbytery, of Lower Marsh Creek, for a long time after Upper Marsh Creek is mentioned. There is no mention of the organization of Lower Marsh Creek on the minutes of the Donegal Presbytery, as far as I remember. Its first minister was a member of the Newcastle Presbytery. It would seem that it was organized by some minister of the *New Side*. As far as I can determine, Rev. Andrew Bay was the first minister. He was a member of the Synod of New York during the separation." (Rev. H. R. Wilson, D.D., to Rev. D. D. Clarke.)

"The first house of worship was a log building, located at the graveyard, on the bank of Lower Marsh Creek. A stone in the yard bears date, 1749. It was rude throughout, benches being used instead of pews. While the congregation worshipped there, it was supplied for a time by a Mr. Balch.

"About the year 1790, the old log house was thrown down, and the present stone edifice erected. This building is about five miles southwest of Gettysburg, in 'Carroll's Tract,' a section of country named after the venerable proprietor and patriot, Charles Carroll of Carrollton. This was a considerable advance in capacity and appearance on the old log house, yet it was unsightly. The seats were straight and high-backed, and the pulpit very narrow and deep, and elevated on the side of the building. It was subsequently placed at the end, and somewhat modernized. The entrance was by four doors, two at each end of the house; the door in front of the pulpit was paved with brick, and had a gradual elevation to the opposite wall. There was no stove or fire used in winter, in the log house, nor in the present one, for many years after its erection.

"Lower Marsh Creek Church was incorporated in 1805. The first trustees were, Elijah Hart, George Kerr, Reynolds Ramsay, Samuel Witherow, William Miller, William Bigham. The Rev. William Paxton, Benjamin Reid, William M'Clean and Moses M'Clean, were appointed a committee to carry out the desire of the congregation in reference to the provisions of the charter.

"The names of but few of the first elders are now known. Among them were Mr. Cotton, James Ferguson, James M'Gaughy, Benjamin Reid, William Hill, William M'Clean, Captain David Wilson, Samuel Witherow, Samuel M'Cullough, John M'Ginley, Abraham Scott. In later times, John Kerr, John Stewart, Hugh M'Gaughy, Amos Maginley, William

M'Gaughy, William M. Scott, who have gone to their reward, while many of their descendants are still in the church of their fathers, and some have taken their place in the eldership.

"From this congregation the following persons have entered the ministry: Samuel Shannon, first lieutenant of the company of Captain David Wilson, an elder, and officer in the War of the Revolution. Mr. Shannon went to Kentucky. John M'Knight, one of the pastors; John Linn of Shearman's Valley; Samuel Waugh of Silvers' Spring; John Slemmons, another of its pastors; Samuel Ramsey, who settled in Virginia; Amos M'Ginley, D.D., of Path Valley; H. R. Wilson, D.D., James Black, Virginia; John Waugh (of John), John Waugh (of David); Rev. John M'Pherrin of West Pennsylvania, it is believed, went from this congregation. All of the above, except Dr. M'Ginley and Mr. Black, have died. Several of the sons of those who were pastors of this congregation are now in the ministry, or preparing for it. We here insert the Obituary of Dr. W. Paxton, as it is found in the Presbytery's Book of Obituaries.

"The Rev. William Paxton, D.D., late pastor of the Presbyterian Church of Lower Marsh Creek, died at his late residence, in Fairfield, Adams County, Pa., on the 16th day of April, 1845, in the 86th year of his age, and in the 53d year of his ministry. He was born in Lancaster County, on the 1st day of April, 1760. Very little is known of his early life; but from what is known, it appears that he remained with his parents until he was nearly thirty years of age, when he commenced his classical education, under the superintendence of the Rev. Nathaniel Sample, with whom, also, he pursued his theological studies. On the 29th day of April, 1789, Dr. Paxton was received under the care of the Presbytery of Newcastle as a candidate; and on the 8th day of April, 1790, he was licensed by the same Presbytery, as a probationer for the Gospel ministry. On the 4th day of October, 1791, the churches of Thom's Creek and Lower Marsh Creek, within the bounds of the Presbytery of Carlisle, requested that he might be appointed a stated supply to them, and the Presbytery of Newcastle gave him permission to preach to their churches for five successive Sabbaths. On the 21st of December, 1791, the churches of Thom's and Lower Marsh Creek, presented calls to the Presbytery of Newcastle for the ministerial services of Dr. Paxton; and on the 4th day of April, 1792, he accepted these calls, and was accordingly dismissed from the Presbytery of Newcastle, to put himself under the care of the Presbytery of Carlisle. On the 7th of June, 1792, he was received under the care of the Presbytery of Carlisle, and on the 3d day of October, 1792, he was ordained to the work of the Gospel Ministry, and installed Pastor of the churches of Thom's and Lower Marsh Creek.

"It cannot be ascertained how long Dr. Paxton was pastor of the church at Thom's Creek; but the church of Lower Marsh Creek, finding themselves able to support him all his time, received the whole of his ministerial services from an early date.

"On the 20th day of January, 1794, Dr. Paxton was united in marriage with Miss Jane Dunlap, of Cumberland County. This lady still lives, waiting for the salvation of God. Dr. Paxton had four children, all of whom, with one exception, preceded their father to the grave.

"On the 19th day of October, 1841, on account of the infirmities of age, Dr. Paxton applied to Presbytery to dissolve the pastoral connexion between him and the Church of Lower Marsh Creek; which connexion, after having existed for a period of forty-nine years, was accordingly dissolved. It may be proper, however, to add, that Dr. Paxton continued to supply the Church of Lower Marsh Creek occasionally, until they obtained their present pastor, so that it may be said that that church was favoured with his ministrations for more than half a century. It is worthy of remark, also, that during the forty-nine years of his pastoral life, Dr. Paxton rarely, if ever, disappointed his people, by a failure in attendance upon the duties of the sanctuary. No inclemency of weather ever prevented him from being in the house of God on the Sabbath, to preach the Gospel to those who might not be prevented by the same cause, from attending upon his ministry.

"The early life of Dr. Paxton was somewhat identified with the struggles of our country for her national independence. He served in three campaigns in the

Revolutionary War, in one of which he was in the neighbourhood, during the battle of Trenton.

"Although Dr. Paxton had not the advantage of a collegiate education, still, by close application, under private tuition, he attained to a standing in literature, science, and theology, rarely equalled by many who have enjoyed that benefit. Accordingly, the Trustees of Dickinson College, in virtue of his attainments in those acquisitions, conferred on him the honorary degree of Doctor of Divinity,—a title which in those days was far more the reward of merit than of favour. Dr. Paxton was possessed of a profound and discriminating intellect. His pulpit performances bore ample testimony to the extent and variety of his acquisitions. His sermons were rich in thought, always exhibiting with great force and plainness the fundamental doctrines of the Gospel.

"In his private intercourse, he was remarkable for affectionate simplicity; he claimed no distinction above the plainest individual; and he seemed to be conscious of no superiority to others, either in understanding or knowledge. His habits were domestic, perhaps to a fault. The circle around his own fireside was so delightful to him, that he seldom sought enjoyment abroad. His door was always open to his acquaintances and friends; he was always particularly pleased with the company of his ministerial brethren, and few ever left his house without feelings of gratitude for his society and hospitality. As a Christian, his object appeared to be, to cultivate and cherish an intelligent piety. Humble and unostentatious in his deportment, his unabating confidence, amidst all the dealings of God with him, was founded on the merits of the blessed Saviour, whose Gospel he was permitted to preach to others. The venerable father is now at rest. With him, we trust, the agonies of dissolving nature were but the prelude to eternal joys. His dying was but the laying down of mortality to put on immortality, and He who is the resurrection and the life, will watch over the sleeping dust in its repose in the grave, and He will, in his own time, burst the bars of the tomb, and that which was born a natural, will be raised a spiritual body, in angelic splendour and beauty."

The Rev. D. D. Clarke, the present pastor of Lower Marsh Creek, was installed in June, 1843.

The following persons compose the Session at this time: James Blythe, Andrew Marshall, John Marshall, James Bigham, R. Cobean, John M'Ginley, J. J. Kerr, A. W. Maginley,—the two first of whom do not act, by reason of infirmity.

Recently, the house has been thoroughly remodelled. The improvements are, a new roof, floor, and pulpit; the seats lowered and sloped in the back. Venetian blinds; carpeting; vestibule, with the entrance by two doors into the vestibule; making it as neat and comfortable as most of the country churches. The congregation, during the present pastorate, has suffered by death and removals, but it has received numerous valuable accessions. Harmony prevails among its members the attendance is good; and the spirit of benevolence has greatly increased.

---

## CHURCH AT GETTYSBURG.

THIS church was originally known as the "Upper Presbyterian Church of Marsh Creek." This is the name which it bears in the Act of Incorporation, passed 13th of September, 1787. The first pastor of the congregation of whom any notice is taken on the records of Presbytery, was the Rev. Mr. M'Mordie, who resigned his charge about the year 1762. The Rev. Mr. Black, who was a successor of Mr. M'Mordie, applied for, and obtained the dissolution of his pastoral relation in 1794. "Of his history," writes the present pastor, the Rev. Mr. Johnston, "I cannot learn anything, excepting that tradition says he formed and sustained a temperance society before the present temperance movements had a being." It may be here stated that intemperance was the prevailing sin of the Church in its early history in this country, and more frequently than any other called for the exercise of discipline.

The congregations of Upper Marsh Creek and Great Conewago were united in 1798, and the Rev. David M'Conaughy was installed their pastor on the 8th day of October, 1800. "In that same year the formation of Adams into a separate county took place, and Gettysburg became the county seat. This town was situated about three miles from the site of the Upper Marsh Creek Church, and within the limits of that congregation. Increasing in wealth and population, and embracing within it a number of Presbyterian families, it was deemed too important a place to be left without the stated preaching of the Gospel by Presbyterians. For a time it was supplied by occasional preaching by Dr. M'Conaughy himself, and also by Dr. Paxton, the talented and eloquent pastor of the adjacent church of Lower Marsh Creek, one or more of the families belonging to whose church, resided in the town. After some years, however, the congregation of Upper Marsh Creek determined to remove their edifice to town, and in the year 1813, Dr. M'Conaughy preached his last sermon in the old church, previous to its demolition. From various causes the new edifice was not ready for occupancy for several years. In the mean time, the congregation were kindly allowed the use of the Associate Reformed Church, then vacant, until a pastor should be procured. Afterwards they worshipped in the court-house, until the completion of their edifice. In the month of August, 1816, the house, having been completed, was solemnly dedicated to the worship of the Triune God. The congregation still retained its original chartered name of 'Upper Marsh Creek,' and still remained in union with Great Conewago, under the same pastoral care as before. In these united congregations Dr. M'Conaughy continued, in the faithful and acceptable discharge of his ministerial duties, until the spring of 1832, when he was dismissed, at his own request, to connect himself with the Presbytery of Washington, within the bounds of which he intended to reside, as President of Washington College."

From the same source to which we are indebted for the extract just given, we derive the following condensed sketch of Dr. M'Conaughy's history and character.*

The Rev. David M'Conaughy was a native of Pennsylvania. He was born in Menallen Township, York County (now Adams), about six miles from Gettysburg, on the 29th of September, 1775. His collegiate education he received at Dickinson College, Carlisle, where he was graduated on the 30th day of September, 1795, during the presidency of the Rev. Dr. Charles Nisbet. He had the Latin Salutatory assigned him, which, according to the usage of the institution, at that time, was considered the first honour. After leaving college, he remained two years under the direction of the Rev. Dr. Nathan Grier, of Brandywine, in the prosecution of his theological studies, when, on the 5th day of October, 1797, he was licensed by the Presbytery of Newcastle to preach the Gospel.

On the 8th day of October, 1800, he was ordained

* A discourse commemorative of the late Rev. David M'Conaughy, D.D., L.L.D., by the Rev. David Elliott, D.D., preached March 21, 1852.

and installed pastor of the united churches of Upper Marsh Creek and Great Conewago.

Dr. M'Conaughy watched over his flock with a shepherd's care, and was ever ready to bestow his labour and exert his influence for the advancement, not only of their spiritual, but also of their temporal interests. He was the pioneer in the temperance reform in his native county. Preparatory to the formation of a society, and with a view of gaining access to all classes, he appointed meetings to be held in the court-house in the evenings, at which he read the temperance essays of Drs. Rush, Beecher, and others. Through his agency the first temperance society in Adams County was formed, of which he was elected the first president.

On the 9th of May, 1832, Dr. M'Conaughy was inaugurated as President of Washington College. The number of students at the time of his accession, was one hundred and nineteen. Under his mild and paternal administration, the number continued to increase, and every year added to the strength and reputation of the institution, in the minds of intelligent and well-informed men.

On the 1st of October, 1849, Dr. M'Conaughy tendered his resignation of the presidency to the Board of Trustees, by whom, after they had ascertained that his purpose to retire was immovably fixed, it was accepted. The high respect and veneration entertained for him by the Board of Trustees, were indicated by the strongly expressive resolutions which were passed immediately upon the acceptance of his resignation.

Dr. M'Conaughy, after the dissolution of his connexion with the college, pursued his mental labours with his accustomed activity. As evidence of this, during the next year after his resignation, he prepared and published a volume of "Discourses, chiefly Biographical, of Persons eminent in Sacred History." These are admirable discourses,—"fine specimens of discriminating thought, lucid arrangement, vigorous style, and the skilful and profitable exhibition of sacred truth."

In the year 1838, he published, for the exclusive use of the senior class in Washington College, "A brief Summary and Outline of the Principal Subjects comprehended in Moral Science." This is a comprehensive and well-digested outline, which, it is to be regretted, he did not fill up, and thus have furnished our colleges with a convenient and religious text-book on that subject. His other publications consist of some half dozen sermons, and a few of his Baccalaureate Addresses. These are all written with his accustomed ability, and were well adapted to the occasion and circumstances which severally called them forth. Since his decease, a couple of tracts from his pen have been issued from the press,—one on the Doctrine of the Trinity, and the other on the Salvation of Infants.

Of Dr. M'Conaughy's early religious experience, and his first introduction into the kingdom of God we have no knowledge, but that he was a man of eminent piety towards God, no one acquainted with his character can entertain a doubt. His piety was intelligent, of a confiding character, cheerful, and eminently spiritual.

He died at his residence in Washington, on Thursday, the 29th of January, 1852, in the seventy-seventh year of his age, and the fifty-fifth of his ministry.

The Rev. James C. Watson, D.D., in June, 1832, became the successor of Dr. M'Conaughy in the churches of Gettysburg and Great Conewago, and continued to be their pastor until August, 1849, when he resigned, and the churches were separated. The Rev. Robert Johnston entered upon his labours as Pastor at Gettysburg, in January, 1850.

The names of the present elders of this congregation, are, George Arnold, Moses McLean, Nicholas Randolph, James M'Alister, Hugh Denwiddie, Robert G. M'Creary.

The present church edifice in Gettysburg, which is large and beautiful, was erected in 1842.

---

## CHURCHES AT BEDFORD AND SCHELLSBURG.

Bedford County, originally part of Cumberland County, was established, March 9th, 1771. It then included the entire southwestern part of the State.

The establishment of Westmoreland in 1773, of Huntingdon in '87, and Somerset in '95, and Fulton in 1850, reduced it to its present limits.

Bedford, the county seat, has, in addition to a Presbyterian church, churches for German Reformed and Lutheran, Methodist, and Catholic congregations.

The Presbyterian interest in this borough and the circumjacent region, was watched over by supplies from Presbytery, from 1763 until about the year 1782, when, as the Records of Presbytery show, there was a congregation in existence of sufficient ability to call a pastor. This call was given to the Rev. Mr. Waugh, and contained an agreement on the part of the congregation, that if Mr. W. should become their pastor, his time should be divided, as follows: one-fourth in Providence Township, five Sabbaths in the year in Colerain Township and Cumberland Valley, and the remainder in the town of Bedford. This call was not accepted.

In 1786, a call from this congregation was given to the Rev. Mr. Bard, who consented to settle as pastor, and continued in this relation until the autumn of 1789. After this, the congregation was supplied by appointments of Presbytery, the Rev. Mr. Bard, also, frequently officiating for it, until 1808, when the Rev. Alexander Boyd accepted the Pastorate of the church, which he retained until 1815. The ruling elders of an early date, were, James Taylor, Sr., David Anderson, David Riddle, John Reynolds,

William Reynolds, and John Ritchey. Mr. Boyd preached at his settlement, in the old court-house, and during his incumbency (1810) the first church edifice was erected.

The next Pastor at Bedford, was the Rev. Jeremiah Chamberlain, a native of Gettysburg, Pennsylvania. Mr. C. took charge of the church in 1819, and resigned his post in 1822, to accept an invitation, which, at the early age of twenty-seven, he had received, to the Presidency of Centre College, Danville, Kentucky. The following extract in relation to him, from a discourse on his life and character by the Rev. Joseph B. Stratton, on the occasion of his death as a victim of murder, in 1851, whilst President of Oakland College, will be read with interest.

" That his character was no ordinary one, the history of his achievements sufficiently indicates. His intellectual endowments and acquirements, without being brilliant or profound, were such as qualified him to be a ready and clear-sighted student, and an able and perspicuous instructor. His life was too crowded with extraneous duties to allow him the opportunity to seek the scholastic eminence, which otherwise would have been easily accessible to him. It was rather as the man of practical energy, of high-toned loyalty to principle, of self-possessed sobriety, of forethought and farsightedness, of fertility of invention and aptness in execution, of firmness tempered by suavity, of strict uprightness and disinterested devotion to whatever his heart and conscience approved, it is rather as the paternal counsellor, the warm-hearted friend, the cheerful companion, the sincere and simple preacher, with the clear doctrine of Scripture ever on his lip, and the tear of emotion often in his eye, as the comforter in sorrow, and the helping brother to all who asked his sympathy or aid—it is in such characters as these, that Dr. Chamberlain won distinction, and merited all he won."

Dr. Chamberlain's successor at Bedford was the Rev. Daniel M'Kinley, who accepted the call given him in 1827, and resigned his pastoral relation in 1831, on account of the delicate state of his health, which unfitted him for the discharge of duty.

Mr. McKinley was succeeded by the Rev. Baynard R. Hall, who served the congregation about six years; the Rev. Elbridge Bradbury, whose pastoral relation, formed in 1839, was dissolved in 1841; the Rev. Alexander Heberton, who was installed in 1843, and resigned in 1845; and the Rev. William Maclay Hall, who was pastor for several years. When Mr. Hall was released from the pastoral care of the church, on account of increasing infirmities, which, not long after, terminated by death the life which he had devoted to the self-denying toils of the ministry, by renouncing a lucrative practice of the Law, the pulpit was supplied for a length of time by the Rev. William L. McCalla, during which period the Schellsburg and Bedford churches were united by Presbytery in one charge. In 1850, Mr. Thomas K. Davis, a licentiate, supplying the pulpit of the church at

Fayetteville, was called to the pastoral charge of the Bedford and Schellsburg churches.

With the following data we have been kindly furnished by the Rev. Mr. Davis.

"The old building in Bedford was torn down about the year 1828, to give place to a more comfortable edifice. This building is of brick, and handsomely situated on the public square. It will accommodate 500 persons. The room in the basement is used for a lecture and Sabbath-school room. The building, although in many respects commodious and fine-looking, contains the lofty pulpit, and high-backed box-like pews of ancient times. The spirit of modern improvement will, doubtless, ere long lower the pulpit, and give a comfort to the seats which they now lack.

"The congregation have a large and conveniently situated burying-ground, not far from the church. They have never as yet secured a parsonage.

"The church numbers eighty-four communicating members at the present time. There are but two ruling elders, Mr. James Rea, Sr., and John Mower, Esq.

"In May, 1833, Mr. James Taylor, Sr., and thirty-eight other members of the Bedford Church, made application and were organized as the Church of Schellsburg. The Rev. James G. Brackenridge was their first pastor. The memory of this devoted man is revered by the people, and the sudden and untimely death of their young minister and his excellent wife, when on a visit to their friends near Taneytown, Md., is still deplored. James Taylor, Sr., and Benjamin Gibbony, were the first ruling elders. The church building which is now used, was erected about the year 1835. It cost nearly $2200. It is pleasantly situated, has a neat appearance, and will accommodate about 400 persons.

"The pastors who succeeded Mr. Brackenridge were, the Rev. Messrs. Samuel Montgomery, David D. Clark, and Geo. S. Inglis. In 1848, this church was connected with that of Bedford, in receiving the services of Mr. M'Calla; and in 1850, the present pastor of the Bedford Church was installed pastor of the Schellsburg charge.

"A part of the Schellsburg congregation now worship statedly in a sanctuary of their own, recently built near 'The Forks,' about equally distant from Bedford and Schellsburg. 'The Stone Church' was commenced during Mr. Inglis's time, and finished in 1851. It is beautifully situated at the western base of Will's Mountain, on the banks of the Raystown Branch, and is an interesting and encouraging field of labour.

"The Schellsburg Church now numbers one hundred members more than the parent church, which sent out the colony in 1833. The elders at present are, Messrs. James Taylor, Jr., John Smith, George W. Hunt, Robert M. Taylor, and James Mullin.

"With the exception of two small congregations in Wells' Valley, and at Green Hill, under the care of the

Rev. Mr. White, and another on Yellow Creek, ministered to by the Rev. Mr. Hill, of the Huntingdon Presbytery, these are the only Presbyterian congregations in the county. We have Romanists in Harman's Bottom, that dark corner of Bedford County, Hicksites in the 'Quaker Settlement,' north of Schellsburg, and Unitarian Baptists of the Christian connexion, in different parts, with multitudes of people in various sections, who are very, very destitute of Gospel blessings. If our Presbytery were not so *far-sighted* as to bestow their attention on distant parts of the land and on other continents, overlooking the home field, which is full of interest and full of importance, we would have a missionary or two preaching sound doctrine and holy living, among the wild mountains and in the pleasant valleys of old Bedford County."

---

## THE CHURCHES OF M'CONNELLSBURG, GREEN HILL, AND WELLS' VALLEY.

It is with the Church of M'Connellsburg, as with most of the other churches of the Presbytery,—no records of its early history can be found. The probability is, that no such records were kept; but if they were, they have perished. It is, however, evident from the minutes of Presbytery, that "The Great

Cove," (as the place was first called,) was a point frequently supplied with the preaching of the Gospel by appointment of Presbytery, as far back, at least, as 1769. There are also still living within the bounds of the congregation, some aged members of it, whose memories are of service in rescuing its history from oblivion. From this source, the Rev. N. G. White, the present pastor of the charge, received aid in the preparation of the subjoined satisfactory sketch.

"The congregation now worshipping in the Presbyterian church in the Borough of M'Connellsburg, was organized some time before the year 1791. I know not the precise date. It was called the 'Presbyterian Congregation of the Great Cove.' Its first elders were William Alexander, William Gaff, and Charles Taggart. To their number were added shortly afterwards, Alexander Alexander (familiarly known as 'Double Alick'), and James White. They worshipped for some time in private houses, mostly in that of John Dickey, who was an Associate Judge of Bedford County nearly fifty years, and was one of the first and most efficient members of the congregation. It was owing chiefly to Judge Dickey's instrumentality, that a small log church was built, about two miles south of the town, which continued to be occupied as a house of worship until the present edifice was erected, in the year 1811. A Mr. Barclay, a Scotchman and member of the congregation, left by will $500 towards the erection of a church in the town. This sum, together with subscriptions of various sorts from different members of the congregation, enabled them to put up the present building. It continued (though occupied all the while) in an unfinished state for four or five years, when a pulpit, pews, and other fixtures were added, putting it in the state in which I found it when I first visited this place.

"Its first pastor was the Rev. Isaac Kellar, who was settled here in the year 1818, and remained about five years as minister of the congregations of M'Connellsburg and Loudon. After his removal, a Mr. Jewett, from one of the New England States, came and established an Independent church, which greatly distracted the Presbyterian congregation. They, however, obtained occasional supplies for several years after which the late Rev. Robert Kennedy, of the Welsh Run Church, was their stated supply, till the fall of 1833. During the winter of 1833–4, I preached to them; in the spring following received and accepted their call, and was ordained and installed on the 11th of June, 1834. Perhaps I may say here, that I was licensed by the Presbytery of Newcastle, on the 2d of October, 1833. The call to me included not only the Church of M'Connellsburg, but certain inhabitants of Green Hill, and Wells' Valley, each of which is supplied with a comfortable and neat church, in which I preach every four weeks. The Session of the church in town, is at present composed of James Agnew, John Jordan, Henry Hoke, and David Agnew.

"The Church at Green Hill was organized on the 12th day of September, 1835, consisting of twenty-one members, and John Jordan was elected and ordained a ruling elder. During the summer of that year, they put up a neat frame church, in which they still continue to worship. The Session of that church is at present composed of James Austin, and James Lyon. William Alexander and Roland Austin have been recently elected elders, and will be ordained in a few weeks.

"The Church in Wells' Valley, which is twenty miles west of M'Connellsburg, never was formally organized. It is composed chiefly of the descendants of Alexander Alexander ('Double Alick', referred to above), who was a member of the Church in town, and whose son John was chosen an elder, and served with great acceptance in that capacity, until his death in 1840. This John Alexander was in every respect a model of a good elder. He was one of the best men I ever knew. And though so modest and retiring in his disposition and habits, as to attract but little notice beyond the narrow circle of his acquaintance, yet few ministers of the Gospel of the present day possess as accurate a knowledge of the Scriptures, and of Systematic and Polemic Theology, as he did. He could repeat verbatim, nearly all of the New Testament, and more than one-half of the old. The Bible was his daily study for half a century, he imbibed its spirit, and he was truly 'clothed with humility.' No man that ever lived in this section of the country, possessed so strongly the confidence of the community, as a man of honesty, integrity, and true piety. Truly 'the memory of the just is blessed.' The elders of this church are, John Wishart and John B. Alexander.

"There are about one hundred and forty communicating members in the Church in M'Connellsburg, about fifty at Green Hill, and about forty in Wells' Valley,—making two hundred and thirty in the whole charge."

---

## CHURCH AT CUMBERLAND, MARYLAND.

We have been favoured with the following sketch by the Rev. John H. Symmes.

"We have no record among us of the date of the organization of the Presbyterian Church in Cumberland, Md., but it is certain that there was preaching here occasionally, by supplies, from the beginning of the present century. The congregation was small and feeble for many years, struggling, as it were, for a mere existence. Among those who ministered in holy things to this feeble church, at different times, were the Rev. Messrs. Hays, Kennedy, Raymond, and S. H. M'Donald. During the time that Messrs. Hays, Kennedy, and Raymond laboured here, the church was able to do very little towards the support of a pastor. Messrs. Hays and Kennedy were successively principals of the Allegany County Academy, in which they taught for many years. From this source they derived their principal support, and it is probable expended upon it their principal labours. Mr. Raymond, at a later date, laboured a part of his time in Cumberland as a missionary, and was aided from the Missionary Fund. The Presbyterians in Cumberland, for many years had no place of worship of their own, but worshipped alternately in the Lutheran church.

"In connexion with the Episcopalians, they at one time erected a house of worship, under an agreement, that each denomination should have the right to worship in it alternately, according to their respective forms. But in process of time, the Presbyterians were denied their interest and privileges in the building; and the Episcopalians very unjustly appropriated the entire property to their own use. Had the Presbyterians appealed to Cæsar to avenge them of their adversary, the Episcopalians would doubtless have been compelled to abide by the terms of the agreement, and restore to the others their privilege, or its equivalent. But the Presbyterians, as usual in such cases, chose rather to suffer wrong.

"In the year 1838, they erected a house of worship for themselves, 45 by 55 feet, with a gallery in the end, and surmounted by a small cupola and a bell. At this time, they were efficiently aided by the indefatigable efforts and labours of the Rev. S. H. M'Donald, who for the space of five or six years acted as their stated supply. He was succeeded by the Rev. B. Wall, who was installed as the first regular pastor of this church, on the second Sabbath of July, 1843.

The present incumbent, the Rev. J. H. Symmes, after labouring here from December, 1844, until the 9th of April, 1845, was on that day installed as pastor of the church, by a committee of the Presbytery. The congregation having increased so that the building was too small for their accommodation, in the autumn of 1846, an addition of 18 feet was made to the rear, and a lecture and Sunday school-room, 26 by 36 feet, mostly in the rear of the church edifice as altered. In 1846, the number of communicants was thirty-five; they now number about one hundred and twenty. The present ruling elders are, John Boward, James M. Smith, M.D, J. P. Agnew, and Abraham Russell."

---

## HAGERSTOWN CHURCH.

The first pastor of this church, as far as we can learn, was the Rev. Thomas M'Pherrin. How long precisely, he was connected with it in this character, we do not know; but, as we find in the minutes of the Presbytery of 1774, a notice of his acceptance of a call from the united congregations of East and West Conococheague and Jerusalem, and then in the minutes of 1779, a notice of the dissolution of his pastoral relation to the people of Hagerstown, it is evident that his connexion with that congregation was of short duration.

In 1788, in compliance with a supplication from Falling Waters, Hagerstown, and Williamsport, the Rev. Mr. Caldwell was appointed by Presbytery "as a constant supply for those places for one year."

In September, 1825, the Rev. M. L. Fullerton was installed as pastor of the church in Hagerstown, on which occasion the Rev. Mr. Elliott preached the sermon from 1 Thess. ii. 4, and the Rev. Mr. Paxton presided, offered up the consecrating prayer, and delivered the charges.

The pastoral relation of the Rev. Richard Wynkoop, which had existed for four years, was dissolved by Presbytery in April, 1838.

The Rev. J. T. Marshall Davie was installed pastor of the congregations of Greencastle and Hagerstown, in October, 1840, and his connexion with the latter congregation, was dissolved in 1842.

Mr. William Love, a licentiate of the Presbytery of Baltimore, was called to the church of Hagerstown, in 1845. At the same time, the Associate Reformed Church of that place was taken under the care of the Presbytery of Carlisle, as "The Second Presbyterian Church of Hagerstown."

In 1846, the First Presbyterian Church and the Presbyterian Church of Hagerstown, were, by a resolution of Presbytery, and on their own request, united, to be known as "The Presbyterian Church of Hagerstown," the name by which it was designated prior to the separation. In the same year Mr. Love's labours among his people ceased, and he was dismissed to the Presbytery of Winchester, Va.

The Rev. Septimus Tustin, who had for several years served as Chaplain to the Senate of the United States, was elected pastor at Hagerstown in 1848, and served in this capacity until 1850. Dr. Tustin afterwards settled in Germantown, near Philadelphia, and now, having temporarily desisted from pastoral labour, by reason of indifferent health, is residing with his son in Washington City.

The Rev. Robert W. Dunlap, who previously had charge of a church in Baltimore, was Dr. Tustin's successor at Hagerstown, and still labours among his attached people with encouraging success.

The building in which the congregation now worship, was the first used by them, and was first occupied in July, 1817. Previous to that time, the congregation worshipped in the German Reformed Church. The church was built by subscription. A list of the subscribers is in the hands of the Session, and embraces the names of nearly all the citizens of the town and surrounding country.

The first Bench of Elders were—John Kennedy, Robert Douglass, John Robertson, Joseph Gabby. The present Session consists of Joseph Gabby, Samuel Steele, William Stewart, William Marshall, Joseph Rench, and James M'Dowell.

The Church at Hagerstown has passed through some stormy scenes, but its present condition is peaceful and prosperous.

## SHERMAN'S CREEK.

THE following sketch of this congregation, is from the pen of the Rev. M. B. Patterson, its stated supply:

"The early history of the Sherman's Creek congregation, is involved in considerable uncertainty as to dates, from a want of authentic records. It can, at present, be learned only from the diverse and sometimes contradictory testimony, gathered from the fading memories of a few of the most aged members.

"It appears that towards the end of the last century, a few Presbyterian ministers had visited this region, of whom nothing more is remembered than their names, which were Rev. Messrs. Boyd, Porter, and Hoge.

"About the beginning of the present century, supplies were sent to this section of country, from the Presbytery of Carlisle, viz., Rev. Messrs. Sharon, Moodey, Wilson, and Brady.

"The majority of the first settlers of this peaceful and retired region, were of Scotch-Irish descent, and warmly attached to the doctrines and order of the Presbyterian Church. In an early day, it was no uncommon thing for persons of both sexes, to travel on foot from ten to fifteen miles, when an opportunity offered of hearing the Gospel. The names of the families are, Adams, Boyd, Finley, Kirkpatrick,

Ickels, M'Cord, M'Clintock, Smiley, Wallace, and White.

"In 1804, a lot of ground was purchased and a house for public worship erected. Its dimensions were twenty-eight feet square. The materials were logs, which were delivered on the ground by the members of the congregation, in fulfilment of a previous contract entered into by subscription. The logs were *raised* in 1804, but the building was not finished till 1805, owing to a prevailing disease.

"In the year 1805, the Sherman's Creek Church was organized by Rev. Joseph Brady, a member of the Carlisle Presbytery, who was regularly called and installed their first pastor. His salary was $400, one-third of which was to be paid by this congregation.

"The following named persons composed its first Session:—John White, Samuel Ickels, James Wallace, and Samuel Smiley. They all served this church in the capacity of ruling elders, till they were removed by death. There are no means of ascertaining at the present time, the number of communicants composing their first organization.

"Near the church a burying-ground was made, in which reposes the dust of many of the early inhabitants of this region.

"In 1808, a session-house was built of logs, which is standing yet.

"This church continued under the pastoral care of Rev. Joseph Brady, until the time of his death, which took place April 24, 1821.

"Mr. Brady was interred in the burying-ground at the Mouth of Juniata; and the three congregations, which he served about twenty years, in token of respect, erected at his grave a suitable monument.

"After the death of Mr. Brady, this church was supplied by Rev. Mr. Lochrain, Prof. M'Clelland, of Dickinson College, and other supplies from Presbytery, till November 12, 1826, when Rev. John Niblock, of the Northumberland Presbytery, was called and installed pastor.

"During Mr. Niblock's time, the church edifice was enlarged by the addition of fourteen feet of frame, and the whole was weather-boarded and plastered.

"April 16, 1829, the Sherman's Creek Congregation was incorporated by an act of the Legislature.

"The pastoral relation between Mr. Niblock and this church was dissolved by death, August 11, 1830. Mr. Niblock was buried in the graveyard at Middleridge Church.

"Rev. Matthew B. Patterson supplied this church from January 1, 1831, until the 22d of November following, when he was installed its pastor.

"In 1833, the General Assembly's collection of Psalms and Hymns was introduced.

"In 1843, the present edifice was erected. The materials are frame. The dimensions are 28 by 36 feet. It is located two miles west of the old site.

"The members of the present Session are, Jesse Kirkpatrick, David Smiley, and Frederick M'Kasky."

## MOUTH OF JUNIATA AND MILLERSTOWN.

THE present pastor of these churches, has kindly furnished us with the following information:

"The church at the Mouth of the Juniata, was organized by the Rev. Joseph Brady, A. D. 1804, who was ordained by the Carlisle Presbytery, Oct. 3, 1804. The church edifice (which was the first in this region), was erected in 1804. The first elders of this church were, Isaac Kirkpatrick, John Woodburn, William Patterson, and George M'Ginnes. Mr. Kirkpatrick is the only one of the first elders, now living in the bounds of this congregation. This church continued under the care of Mr. Brady till his death, which took place April 24th, 1821.

From this period it was supplied with the word and ordinances, by Messrs. Lochrain, Tod, and other persons appointed by Presbytery, till Rev. John Niblock was installed its pastor, Nov. 21, 1826. In 1826, Wm. Irwin, John Hearst, Samuel Willis, James Wilson, Jacob Steel, and Robert Galey, were elected and ordained elders.

This congregation was incorporated by the Legislature, during the session of 1828–9.

Mr. Niblock died Aug. 11, 1830.

Rev. M. B. Patterson, who was received by the Carlisle Presbytery, Sept. 27, 1831, supplied this church from Jan. 1st, 1831, till the following November 22d, when he was installed its pastor. The pastoral relation was dissolved in 1844 or '45.

The church edifice at the Mouth of the Juniata, having become very much out of repair, and the location being one difficult of access, it was determined by the congregation to erect a new house of worship, which they did, in the village of Petersburg, one mile distant from the old church. The building was completed in 1841. Its dimensions are forty by fifty feet.

In 1845, John Mineer and Thomas White were elected and ordained elders.

The Rev. Charles B. Maclay, who was licensed by the Carlisle Presbytery, April, 1846, and ordained June 2, 1847, supplied this church from April, 1846, till Nov. 1847, when he was installed its pastor. The pastoral relation was dissolved Oct., 1848.

Mr. Hezekiah Hanson, who was licensed by the Carlisle Presbytery, Oct. 4th, 1848, commenced to supply this church, Dec. 26, 1848, received a call, and was ordained August 22d, 1849.

The church edifice in Petersburg was repaired in 1850–51.

The old church at the Mouth of the Juniata, is used occasionally during the summer; its dimensions are about 25 by 30.

The present elders of this church are, Isaac Kirkpatrick, Thomas White, William Irwin, and Jacob Steel.

The Presbyterians of Millerstown and vicinity

erected a small house, in which they worshipped until after their present house was erected. The land upon which the first house was built, was conveyed, on the 4th of May, 1808, to Thomas Cochran, William North, and Amos Jordan, and their successors in office for ever, as trustees of the Millerstown Presbyterian Congregation.

According to the most reliable information we can obtain, there was no regular church organization, until the Rev. N. R. Snowden, in 1818, organized the present congregation. Mr. Snowden, shortly after, was installed pastor over the united congregations of Millerstown, Liverpool, and Buffalo. The elders who were then elected and ordained, were William North, John Black, and Joseph Castles. About two years after, owing to some dissatisfaction, the pastoral relation between Mr. Snowden and the congregation was dissolved. The congregation was supplied with the word and ordinances, from this period, by Messrs. Hill, Grey, Lochrain, and other appointments from the Huntingdon Presbytery, till November, 1829, when Mr. B. E. Collins, a licentiate of the Philadelphia Presbytery, was engaged to preach as a supply, which he did until he was installed pastor, November 29, 1832. In June, 1830, Thomas Cochran and Isaac M'Cord, were elected and ordained elders of this congregation. In consequence of the smallness of the house, the congregation determined to erect a new house of worship, in a more central part of the town. The building, 45 by 50 feet, was finished and opened for worship, in 1832. Mr. Collins continued as pastor of this church until April, 1839, when the pastoral relation was dissolved. The congregation was supplied from this time by Messrs. Williamson and McDonald, till Rev. George D. Porter, who was elected pastor, entered upon his duties, November 17, 1844. This church, being under the care of the Presbytery of Huntingdon, was transferred to the care of the Presbytery of Carlisle, by the Synod of Philadelphia, at their meeting held in Philadelphia, October, 1845. Mr. Porter was installed pastor of this church, September 12, 1846, and continued as such until June 10, 1851, when the relation was dissolved at an adjourned meeting of the Carlisle Presbytery, held in Greencastle, June 10th, 1851.

Rev. H. Hanson, who was labouring at Petersburg, Perry Co., being invited by this congregation, entered upon his ministerial duties, June 29, 1851.

The present members of Session are, H. Hanson, Mod.; Elders, Samuel Black, William Kip, W. J. Jones, George Rothrock, Jacob Kip, and John Shammo.

---

## LANDISBURG, BLOOMFIELD, AND BUFFALO.

THE churches of Landisburg, Buffalo, and Bloomfield, were organized about the year 1823. "Formerly," says the Rev. Mr. Dickey, "the Presbyterians within the bounds of the two former congregations, were a part of the Centre Church, then under the care of the Rev. John Linn. At what time houses of worship were built and a church organized, I am unable to say, as I have not access, at present, to the sessional records of either church. It was probably soon after the death of Mr. Linn. For a few years, the churches of Landisburg and Buffalo were united with the Centre and Upper Churches, and were under the pastoral care of the Rev. James M. Omstead. Afterwards, Mr. Omstead having resigned his pastoral charge, a new connexion was formed with the Church in Bloomfield, and the present pastor was called and installed in 1834. The original elders in the Landisburg Church were, Samuel Linn, Francis Kelly, John Deven, and James M'Clure. Those in the Buffalo Church, were, Charles Elliot, Robert Elliot, Andrew Linn, George Baker, Robert Irvine, and John Sanderson. Both churches possess neat and comfortable houses of worship; the buildings are of frame, and tastefully furnished. The present Buffalo Church is a new building, with a belfry and bell, and is located in the vicinity of Ickesburg. The present elders in Buffalo Church, are, Robert Elliot, George Baker, and John M'Kee. In Landisburg, James M'Clure, Parkinson Hench, Henry Fetter, and John Linn.

The Bloomfield Church was originally formed out of the Ridge Church, about four miles distant, which has now become extinct. The church was built in 1834, and is a substantial brick building, with a basement story for a Sunday-school and Lecture-room. The original elders were Wm. M. M'Clure, Jeremiah Madden, James M'Chord. The elders at present, are, John Campbell, and Finlow M'Cowan.

---

NOTE.—It was our intention to give a running sketch of the churches of Thom's Creek and Piney, Williamsport and Hancock, and Great Conewago. As, however, our volume has already far exceeded, in the number of its pages, what was originally designed, and, especially, as up to a point which admits of no delay, we have failed to receive the data which are necessary to make such a sketch at all satisfactory, we are reluctantly obliged to abandon this purpose.

# APPENDIX.

# APPENDIX I.

---

### CALL FROM THE BIG SPRING CONGREGATION TO THE REV. SAMUEL WILSON.

Big Spring, Cumberland County,
21st March, 1786.

WE, the subscribers of this paper, and members of the Congregation of Big Spring, do hereby bind and oblige ourselves annually to pay Mr. Samuel Wilson, Preacher of the Gospel, on his being ordained to be our minister, and for his discharge of the duties of said office, the sum of one hundred and fifty Pounds, Pennsylvania Currency, in specie, and allow him the use of the dwelling-house, barn, and all the clear land on the glebe, possessed by our former minister, also plenty of timber for rails and fire-wood, likewise a sufficient security for the payment of the above-mentioned sums during his incumbency. As witness our hands:—

| | |
|---|---|
| Alexander Laughlin, | Alexander Thompson, |
| John Davidson, | Rannel Blair, |
| Robert Shannon, | Samuel Finley, |
| David Williamson, | Samuel Cunningham, |
| Thomas Buchanan, | John Eawing, |

| | |
|---|---|
| Robert Bovard, | James Laughlin, |
| Solomon Lightcap, | Atchison Laughlin, |
| Joseph Pollock, | Robert Hutchison, |
| James Jack, | John Mitchell, |
| William Dening, | Samuel Mathers, |
| Andrew Bell, | Jermon Jacobs, |
| John Allison, | John Reed, |
| John Bell, | John Hodge, Senr., |
| Robert Patterson, | William Dinison, |
| David Ralston, | James Irvine, |
| John M'Geehen, | John Brown, |
| Hugh Laughlin, | John O'Neal, |
| John Bell, | William Douglass, |
| Jeremiah M'Kibbin, | Alexander Officer, |
| James Graham. | James Officer, |
| Joseph Partes, | Thomas Espey, |
| Charles Leeper, | James Gillespie, |
| George M'Geehen, | Samuel Hathorn, |
| Hugh Patton, | James Johnston, |
| Margaret M'Kain, | Alexand. Lechey, |
| William Giffin, | Catherine Brown, |
| William Hodge, | Margaret M'Clure, |
| Alexander M'Geehen, | James Armstrong, |
| William M'Cracken, | James Stewart, |
| Robert Bell, | Robert Lusk, |
| William M'Farland, | Andrew M'Elwain, |
| Samuel M'Cormick, | Mary M'Elwain, |
| William Laughlin, | James M'Elwain, |
| Thomas Jacobs, | Thomas Alison, |
| Andrew Walker, | John Wallace, |
| John M'Clintock, | Joseph M'Donnel, |
| Andrew Thompson, | Robert Gillespie, |

Nathanael Gillespie,
Samuel Mitchell,
John Mitchell,
Alexander Elliott,
John Munro,
John Reed,
Samuel Fenton,
Andrew Deniston,
John M'Farland,
John Purdy,
James Brandon,
James Shannon,
Hugh Smith,
John Shannon,
Thomas Mathers,
John Patton,
John Porterfield,
Jared Graham,
Margaret M'Farland,
William Brisbane,
James M'Farland,
Richard Woods;
William Nicholson,
William Stevenson,
David Ramsey,
Paul Martin,
Robert M'Comb, Jun.,
Andrew Bell,
William Thompson,
David Sterret,
Adam Carnahan,
James M'Guffin,

L. Work,
James Carson,
William Thompson, Jr.,
John Murain,
Daniel Boyle,
William Himter,
Robert Patterson,
Widow Preaugh,
James Huston,
Robert Mickey, Sen.,
Robert Mickey, Jun.,
James Mickey,
Elizabeth Kilgore,
William Kilgore,
Samuel Weaver,
George Weaver,
John M'Cune,
John M'Farland,
James Johnston,
Samuel Lindsey,
Matthew Wilson,
Samuel Wilson,
William Lindsey,
John Whitin, Jun.,
Elizabeth M'Cullough,
Thomas Grier,
Ann Brouster,
John Lusk,
David Lusk,
Alexander M'Bride,
William Milligan,
Agnes Irwine,

James Aumer,
William Wilson,
James Wilson,
Francis Donald,
George Little,
James M'Cune,
John Brown,
William Hunter,
Adam Bratton,
William Walker,
Joseph Walker,
Robert Walker,
John Carson,
Isabella M'Cune,
Patrick M'Farland,
Abigail Flinn,
John Coply,
Patrick Murdock
Thomas Appleby,
John Brown,
William Adams,
William Ferguson,
John Graham,
Berry Kilbourne,
James Mitchell,
Thomas Moore,
Caleb Ardle,
William Smith,
James Laughray,
David Graham,
William Patton, Jun.,
Joseph Pierce,
Joseph Hays,
Matthew Davidson,
George M'Geehen,
James M'Geehen,
Benjamin M'Geehen,
Jacob Atchison,
Joseph Van Horn,
John Robinson,
John M'Cune,
Richard Nicholson,
James Nicholson,
Samuel M'Elhenny, Jr.
Samuel M'Elhenny, Sr.
John Gourril,
Samuel Morrow,
John Bell,
William Carnahan,
William Bryson,
Hugh Allen,
John Sumar,
John Clark,
William Clark,
James Hamilton.
Hannah Bovard.
Number of Pew-Holders, 204.

# APPENDIX II.

## CALL FROM THE CONGREGATIONS OF CARLISLE AND LOWER PENNSBOROUGH TO THE REV. JOHN STEEL.

"Whereas at the union of the congregations of Carlisle and Lower Pennsborough in April, 1764, it was agreed that each congregation should pay seventy-five pounds to Mr. John Steel, our minister, as stipends, yearly and every year from time of said union, and said agreement was signed by six men of each congregation in the name and behalf of said congregations,

"Now in order to give ease and relief to said six men who signed in behalf of the congregation of Lower Pennsborough, and at the same time to secure to our said minister his yearly stipends, said congregation have this day concluded that forty-two men shall give their promissory note to said John Steel for his yearly stipends, and that said forty-two men shall be a fix'd committee of said congregation, and have power to regulate seats and order all the other affairs of said congregation.

"Therefore, in consequence of said agreement, and to answer the above said ends, we the subscribers, with the consent and by the appointment of said congregation, do offer ourselves and accordingly become jointly bound to Mr. John Steel, our present minister, to pay him, yearly and every year, the sum of seventy-five pounds, good and lawful money of Pennsylvania, at or upon the first day of April, in every year following the date hereof, including the stipends of seventy-five pounds due to our said minister for the year past, April, 1768, and what arrears may be due to our said minister for the years 1765 and 1766,—all which we bind ourselves to pay or cause to be paid unto said John Steel, according to the true intent and meaning of the agreement made at the union of said congregations, as witness our hands this twentieth and seventh day of June, 1768.

Moses Star,
James Crawford,
Joseph M'Clure,
——— Abernethy,
Andrew Armstrong,
John Caruthers,
John M'Teer,
James M'Curdy,
William M'Cormick,
John Carothers,
James Nailer,
James Oliver,
Samuel Fisher,
John Dickey, Sen.,
Thomas Donaldson,
William M'Teer,
Thomas M'Cormick,
David Hoge,
William Orr,
John Nailer,
John Trindle,
William Gray,
Christopher Quigly,
Edward Morton,
Samuel Geddis,
Andrew Ervin,
James Caruthers,
Jonathan Hoge,
Samuel Huston,
John Semple,
John M'Cormick,
William Trindle,
Alexander Trindle,
Hugh Laird,
Thomas Stewart,
James M'Teer,
Patrick Holmes,
David Bell,
Nathanael Nelson,
William Geddis,
Matthew Loudon.

# APPENDIX III.

## SOME ACCOUNT OF THE SCHISM IN THE PRESBYTERIAN CHURCH OF THIS COUNTRY, A CENTURY AGO.

In the beginning of the last century there was a sad declension of religion in this country, as there was also in Great Britain. Of this there is evidence from various sources. According to the testimony of the Rev. Samuel Blair, "a very lamentable ignorance of the essentials of true practical religion, and of the doctrines relating thereto, very generally prevailed, in Pennsylvania." There was, also, necessity, in 1735, for a solemn injunction from the Synod of Philadelphia, to the Presbyteries under its jurisdiction, carefully to guard the doors of admission to the ministerial office and to church membership, against unworthy and unfit candidates.

Such was the state of religion, likewise, in the Congregational Churches of New England. "There is," said Dr. Increase Mather, in 1721, "a grievous decay of piety in the land, and a leaving of her first love, and the beauties of holiness are not to be seen as once they were."

About the year 1732, the work of God was signally revived. This was the case simultaneously in America, England, and Scotland. The first of the gracious visitations with which this country was blessed, occurred at Freehold, New Jersey, under the ministry of the Rev.

John Tennent. Soon there was a similar manifestation of the Spirit's presence and power, in Lawrence, Hopewell, and Amwell, three contiguous towns in New Jersey, under the ministry of the Rev. John Rowland; in Newark and Elizabethtown; in Philadelphia, under the ministry of Mr. Whitefield; in New Londonderry (Fagg's Manor), in Pennsylvania, under the ministry of the Rev. Samuel Blair; and in New Providence, Nottingham, White Clay Creek, Neshaminy, and other places of this region, as well as throughout New England.

That this revival was a genuine one, is evident, from the testimony in its favour of such men as Edwards, Cooper, Colman, and Bellamy, in New England, and the Tennents, Blair, Dickinson, and Davies, in the Presbyterian Church. This is evident, also, from the experience of its subjects which was in general answerable to the truth, and from its results, as exhibited in the external fruits of holiness in the lives of the large majority of those, to whom its special influence extended. It cannot be denied, indeed, that in some degree, and in some localities, fanaticism prevailed, and that there was an unwarrantable dependence placed upon bodily agitations, as evidential of conversion, and that there was a harshness and censoriousness, utterly incompatible with the spirit of the occasion, manifested by ultraists, toward all who would not follow them to their dangerous extremes. Equally undeniable is it, however, that the genuineness of the great and extensive awakening now referred to, is not to be questioned, because of some of the evils and irregularities with which it was attended and followed, for from these, perfect exemption cannot be expected for any movement, in a world such as this, where wheat is being sown as well as tares, and where every light produces its shadows. Of these errors, there may be specified in addition to those already noticed, "a strong leaven of enthusiasm, manifesting itself in the regard paid to impulses, inspirations, visions, and the pretended power of discerning spirits,—and the disregard shown to the common rules of ecclesiastical order, by itinerant preachers and lay exhorters, who went into the parishes of settled ministers, and without their knowledge, or against their wishes, insisted on preaching to the people."

In relation to this revival, there was, as was to be expected from what has been already stated, a wide difference of opinion among the ministers of Synod. Some regarded it as the work of God, and were active in furthering it, but others, and the more numerous party, withheld from it all co-operation, and pronounced it a mere fermentation of unsanctified feeling, which could not issue in any good results either God-ward or man-ward. As was natural amongst persons occupying such opposite stand-points, irritation arose, both among the ministry and laity. Those favourable to the work in progress, viewed all who were adverse, to it, as fighting against God, and as having the root of their hostility in unrenewed hearts; and those opposed to this work, condemned the terrific style of preaching employed in its promotion, and accused the more prominent actors in the movement, of exhibiting a spirit of malignant denunciation and misrepresentation, and of helping to obscure the true idea of religion, by encouraging the belief, that it exists rather in violent excitement and rapture than in principle carried into obedience.

There was, however, another ground of dissension among the ministers of the Synod, beside that just noticed. The Rev. William Tennent established a classical school at

Neshaminy, in Bucks County, Pennsylvania, about twenty miles north of Philadelphia. The object of this institution, (which afterwards became the celebrated LOG COLLEGE), was, to furnish candidates for the ministry an opportunity for securing the requisite literary qualifications for this office, without the inconvenience and expense of becoming students of a college in New England or Europe. Back of this, however, there was another desideratum aimed at, which was this,—that the Presbyterian Church of this country, might be able to rely upon a ministry educated at home, rather than be under the necessity of receiving ministers from foreign lands, who, at that time, to say nothing of the chances of imposition which existed, were not, generally, even when able to show their credentials, such men as the Church could with much hope of benefit, welcome to her communion. The competency of Mr. Tennent to conduct such a school, so as to accomplish the first of these objects, at least, was demonstrated by the very satisfactory examination which his son Gilbert, one of his students, sustained before the Presbytery of Philadelphia. Notwithstanding this proof, however, the Synod resolved, 1738, that in order to prevent the admission of uneducated men into the ministry, every candidate for the sacred office, before he was taken on trial, should be furnished with a diploma of graduation from some European or New England college, or with a certificate of competent scholarship from a committee of Synod. The same year, the Presbytery of New Brunswick was formed. At the next meeting of Synod, a remonstrance was presented by this Presbytery against this resolution, and it was modified so as to express the determination of Synod, "that every person who proposes himself to trial, as a candidate for the ministry, and who has not a diploma, or the usual certificate from a European or New England University, shall be examined by the whole Synod, or its commission, as to those preparatory studies which we generally pass through at college, and if they find him qualified, they shall give him a certificate, which shall be received by our respective Presbyteries, as equivalent to a diploma or certificate from the college, &c." But as thus modified, the resolution was no more acceptable than in its original form, to those who from the beginning had resisted it, and therefore a protest was entered against it, signed by William Tennent, Senr., Gilbert Tennent, William Tennent, Jr., Charles Tennent, Samuel Blair, and Eleazer Wales. We pretend not to state all the reasons, which influenced these ministers in their opposition to the action of Synod in this matter, but it is plain that they regarded it as inconsistent with the rights of Presbyteries, as calculated, if not intended, to disparage or destroy the Log College, and as tending to frustrate their design, in having a Presbytery set off in New Jersey chiefly composed of the friends of this Institution, which was, to license such men as they should deem properly qualified, and to make fervent piety the first and principal qualification for the ministry.

The Presbytery of New Brunswick having, in 1738, in contravention of the authority of Synod as expressed in its late act, licensed Mr. John Rowland to preach the Gospel, when the records of this Presbytery came to be reviewed by the Synod, that body declared, by "a great majority," the licensing of Mr. Rowland "to be very disorderly, and admonished the said Presbytery to avoid such divisive courses for the future, and determined not to admit the said Mr. Rowland to be a preacher of the Gospel within our bounds, nor to encourage any of our people to accept him until he submit to such examinations as were appointed by this Synod for those that have had a private education." In anticipation of this result, the Presbytery came prepared with an "Apology for dissenting from two acts or new religious laws passed at the last session of the Synod." Afterwards, in the same year, the New Brunswick Presbytery continued to disobey the Synod, and licensed Mr. M'Crea, and in 1740, they licensed Mr. William Robinson, and Mr. Samuel Finley, having no respect, in either case, to the requisition of Synod.

The effect of this controversy throughout the presbyteries and congregations of the Church was, of course, disastrous, and hence, in 1740, an effort was made to compromise the difficulty, by repealing the first act of Synod in relation to itinerant preaching, and by so modifying the second act in relation to the examination of candidates, as to meet the views of the New Brunswick brethren. It was also proposed by Mr. Dickinson, that the matter in dispute should be referred to some ecclesiastical body in Scotland, Ireland, or England, or to the ministers of Boston. After this, a member of the New Brunswick Presbytery proposed, "that the Synod might appoint two of their number to be present at the examination of candidates for the ministry, who, if they found them (the presbyteries), guilty of malconduct, might accuse them to Synod; but when it was ascertained that an objection of these delegates to the competency of a candidate would refer the question of his licensure to the Synod, the Brunswick brethren declined.

The failure of these efforts at accommodation, increased the unhappy state of feeling which had been growing in the Synod and Church, and at this point this feeling was greatly aggravated by the reading of formal papers of complaint, by Mr. Gilbert Tennent and Mr. Blair, against their brethren, before Synod. The same effect, in a high degree, was produced, by Mr. Tennent's famous Nottingham Sermon (called so because it was preached at that place), in which he describes the body of the ministers of that generation as letter-learned Pharisees, plastered hypocrites, having the form of godliness, but destitute of its power. The division which thus already virtually existed, was consummated at the meeting of Synod, June 1st, 1741, when a *protestation*, read by the Rev. Robert Cross, and signed by twelve ministers, and seven elders, was adopted, to the effect, that "the former protesting brethren, whether they were the major or minor number, had no right to sit, or to be looked upon as the Synod." The day after this rupture, the Presbytery of New Brunswick held a *pro re nata* meeting in Philadelphia, with four members, and seven correspondents, and resolved that in view of what had taken place, it was the bounden duty of the exscinded brethren, to form themselves into distinct presbyteries for carrying on the government of Christ's Church. This revolution led to the attaching Mr. William Tennent, Sen., and Richard Treat, to the Presbytery of New Brunswick, and the erection of a new Presbytery to be called Londonderry, both of which Presbyteries were to meet in the ensuing August, at Philadelphia, in the capacity of a Synod.

After several unsuccessful efforts for reconciliation, at a meeting of Synod, in 1743, an overture was presented from the Presbytery of New York, proposing that for certain reasons, and on certain terms, a reunion should take place between the Synod and the ejected members, and all past differences be buried in oblivion, but this proposal was unanimously rejected. In 1744, no member of the New

York Presbytery appeared in Synod, and no new effort was made to heal the schism. In 1745, a committee was appointed to draw up a plan of union. To this plan the New York brethren immediately refused to accede. The consequence was the erection of another Synod, under the name of the Synod of New York, which met as a separate and independent body, at Elizabethtown, September, 19, 1745. In May, 1758, a union was effected between this Synod and that of Philadelphia, on a plan devised by committees appointed by these respective bodies for this purpose, and unanimously agreed to by them.

Thus, after seventeen years' duration, ended this unhappy schism in the Presbyterian Church,—a schism which made its influence to be felt throughout the presbyteries and congregations, and which, it is scarcely necessary to add, was not produced by any diversity of opinion as to doctrine or discipline, or the form of church government, but by loss of confidence and alienation of feeling, arising from the different views entertained of the revival which then prevailed, and of the place for receiving, and the tribunal for testing, literary qualifications of candidates for the ministry. We regret that our statement of the subject must be so compendious as to be unsatisfactory, but those who wish to examine it thoroughly, can do so by reference to Dr. Alexander's "Log College," and Dr. Hodge's "History of the Presbyterian Church," from which the facts we have presented, have been gleaned.

# APPENDIX IV.

## HISTORY OF THE FRANKLIN COUNTY BIBLE SOCIETY.

THE Franklin County Bible Society was organized at Chambersburg, December 12th, 1814, some time before the formation of the American Bible Society.

The first officers of this Institution were:—The Rev. John McKnight, D.D., President; the Rev. James Hoffman, and James Riddle, Esq., Vice-Presidents; the Rev. John Lind, Secretary; the Rev. David Elliott, Clerk; John Findlay, Esq., Treasurer; and the Rev. Messrs. David Denny, John F. Moeller, John Moodey, Robert Kennedy, Mr. James McFarland, Mr. John Colhoun, Edward Crawford, William M. Brown, and George Chambers, Esq'rs, other Managers.

In pursuance of appointment, the Rev. John Lind delivered a discourse before the Society, at Chambersburg, February 17th, 1815; and the Rev. David Elliott, by like appointment, rendered the same service, at the same place, November 14th, 1815.

In April, 1816, public attention was invited to the consideration of the propriety of uniting the friends of the Bible cause, and a meeting was desired at New York for the purpose. This measure was approved of by the Franklin County Bible Society, and on the 11th of April, 1816, Matthew St. Clair Clarke, Esq., one of its members, was appointed a delegate to represent this Society at New York. Mr. Clarke fulfilled his appointment, and assisted in organizing the American Bible Society, in May, 1816.

The Franklin County Bible Society was for many years very active and efficient in ascertaining and supplying those destitute of the Bible, within the limits of Franklin County, and still is faithful to the purpose of its existence.

Of its officers at its organization, but three survive, viz., Rev. John Moodey, D.D., Rev. David Elliott, D.D., and Judge Chambers.

THE END.

www.ingramcontent.com/pod-product-compliance
Lightning Source LLC
LaVergne TN
LVHW010208110826
845151LV00002B/642
*9781425535926*